Reflections
on
Human Development

Mahbub ul Haq

(1934–1998)

Educated at Cambridge and Yale as an economist, Dr. Mahbub ul Haq enjoyed a distinguished career as an eminent policy-maker and a world-renowned scholar and author. He served in various high-level capacities, including being the chief architect of World Bank's focus on poverty reduction strategies and a close associate of World Bank's President, Robert S. McNamara (1970–82); Finance and Planning Minister of Pakistan (1982–88); Special Adviser to UNDP Administrator, and founder and author of UNDP's annual *Human Development Reports* (1990–95). In 1995, Dr. Haq took over as founder and President of the Human Development Centre in Islamabad, President of the Foundation for Advancement of Science and Technology (FAST), and Chancellor of the National University of Computer and Emerging Sciences.

Dr. Haq was the author of several internationally famous books, including *The Strategy of Economic Planning* (Oxford, 1963), *The Poverty Curtain* (Columbia, 1976), *Reflections on Human Development* (Oxford, 1995), *The Tobin Tax* (editor, Oxford, 1995), besides authoring the *Human Development Reports* (1990–95, Oxford) and reports on *Human Development in South Asia* (1997–98, Oxford).

Reflections
on
Human Development

Mahbub ul Haq

DELHI
OXFORD UNIVERSITY PRESS
CALCUTTA CHENNAI MUMBAI
1999

Oxford University Press, Great Clarendon Street, Oxford OX2 6DP

Oxford New York

Athens Auckland Bangkok Calcutta
Cape Town Chennai Dar es Salaam Delhi
Florence Hong Kong Istanbul Karachi
Kuala Lumpur Madrid Melbourne Mexico City
Mumbai Nairobi Paris Singapore
Taipei Tokyo Toronto

and associates in

Berlin Ibadan

© Oxford University Press, Inc. 1995
Oxford India Paperbacks 1998

ISBN 0 19 564598 7

Printed in India at Saurabh Print-O-Pack, Noida, U.P.
and published by Manzar Khan, Oxford University Press
YMCA Library Building, Jai Singh Road, New Delhi 110 001

To

Toneema and Farhan

Let knowledge be thy sword
And wisdom thy only shield

Contents

Foreword

Paul Streeten

*I*t was in 1965, when I worked in the British Ministry of Overseas Development in London, that I first met Mahbub ul Haq. Then the chief economist in the Pakistan Planning Commission, he had come to London to present the Pakistani case. I was immediately impressed by his quick grasp of complex issues, his tough backbone, his sense of humour and his gentle but firm and enthusiastic manner of presenting his case to hardened British civil servants. Later, at a conference in Williamsburg on the widening international income gap, organized and led by the wonderful Barbara Ward, he shone again, particularly in presenting a brilliant parody of a typical American aid official.

In the late 1970s, we worked together in the World Bank on "basic needs", a conceptual forerunner of human development. In addition to his major substantive contribution, Mahbub ul Haq wrote the foreword to our joint book, *First Things First: Meeting Basic Needs in Developing Countries*. Our ways then parted for about eight years. He went back to Pakistan to be a cabinet minister, I went on to Boston University. I was delighted when, out of the blue, he asked me to join him again in 1989, this time at the UNDP—where he had become Special Adviser to the Administrator—to work with him on the *Human Development Report*. As at the World Bank, he had gathered a splendid small team. His leadership was inspiring. Many reflections on this work are gathered in this volume.

We had endless debates. We defined human development as widening the range of people's choices. Human development is a concern not only for poor countries and poor people, but everywhere. In the high-income countries, indicators of shortfalls in human development should be looked for in homelessness, drug addiction, crime, unemployment, urban squalor, environmental degradation, personal insecurity and social disintegration. The indicators for the advanced countries are, of course, different from those in poor countries—though, alas, to John Kenneth Galbraith's complaint about private affluence amid public squalor has been added that of private affluence amid private squalor. A walk through the streets of New York or London provides plenty of evidence.

Suicide rates are more controversial. Suicides can be regarded as indicating more options and therefore as positive, particularly those of terminally ill, elderly patients. But they can also be regarded as a sign of the breakdown of the social fabric, a failure to uphold the moral values of the family or the sanctity of life.

We got into terrible trouble when Mahbub wanted to say that development means enlarging the choices not of trees, but of people. How about choices in advanced countries? We have come to accept divorce as a normal feature of life, one that enlarges people's range of choices, though we debated whether it should be bracketed with cancer and AIDS as a curse of our times or celebrated along with aspirin and anaesthetics as a welcome liberation from past miseries. We searched for a "green" Keynes, born in the South, and preferably a woman.

I have sometimes thought that the human race consists of two types: molluscs and mammals. Molluscs are those with a hard veneer, unyielding and tough, but when you push through their exterior, you find a squishy, soft, mushy mess underneath. Mammals are soft and warm and yielding outside, but underneath lies a firm, strong backbone. In negotiations, the molluscs are sometimes deceived into thinking that the mammals are pushovers. But they should beware. Mahbub ul Haq is a mammal. His gentle appearance conceals a tenacity and strength of character that he has demonstrated both inside his own government and in foreign negotiations. A testimony to his flexibility in the light of new evidence is the plaque he had on the wall in his World Bank office, which read, "It is too late to agree with me; I've changed my mind." He gave it, I believe, to Maurice Strong, who urgently asked for it.

Mahbub ul Haq's powers of persuasion are formidable. In 1971, he saved the 1972 United Nations Stockholm Conference on Human Environment, organized by Maurice Strong. The developing countries wanted to pull out. But at a meeting in Founex, near Geneva, Mahbub single-handedly turned around the negative attitudes of the delegations from the developing countries, committing them to wholehearted support of the conference. He did this by marrying the concerns of environment and development into a single concept of an environmentally sound, people-centred development paradigm—a forerunner of the current concept of sustainable human development. It was a gigantic achievement. The Founex Report, written principally by him, has proved to be a seminal document.

The concept of basic needs, as we understood it, was not (as is sometimes thought) centred on the possession of commodities. Instead, it was concerned with providing all human beings, but particularly the poor and deprived, with the opportunities for a full life. Human development goes beyond basic needs in that it is concerned with all human beings—not only the poor and not only in poor countries—and not only basic needs. Human development applies to the advanced countries as much as to the middle-income and low-income countries.

Human development puts people back at centre stage, after decades in which a maze of technical concepts had obscured this fundamental vision. That is not to say that technical analysis should be abandoned. Far from it. Mahbub ul Haq has always emphasized the need for the highest professional standards and is himself a fine practitioner of economic techniques. But he reminds us that we should never lose sight of the ultimate purpose of the exercise of development: to treat men, women and children—present and future generations—as ends, to improve the human condition, to enlarge people's choices.

Human development is not once, twice or thrice, but six times blessed.

First, and above all, it is an end in itself that needs no further justification. The human development approach pioneered by Mahbub ul Haq reminds us of this truth, which is sometimes forgotten in the preoccupation with technicalities.

Second, human development is a means to higher productivity. A well-nourished, healthy, educated, skilled, alert labour force is the most important productive asset. This has been widely recognized. Yet Hondas, beer and television are often accepted without question as final consumption goods, while investments in nutrition, education and health services must be justified on grounds of productivity.

Third, it slows human reproduction by lowering the desired family size. This is generally regarded as desirable. It is paradoxical that a policy that reduces infant mortality and raises health standards generally should lead to slower population growth. One might think that more survivors would mean more mouths to feed. But evidence shows that people try to overinsure themselves against infant deaths, and that fewer child deaths lead to a smaller desired family size. It is true that there is a time lag of about two decades between a drop in child mortality and lower fertility rates. But other components of the human development strategy—such as better and longer education for girls—pay off sooner in smaller families.

Fourth, human development is good for the physical environment. The poor are both a cause (though not as significant a cause as the rich) and the main victim of environmental degradation. Deforestation, desertification and soil erosion decline when poverty declines. How population growth and population density affect the environment is more controversial. The conventional view is that they have a detrimental effect. But recent research has shown that rapid (though not accelerating) population growth and high population density (particularly if combined with secure land rights) can be good for soil and forest conservation. More people in Guinea have meant more trees, not fewer. In Nepal, increased erosion was the result of depopulation; terraces could not be maintained for lack of people. In the Kakagema District in Kenya, the density of trees varies with the density of the population. A study of the Machakos District in Kenya found a fivefold increase in population associated with a shift from highly degrading to much more sustainable agriculture.

Fifth, reduced poverty contributes to a healthy civil society, increased democracy and greater social stability. China has witnessed a rapid reduction in poverty while maintaining an autocracy, but with successful human development, the call for freedom cannot be suppressed for long.

Sixth, human development has political appeal, for it may reduce civil disturbances and increase political stability, though this will depend on the relation between aspirations and material improvements. If aspirations move too far ahead of material improvements, political instability may result.

At first blush, there appears to be a unity of interest between those who emphasize human development's productivity aspect, the human resource developers, and those who stress its ends, the humanitarians. Although their motives differ, both have the same cause at heart, and

REFLECTIONS ON HUMAN DEVELOPMENT

they should embrace each other, for example, when it comes to promoting education. The ends presumably are the same in both camps.

Although there can indeed be harmony among some of these objectives, there can also be conflict. Humanitarians, those who emphasize people as ends, are concerned also with the unproductive and the unemployable: the old, the disabled, the chronically sick. These people suffer from a double disadvantage: they face greater difficulties both in earning income and in converting income into well-being.

There may be a bonus for the community looking after them—however—if not higher production, at least lower reproduction. If parents know that the community will care for them if they become disabled or infirm, an important cause of the desire for large families, particularly for many sons, disappears. Discrimination against females will also decline. But these benefits are incidental. The main point is that the disabled also are people, worthy of our concern.

Another example of a possible conflict arises in the case of women. Those who advocate women's freedom and the abolition of discrimination on grounds of efficiency and productivity will welcome the benefits for men also. But those who are concerned with women's rights as an end will advocate policies that reduce the benefits to men and involve sacrifices by them. Men's support for the policies will tend to vary according to which aspect is stressed.

Those who see nutrition, education and health as ends in themselves rather than as means to higher productivity will argue for projects and programmes that enhance those ends, even when conventionally measured rates of return on these investments turn out to be zero. It amounts to standing the conventional approach on its head—or rather, back on its feet.

The item in UNDP's *Human Development Report* that has caught the public's eye and caused the most controversy is the Human Development Index (HDI). The concept of human development clearly is much wider and richer than what can be caught in any index or set of indicators. That is also true of other indicators, such as those of temperature. Why try to catch a vector in a single number?

Such indexes are useful in focusing attention and simplifying problems. They are eye-catching. They have considerable political appeal. They have a stronger impact on the mind and draw public attention more powerfully than a long list of indicators combined with a qualitative discussion. The strongest argument in their favour is that they show up the inadequacies of other indexes, such as gross national product (GNP), contributing to an intellectual muscle therapy that helps us to avoid analytical cramps. They can serve as mental finger exercises. They redirect our attention from one set of items to others—in the case of the HDI, to the social sectors: nutrition, education and health. But again, it should be remembered that human development is a much richer concept than can be caught in any index, whether GNP, the HDI or any other.

The Human Development Index comprises (1) the logarithm of gross domestic product (GDP) per head, calculated at the real purchasing power, not at exchange rates, up to the international poverty line (after 1990 this was modified in various ways); (2) literacy rates (and, since the 1991 report, mean years of schooling); and (3) life expectancy at birth. These disparate items are brought to a common denominator by measuring the distance between the best and the worst performers and producing a ranking of countries. Critics have said that not only the weights of the three components are arbitrary, but also what is excluded (such as freedom and human rights) and what is included.

As we have seen, one of the great drawbacks of income per head is that it is an average that can conceal great inequalities. But the other components of the Human Development Index, life expectancy and literacy, also are averages. They can conceal vast discrepancies between men and women, boys and girls, rich and poor, urban and rural residents and different ethnic or religious groups. The HDI has in fact been disaggregated by sex, region and ethnic group for a few countries for which data were available, with illuminating results. It has also been adjusted for sex disparities. This is done by first adjusting the HDI ranking by expressing the value of each component of the index for females as a percentage of the value for males. These percentages, calculated separately for income, educational attainment and life expectancy, are then averaged and the country's general HDI is multiplied by this factor to yield a sex-disparity-adjusted HDI. This procedure makes a considerable difference to the rankings of countries. Japan moves down from 3 to 19, Canada from 1 to 9, Switzerland from 2 to 17 and Hong Kong from 22 to 30. But, Sweden moves up from 4 to 1, Denmark from 15 to 4, Finland from 16 to 3 and New Zealand from 18 to 8.

Disaggregation is also possible by other categories—for example, income group, residence (urban, rural), ethnic group, region and continent. *Human Development Report 1993* disaggregated the HDI by ethnic group for a small group of countries.

There are, however, several reasons why even non-disaggregated and non-sex-disparity-adjusted human indicators are less misleading than income per head, and why the HDI should be given legitimacy.

First, the distribution of literacy and life expectancy is much less skewed than that of income. There is a maximum of 100% literacy, and, despite all the achievements of modern medicine, the maximum life span has not been extended significantly. But for income, the sky is the limit. A very few very high income earners can raise the average. (The median or the mode would eliminate some of the distortions, but normally they are not available.)

Second, therefore, the average of a human development indicator tells us something about the distribution. There cannot be high averages if many people are not participating. Thus, because the non-poor gain access to public services before the poor, reductions in infant mortality, for example, indicate improvements for the poor. As Sudhir Anand and Amartya Sen have shown, for life expectancy the average may actually be better than a figure corrected for unequal distribution, for the following reason. Because, all things equal, women live longer than men, an equal life expectancy may indicate a systematic anti-female bias in the distribution of health care, food, education and other ingredients of life. Correcting for distribution in life expectancies can then be *inegalitarian* in its impact on equality of treatment. Since it is easier to extend the life expectancy of females than that of males if we start from the *same* level of life expectancy, concentrating on the *average* life expectancy would in this case be fairer than using life expectancy corrected for distribution.

Third, any upward move in a human development indicator can be regarded as an improvement. Some might object if the literacy of only boys or the life expectancy of only men is increased for a certain period, but unless it can be shown that such increases worsen the fate of girls and women by, for example, increasing the ability and desire to discriminate against them, to object would smack of envy. (The social and economic returns to educating girls are, however, likely to be greater than those to educating boys.)

There is evidence that the lower the level of women's education, the greater the discrimination against them. In this case, an equal improvement in everybody's education reduces anti-female bias.

Fourth, whereas high incomes for some can cause relative deprivation for others, that is not true for human development. If anything, improving the health and education of anyone benefits the entire community.

Fifth, international income gaps may be inevitably widening, but to aim at reducing international gaps in human development is both feasible and sensible. In fact, progress in human development terms presents a more cheerful picture than progress in income terms. Since 1960, average life expectancy has increased by 16 years, adult literacy by 40% and nutritional levels by more than 40%, and child mortality rates have been halved. The international gap in these indicators, unlike that in income per head, is closing. While average income per head in the South is 6% of that in the North, life expectancy is 80%, literacy 66% and nutrition 85%.

Sixth, human development indicators show the troubles of over-development—or, better, maldevelopment—as well as those of under-development. Diseases of affluence can kill, just as the diseases of poverty can. Income statistics, by contrast, do not reveal the destructive aspects of wealth.

Seventh, indicators that measure impact rather than inputs distinguish between goods and "anti-bads" (regrettable necessities), which, though requiring production, add nothing to human welfare. These anti-bads include food requirements arising from unwanted pregnancies and feeding children who die, or from long walks to collect water and fuel, or from excess work or the need to walk between unconsolidated plots or in looking for work. For urban dwellers, they include high housing and transport costs.

Eighth, the index contributes, as we have seen, to intellectual flexibility. It presents a kind of analytical muscle therapy that cures us of cramps of obsession with a single measure such as GNP. Let many possible indexes bloom, so as to show the complex and multiple dimensions of the human condition. In the *Human Development Report*, many additional indicators highlight the human condition. Food security, ratios of military to social spending, population without access to safe water or sanitation, female-male gaps, incidence of AIDS, access to newspapers and telephones, drug-related crimes and many other concrete statistical indicators carry the discussion beyond the usual level.

Ninth, and most important, there is considerable political appeal in a simple indicator that identifies important objectives and contrasts them with other objectives. It draws the attention of policy-makers to the social sectors.

A separate index can cover human freedom and human rights, clearly important aspects of human development. For life expectancy and literacy could be quite high in a well-managed prison. Basic physical needs are well met in a zoo. China shows remarkable progress in human development, but without freedom and human rights.

Should a freedom index be integrated into the Human Development Index? There are some arguments in favour of this, but the balance of arguments is probably against it. First, freedom is so important (and, opportunity costs apart, costless) that no trade-off should be possible between loss of freedom and gains in other indicators. Second, political conditions are much more volatile than changes in education and health. Human development indicators tend to be fairly stable. Once a mother knows the importance of education for her children, or of hygienic behaviour, this knowledge is not lost even when incomes drop. Political indicators, however, can change overnight with a political coup. Third, measuring freedom and human rights is more subjective and less reliable than measuring life expectancy or literacy.

One of the most interesting questions is how freedom is related to human development as more narrowly interpreted. This relationship can be examined only if freedom and human development are recorded by separate indexes. Thus, we might formulate a hypothesis, to be tested using the separate indexes, that freedom, though not a necessary condition of human development, is entirely consistent with it even at quite low levels, and that human development, once it has reached a certain stage, leads inevitably to a call for freedom by the people. Here is a message of hope.

Mahbub ul Haq has the imagination to contemplate alternative ways of looking at human welfare and the political wisdom to recognize the need to draw policy-makers' attention to human priorities. His proposal of a 20:20 contract between aid donors and recipients illustrates these qualities. His proposal sets quantitative targets: donors would allocate at least 20% of aid, and developing countries at least 20% of government expenditure, to social and human development.

An international central bank, an international investment trust and a progressive global income tax are among the ideas to which he has given concrete shape. He combines vision with attention to detail—an uncommon combination. Not afraid to be cast as a utopian, he fills in his and our fantasies with information and detail.

Mahbub ul Haq strengthened the human development approach by adding several dimensions of security: shifting the concept away from military, territorial and national security and towards human security (which can often be increased by reducing defence expenditure), a necessary condition for human development. Ethnic conflict, civil wars, external aggression and genocide are now seen as having economic and social roots in the extreme human insecurity that arises from hunger, poverty, unemployment, discrimination, social exclusion and social disintegration. Mahbub ul Haq has argued that tackling the root causes of poverty by preventive action—rather than by intervention after conflicts have broken out into open wars—can be much more effective and save many lives. An entire chapter of this book is devoted to this emerging concept of human security, to which Mahbub ul Haq has contributed so much.

State sovereignty, which still dominates the world order, has become inadequate and indeed dangerous. In peacekeeping, the unrealistic distinction between external aggression and internal oppression must be abandoned. The predominant threat to stability is conflict within countries, not conflict between them. There is an urgent need to strengthen international human rights law. Many of the most serious troubles come from within states—either because of ethnic strife or because of repressive measures by governments. Conditions that lead to tyranny at home sooner or later are likely to spill over into a search for enemies abroad. Consider the Soviet Union's invasion of Hungary and Czechoslovakia, the South African government's interventions in Angola and Mozambique and Iraq's invasion of Kuwait. An ounce of prevention is better than a ton of punishment. And prevention of aggression is an important task for the United Nations. The creation of a UN rapid deployment force would be a significant contribution to peace.

These issues and others are covered in this book, which illustrates brilliantly the insights that can be achieved by a cool head combined with a warm heart.

Preface to the Expanded Edition

*F*our years have elapsed since I wrote the first edition of this book in mid-1994. A great deal of intellectual ferment and further evolution has taken place in the field of human development. From a mere idea, human development is becoming an intellectual movement and a practical strategy. I felt that it was important to expand the book to trace this fascinating evolution.

This second expanded edition has the following additions: (a) a long epilogue at the end of the book (p. 205) which follows the trail of human development ideas and practices over recent years of an unprecedented explosion in thinking on this subject; (b) revised and updated statistical tables in the Human Development Profile of Nations (pp 231–64); (c) new statistical tables on Human Development Indicators for South Asia (pp 265–80); and (d) updated and expanded Selected Bibliography to include a great deal of recent writings in the human development field, particularly for South Asia.

It appears that human development is an idea whose time has come. People-centred strategies have increasingly become the focus of all development dialogue. I sincerely hope that this revised edition makes a modest contribution to this exciting debate.

My grateful thanks to several colleagues and associates: Salma Mahdi for some indispensible help with statistical tables; Adeel Malik for meticulously updating the bibliography; Masooda Bano for much logistical support; and Bazme Sukhanwar for valuable assistance with the preparation of the manuscript. Their labour of love has been a precious gift.

My publishers Oxford University Press have proved to be more than human in bearing many delays caused by my hectic schedule. I cannot thank Nitasha Devasar enough for her patience, perseverance and professional skill.

My own family—Bani, Toneema and Farhan—has always shared all my intellectual enterprises. They share this further evolution of ideas as well.

Mahbub ul Haq

15 June 1998
Islamabad

Preface

This book traces my intellectual journey—and the world's—through a profound transition in development thinking in recent decades. In it, I reflect on the quiet emergence of human development as a major focus of economic thinking. Only 30 years ago, it would have been heresy to challenge the economic growth school's tacit assumption that the purpose of development is to increase national income. Today, it is widely accepted that the real purpose of development is to enlarge people's choices in all fields—economic, political, cultural. Seeking increases in income is one of the many choices people make, but it is not the only one.

My writings reflect this evolution in economic thought. My first book, *The Strategy of Economic Planning* (Oxford University Press, 1963), was a defence of the classical growth school in the context of Pakistan's development planning. But when rapid economic growth during the 1960s failed to translate into improvements in the lives of Pakistan's masses, I was forced to challenge many of the premises of my initial work. My second book, *The Poverty Curtain* (Columbia University Press, 1976), laid out a case for putting equality of opportunity, within nations and between them, at the centre of the development dialogue. This theme was carried forward through *First Things First* (World Bank, 1982), which I edited with Paul Streeten, as well as in the annual *Human*

Development Report that I helped launch in 1990 under the sponsorship of the United Nations Development Programme (UNDP).

My sincere tribute goes to William H. Draper III, the Administrator of UNDP (1986–93). He showed great vision in 1989 in taking a chance on an untested idea—the *Human Development Report*. And he protected the intellectual independence and professional integrity of the report despite considerable international pressure. This was the essence of real leadership—a tradition that his successor, James Gustave Speth, has continued while combining it with admirable intellectual contributions to the substance of the development debate on this subject. Although I have written this book while serving as Special Adviser to the Administrator of UNDP, UNDP carries no responsibility for my views. I carry this burden alone.

So many friends and colleagues have helped in the evolution of my thinking that it is impossible to acknowledge them all. Paul Streeten has added to the many intellectual debts I owe him by contributing a thoughtful foreword to this book. Others who have contributed so generously to the ideas in this book include Amartya Sen, Frances Stewart, Gustav Ranis, Meghnad Desai, Keith Griffin, Wouter Tims, (the late) Jim Grant, Richard Jolly, Hans Singer and Dragoslav Avramovic. The list could be much longer, and I offer quiet thanks to those not mentioned.

Many colleagues helped me in the compilation of this book, particularly Inge Kaul, Selim Jahan, Saras Menon and Laura Mourino, to whom I owe my sincere thanks. Linda Pigon-Rebello, my executive assistant, has been invaluable in completing this book. I could never have finished it without her untiring and selfless help. Renu Corea did an outstanding job of desktopping composition and gave much help to the manuscript. I also thank Bruce Ross-Larson for his editing, Gerry Quinn for his cover design, Alison Strong for proofreading and Kim Bieler and Heather Cochran for producing the camera-ready copy.

The statistical annex at the end of this book is based on data derived from various *Human Development Reports* (1990–94) as well as from the extensive data base system of UNDP. I am grateful to UNDP and to the Department of Information, Ministry of Foreign Affairs of Denmark, for their gracious support for this book.

I must acknowledge my deep debt to my wife, Bani, a constant intellectual companion and an integral part of all I have accomplished in my life. She contributes so generously to my thinking and yet expects so little credit in return.

I have dedicated the book to my two children, Toneema and Farhan, whose human values I greatly respect and who are likely to find themselves in the midst of this exciting debate on human development in the 21st century.

Mahbub ul Haq
New York
7 April 1995

Part 1

Towards a New Development Paradigm

The white Rabbit put on his spectacles. "Where shall I begin, please your Majesty?" he asked.

"Begin at the beginning," the King said gravely, "and go on till you come to the end: then stop."

— Alice in Wonderland

Chapter 1

The Missing People in Development Planning

"Well! I've often seen a cat without a grin," thought Alice; "but a grin without a cat! It is the most curious thing I ever saw in all my life!"

— Alice in Wonderland

The most difficult thing in life is to discover the obvious. It took Newton to question why an apple falls down rather than up and to discover the law of gravity. It took Einstein to point out that time and space are relative, not absolute, which led to the theory of relativity. It took Keynes to observe that if every individual tries to save without investing, the nation as a whole may not be able to save because total output will decline. So, what is considered economically rational behaviour at the disaggregate level may not be all that rational at the aggregate level, an observation that culminated in the General Theory. And it took Churchill to thunder in the midst of the Second World War: "There is no finer investment than putting milk in babies."

In the same spirit, after many decades of development, we are rediscovering the obvious—that people are both the means and the end of economic development. Often, this simple truth gets obscured because we are used to talking in abstractions, in aggregates, in numbers. Human beings, fortunately too stubborn to lend themselves to becoming a mere abstraction, are conveniently forgotten.

Economists, in discussing the means of development, often talk about investment capital. Physical capital has taken centre stage, to the exclusion of many other factors of production. Human capital is measured neither quantitatively nor qualitatively. Nor does it receive the attention it deserves. Many societies, despite an abundance of financial capital, have been unable to develop. The recent experience of the OPEC nations is an illustration. Human capital—human institutions and skills—was missing in most of these nations, and without it their vast windfall gains could not be translated into real development. A few of these countries, such as Kuwait, did develop, by converting their temporary gains into permanent income. But that transformation required human initiative and human capital—above and beyond financial savings.

Societies with similar natural resource endowments often have developed very differently because of differences in their human capabilities. Look at the different problems and development paths of African, Asian and Latin American countries today. We have seen neighbours achieve vastly different outputs from similar investments, with growth rates varying from 3% in one country to 7% in another. The critical difference: human skills and enterprise—and the institutions that produce them. Yet our preoccupation as economists is largely with saving and investment, exports and imports—and, of course, with that most convenient abstraction of all: the gross national product. When we do come to recognize the contributions of human beings as a means of development, we tend to treat them as almost residual elements.

The lack of recognition given to people as an end of development is even more glaring. Only in the past two decades have we started focusing on who development is for, looking beyond growth in gross national product (GNP). For the first time, we have begun to acknowledge—still with a curious reluctance—that in many societies GNP can increase while human lives shrivel. We have begun to focus on human needs, the compilation of poverty profiles, and the situation of the bottom 40% of society often bypassed by development. We have started to measure the costs of adjustment not only in lost output, but also in lost lives and lost human potential. We have finally begun to accept the axiom that human welfare—not GNP—is the true end of development.

But there has been little consistent, comprehensive analysis of how to integrate people into development as both a means and an end. What are the concrete implications for economic planning of placing people at the heart of development? Three specific implications deserve exploration: the human dimensions in development planning, in the adjustment process and in international decisions.

The human dimension in development planning

Most development plans would look very different if their preoccupation were with people rather than with production. They would contain at least five distinct elements conspicuously lacking in most plans today.

1. They would start with a human balance sheet. What human resources exist in the country? How educated are its people? What is the inventory of skills? What is the profile of relative income distribution and absolute poverty? How much unemployment and underemployment are there? What are the urban-rural distribution and the level of human development in various regions? Has the country undergone a rapid demographic transition? What are the cultural and social attitudes and the aspirations of the people? In other words, how does the society live and breathe? Often, the first chapter of a development plan presents macroeconomic aggregates of GNP, saving, investment and other components of national income accounts. Instead, that first chapter should contain a comprehensive human balance sheet. We cannot plan for people if we start with imperfect knowledge about them. A lack of statistical data is no excuse. Once the importance of the human factor is recognized, adequate investment must be made in compiling comprehensive balance sheets in human terms.

2. Plan targets must first be expressed in basic human needs and only later translated into physical targets for production and consumption. This means that there will have to be a clear exposition of the targets for average nutrition, education, health, housing and transport—as a very minimum. There must be an open discussion of what level of basic needs a society can afford at its current per capita income and at its projected incomes. The basic needs targets will then have to be built into detailed planning for production and consumption. In other words, we must proceed from ends to means, not the other way around.

3. An essential corollary of incorporating the human dimension into development planning is that both production and distribution objectives should be integrated and given equal emphasis. The development plan must specify not only what is being produced but how it is likely to be distributed and what concrete policies will be applied to ensure that national production is equitably distributed. That requires action programmes and delivery mechanisms to increase the productivity of the poor—particularly small farmers and small entrepreneurs. It also requires that employment planning accompany production planning, since the only effective means of improving distribution in many poor societies is to create adequate employment opportunities. Of course, the integration of concerns for production and distribution also implies the redistribution of productive assets—especially land, if the existing distribution is badly skewed—and the creation of social safety nets for the poorest.

4. A human development strategy must be decentralized, to involve community participation and self-reliance. It is ironic to declare human beings the ultimate objective of economic planning and then to deny them full participation in planning for themselves. Many developing countries are confused on this subject. Laudable objectives of human development adopted in national plans are often frustrated because the beneficiaries are given little say in planning and implementation.

5. Development plans must contain a human framework for analysing their performance. A comprehensive set of social and human development indicators needs to be developed to monitor plan progress. Besides GNP growth rates, the human story must also be brought out in annual assessments of how many people experienced what growth rates and of how the relative and absolute poverty levels changed every year. In some countries, GNP may have stagnated, but a lot of human capital may have been built up, strengthening the potential for future growth and making the measures of actual growth an unfair basis for comparison with other countries.

These elements should appear in every economic plan of the developing countries. The first part of the plan should consist of an elaboration of these five elements, and the conventional national income accounts and sectoral targets should be moved to the second part of the plan. If development plans are recast along these lines, they may not only become more meaningful, they may finally be read by the people they are meant for. One incidental benefit will be that all plans will not look the same. They will carry the flesh and colour of their people and their societies. There may even be some dents in the enormous egos of those professional consultants who travel from country to country delivering development planning models with the press of an electronic button.

These changes are not minor. They are basic. And although the difficulties are enormous, the task is challenging, exciting and worthwhile. Let us remember: many of these difficulties were encountered in the initial construction of national income accounts. So, after the difficulties of the initial effort are overcome, human balance sheets too should become commonplace.

The human dimension in the adjustment process

For some time, an excited debate has been going on over whether the adjustment process is consistent with human development. It is time we settled this debate: any adjustment process is a dismal failure if it does not protect and advance human development.

The presumed conflict between adjustment policies and growth with human development has dominated international discussion for the past few years. On the conceptual level, that seems strange, for there has been less intellectual investment in this issue than it deserves. One school of thought believes that adjustment policies and growth with human development are antithetical and cannot be made compatible in a national policy framework. It argues that adjustment requires short-term demand management, while growth requires long-term supply expansion. It argues that adjustment policies require the correction of price distortions, a greater role for the market mechanism and less government intervention—a conscious withdrawal of the government presence from the economy. By contrast, human development requires more government intervention and a greater government presence, particularly in education and health.

Let us examine this thesis carefully, because the presumed conflict between adjustment policies and growth with human development may be more apparent than real. Resource allocation is less than perfect in most developing countries today. If demand management is improved, if price distortions are corrected, if unnecessary public intervention is reduced, and if inefficient and corrupt economic and administrative controls are done away with, the resources badly needed for both growth and human development would be released.

Pakistan has shown that correct adjustment policies can release resources to achieve both higher growth and better allocations for human resource development. While undertaking adjustment from 1980 to 1986, Pakistan did not reduce its expenditures on education and health. It increased them—from 8.6% of government expenditure in 1980 to 14.2% in 1986. Thus, Pakistan achieved adjustment neither at the cost of growth—gross domestic product (GDP) grew about 6.5% a year during this period—nor at the cost of human development.

During 1980–86, 25% of Pakistan's government budgetary resources were released through various adjustments that allowed for greater investment in energy development, health, education and other human resource development programmes. Many public industries that had been nationalized in the 1970s and were running inefficiently were returned to private control. Economic controls, government regulations, and price distortions and subsidies were reduced. The many subsidies that persist in developing countries favour the rich and the powerful and, generally, the urban elite. Their reduction often enables countries to pursue programmes that are more populist or that benefit a large majority.

Far from being antithetical, adjustment and growth with human development offer an intellectual and policy challenge in designing suitable programmes and policies. And failures on the policy front should not be explained away by the supposed incompatibility of these objectives at the conceptual level. The challenge of combining these two concerns is like that of combining the conflicting viewpoints of the growth school and the distribution school in the early 1970s. The first school of thought contended that developing countries must pursue GNP growth above all else. Otherwise, they could only redistribute poverty. The other school of thought argued just as vehemently that if GNP growth were the only god worshipped, serious concentrations of income and wealth would result, and the quality of human life could diminish even as national production increased.

The intellectual challenge: to combine growth and distribution policies in the national planning framework. A group working at the Sussex Institute in Britain—financed largely by the World Bank (under Robert S. McNamara at that time), led by Hollis Chenery and bringing together such outstanding intellects as Hans Singer, Dudley Seers and Richard Jolly—produced a fresh analysis on the subject. The breakthrough was simple, as most truths are: Yes, increased productivity is necessary. But let us ask the question, increased productivity of whom and for whom? Not only should a strategy be designed for the redistribution of productive assets and public social services, the productivity of the majority of the poor should be increased.

With that intellectual breakthrough, national policy-makers focused on recasting their development planning strategies. The measurement of poverty profiles and the delineation of policy action to increase the productivity of the poor became as much a planning staple as GNP growth measurement and policies to increase national production. McNamara, with his vision and dynamism, took up the banner of increasing the productivity of the poor and bent all the policies and lending programmes of the World Bank towards this concern. Through his persistent and persuasive advocacy, he managed to influence the policies of all the other international development institutions, as well as the thinking of the world at large.

We must now generate a similar intellectual ferment around the concerns of adjustment and growth with human development. Let research institutions step forward and undertake serious analytical work to achieve a synthesis between these essentially compatible concerns.

A second challenge is to pursue this synthesis in national policy. It does little credit to the developing countries to find constant alibis in the deteriorating international environment for a lack of action on issues that are essentially structural and that only national planners and policy-makers can address. Sometime back, Tanzania's President Julius Nyerere asked in legitimate despair, must we starve our children to pay our debts? It is at least as pertinent to ask, must we starve our children to increase our defence expenditure? The sad reality is that spending on education and health as a proportion of central government spending declined from 21% in 1972 to 9% in 1982 in low-income developing countries, while during the same period, the defence expenditures of all developing countries increased from $7 billion to more than $100 billion. It is therefore pertinent to ask, when our children cry for milk in the middle of the night, shall we give them guns instead?

Defence expenditures are not the only source or evidence of irrationality in domestic resource allocation in the developing countries. The margins of public inefficiency and corruption often exceed 20% of the public budget in many developing countries. Yet there is endless quibbling about small reductions in foreign assistance, when tighter economic management could release substantially more resources for legitimate growth and human development needs.

When Pakistan confronted the necessity for an immunization programme for children, what did it take? In one of the most dramatic stories of increasing child survival, the new programme brought immunization coverage for Pakistani children from 5% in 1983 to 75% in 1988 and now prevents 100,000 infant deaths every year. Did it take more assistance from abroad? Did it take reducing growth rates? No. It took postponing for five years the decision to build an expensive urban hospital. That, by itself, financed the entire expenditure on the immunization campaign.

And what did it take to spread public services and infrastructure to rural areas, with 70% of the people? Only 10% of the public spending was going to the rural areas, because even the rural elite live in the urban areas. Yet Pakistan electrified half its villages between 1983 and 1988 by periodically suffering one or two hours of load-shedding of electricity in the cities.

These political choices are difficult. But much can be accomplished by shifting internal priorities. Easing regulation, lowering subsidies, reducing public expenditures on inefficient industries and making other shifts in internal priorities enabled Pakistan to increase both growth and human development. Nonetheless, enormous scope remains for improving Pakistan's economic management and diverting more resources towards growth and human development. Those who postulate a basic conflict between these goals in developing countries often assume that the allocation of resources is already optimal. They are obviously wrong.

The human dimension in international decisions

If the human dimension is to show up fully in development policy decisions, the first and biggest battle lies within the corridors of power of the developing countries. But full awareness of the issue must also be woven into international decision-making and the programmes and practices of bilateral and multilateral donors. At least four issues deserve attention.

First, an annual review of national development plans and coordinated advice on economic planning are currently considered the prerogative of the World Bank, the International Monetary Fund and the regional development banks. The United Nations specialized agencies dealing with micro human development issues—UNESCO, WHO, UNICEF, UNDP, UNFPA, ILO and so on—are normally denied this privilege. And they generally are not invited to the consortiums and consultative groups to review country performance. If human development is to take centre stage, the World Bank and the regional development banks will have to descend from their macroeconomic concerns with national income accounts and production planning to human development issues. In the 1970s, under the leadership of McNamara, that was beginning to happen, but the path is less sure today. In addition, it is necessary to involve the concerned United Nations agencies in these annual reviews and policy advice, through their regular participation in the annual World Bank missions and in country consortiums and consultative groups. Today, there is a curious divide between the Bretton Woods and UN institutions, reflected in the divide between financial and human issues. It should be possible to find pragmatic ways of bridging this divide.

Second, the designing of conditionality for loans must change. Besides macroeconomic conditionality for budgetary and balance of payments measures, or sectoral conditionality for necessary policy or institutional changes, there must be conditionality for protecting minimum nutritional standards, maintaining minimum employment levels, and setting expenditure floors for education and health. It would be appropriate for the World Bank and the IMF to reconsider their conditionality packages to include the human dimension and to fully involve the UN agencies in such a review.

Third, external lending for human development programmes, such as education and health, is generally a low percentage of total international assistance relative to the priority given to these concerns in national development planning, inadequate as it is. And in view of the general constraints on financial resources, liberal forces normally must fight hard domestically to maintain a high priority for human resource development sectors. These sectors are intensive users of domestic resources, with a low foreign exchange component and high recurring expenditure. Finance ministers are generally reluctant to finance them for that reason, and their reluctance is reinforced when international donors give a low priority to these sectors in their allocations. The need is clear for a stronger link between advice and performance.

Fourth, a concrete proposal. The problems of human development are perhaps most acute in the populous nations of South Asia (chapter 7). Seven countries—Bangladesh, Bhutan, India, Maldives, Nepal, Pakistan and Sri Lanka—have recently organized themselves into the South Asian Association for Regional Co-operation, or SAARC. The region has more than one billion people—mostly uneducated, with low nutritional levels and high mortality rates. While the region has done well in conventional GDP growth terms, its record in human development terms is fairly poor. About 80% of the world's absolute poor live in this region. Why not prepare and implement a human development plan for SAARC for the year 2000? (See chapter 7.)

National development planners could prepare national targets for nutritional levels, literacy, health indicators and population growth, to be endorsed by the annual SAARC summit. International support and financial resources could then be mobilized for a SAARC plan. While the days of the Marshall Plan are long gone, a realistic plan for the human development of more than a billion people is likely to capture the imagination of reluctant legislatures and people in the industrial nations. It will become even more exciting if it is linked with mutually agreed and phased reductions in military expenditures, now exceeding $20 billion a year.

The human dimension of development is not just another addition to the development dialogue. It is an entirely new perspective, a revolutionary way to recast our conventional approach to development. With this transition in thinking, human civilization and democracy may reach yet another milestone. Rather than the residual of development, human beings could finally become its principal object and subject—not a forgotten economic abstraction, but a living, operational reality, not helpless victims or slaves of the very process of development they have unleashed, but its masters. After many decades of development, establishing this supremacy of people in economic development is an exciting challenge. It implies moving towards a new human development paradigm, analysed in the next chapter.

Chapter 2

The Human Development Paradigm

> *"That's very important," the King said, turning to the jury. They were just beginning to write this down on their slates, when the White Rabbit interrupted: "Unimportant, your Majesty means, of course," he said in a very respectful tone, but frowning and making faces at him as he spoke.*
>
> *"Unimportant, of course, I meant," the King hastily said, and went on to himself in an undertone, "important—unimportant—unimportant—important—" as if he were trying which word sounded best.*
>
> — Alice in Wonderland

The rediscovery of human development is not a new invention. It is a tribute to the early leaders of political and economic thought. The idea that social arrangements must be judged by the extent to which they promote "human good" dates at least to Aristotle (384–322 B.C.). He argued that "wealth is evidently not the good we are seeking, for it is merely useful and for the sake of something else." He distinguished a good political arrangement from a bad one by its successes and failures in enabling people to lead "flourishing lives".

Immanuel Kant (1724–1804) continued the tradition of treating human beings as the real end of all activities when he observed: "So act as to treat humanity, whether in their own person or in that of any other, in every case as an end withal, never as means only." And when Adam Smith (1723–90), that apostle of free enterprise and private initiative, showed his concern that economic development should enable a person to mix freely with others without being "ashamed to appear in publick", he was expressing a concept of poverty that went beyond counting calories—a concept that integrated the poor into the mainstream of the community. A similar strain was reflected in the writings of the other founders of modern economic thought, including Robert Malthus, Karl Marx and John Stuart Mill.

After the belated rediscovery of human development, it is necessary to give this paradigm some firmer conceptual, quantitative and policy moorings—here and in the next six chapters.

The basic purpose of development is to enlarge people's choices. In principle, these choices can be infinite and can change over time. People often value achievements that do not show up at all, or not immediately, in income or growth figures: greater access to knowledge, better nutrition and health services, more secure livelihoods, security against crime and physical violence, satisfying leisure hours, political and cultural freedoms and a sense of participation in community activities. The objective of development is to create an enabling environment for people to enjoy long, healthy and creative lives.

Income and human choices

The defining difference between the economic growth and the human development schools is that the first focuses exclusively on the expansion of only one choice—income—while the second embraces the enlargement of all human choices—whether economic, social, cultural or political. It might well be argued that the expansion of income can enlarge all other choices as well. But that is not necessarily so, for a variety of reasons.

To begin with, income may be unevenly distributed within a society. People who have no access to income, or enjoy only limited access, will see their choices fairly constrained. It has often been observed that in many societies, economic growth does not trickle down.

But there is an even more fundamental reason why income expansion may fail to enlarge human options. It has to do with the national priorities chosen by the society or its rulers—guns or butter, an elitist model of development or an egalitarian one, political authoritarianism or political democracy, a command economy or participatory development.

No one will deny that such choices make a critical difference. Yet we often forget that the use of income by a society is just as important as the generation of income itself, or that income expansion leads to much less human satisfaction in a virtual political prison or cultural void than in a more liberal political and economic environment. There is no automatic link between income and human lives—a theme explored at length in the subsequent chapters. Yet there has long been an apparent presumption in economic thought that such an automatic link exists.

It should also be recognized that accumulating wealth may not be necessary for the fulfilment of several kinds of human choice. In fact, individuals and societies make many choices that require no wealth at all. A society does not have to be rich to afford democracy. A family does not have to be wealthy to respect the rights of each member. A nation does not have to be affluent to treat women and men equally. Valuable social and cultural traditions can be—and are—maintained at all levels of income.

Many human choices extend far beyond economic well-being. Knowledge, health, a clean physical environment, political freedom and simple pleasures of life are not exclusively, or largely, dependent on income. National wealth can expand people's choices in these areas. But it might not. The use that people make of their wealth, not the wealth itself, is decisive. And unless societies recognize that their real wealth is their people, an excessive obsession with creating material wealth can obscure the goal of enriching human lives.

The human development paradigm performs an important service in questioning the presumed automatic link between expanding income and expanding human choices. Such a link depends on the quality and distribution of economic growth, not only on the quantity of such growth. A link between growth and human lives has to be created consciously through deliberate public policy—such as public spending on social services and fiscal policy to redistribute income and assets. This link may not exist in the automatic workings of the market-place, which can further marginalize the poor.

But we must be careful. Rejecting an automatic link between income expansion and flourishing human lives is not rejecting growth itself. Economic growth is essential in poor societies for reducing or eliminating poverty. But the quality of this growth is just as important as its quantity. Conscious public policy is needed to translate economic growth into people's lives.

How can that be done? It may require a major restructuring of economic and political power, and the human development paradigm is quite revolutionary in that respect. It questions the existing structure of power. Greater links between economic growth and human choices may require far-reaching land reform, progressive tax systems, new credit systems to bank on the poor people, a major expansion of basic social services to reach all the deprived population, the removal of barriers to the entry of people in economic and political spheres and the equalization of their access to opportunities, and the establishment of temporary social safety nets for those who may be bypassed by the markets or public policy actions. Such policy packages are fairly fundamental and will vary from one country to another. But some features are common to all of them.

First, people are moved to centre stage. Development is analysed and understood in terms of people. Each activity is analysed to see how much people participate in it or benefit from it. The touchstone of the success of development policies becomes the betterment of people's lives, not just the expansion of production processes.

Second, human development is assumed to have two sides. One is the formation of human capabilities—such as improved health, knowledge and skills. The other is the use people make of their acquired capabilities—for employment, productive activities, political affairs or leisure. A society needs to build up human capabilities as well as ensure equitable access to human opportunities. Considerable human frustration results if the scales of human development do not finely balance the two sides.

Third, a careful distinction is maintained between ends and means. People are regarded as the end. But means are not forgotten. The expansion of GNP becomes an essential means for expanding many human options. But the character and distribution of economic growth are measured against the yardstick of enriching the lives of people. Production processes are not treated in an abstract vacuum. They acquire a human context.

Fourth, the human development paradigm embraces all of society—not just the economy. The political, cultural and social factors are given as much attention as the economic factors. In fact, study of the link between the economic and the non-economic environment is one of the most fascinating and rewarding aspects of this new analysis, as subsequent chapters explore (particularly chapter 5).

Fifth, it is recognized that people are both the means and the ends of development. But people are not regarded as mere instruments for producing commodities—through an augmentation of "human capital". It is always remembered that human beings are the ultimate end of development—not convenient fodder for the materialistic machine.

Essential components of human development

There are four essential components in the human development paradigm: equity, sustainability, productivity and empowerment. Each of them needs to be understood in its proper perspective, since they distinguish the human development paradigm from the more traditional economic growth models.

REFLECTIONS ON HUMAN DEVELOPMENT

Equity

If development is to enlarge people's choices, people must enjoy equitable access to opportunities. Development without equity means a restriction of the choices of many individuals in a society. Depending on how inequitable the development process is, it can disenfranchise whole sections of society.

Equity should be understood as equity in opportunities, not necessarily in results. What people do with their opportunities is their own concern: equity in opportunities may not always lead to similar choices or to similar results. In fact, the diversity of outcomes in life demonstrates that equal opportunities often lead to unequal results. Still, equity in access to political and economic opportunities must be regarded as a basic human right in a human development paradigm.

Equal access to opportunities is based on the philosophical foundations of the universalism of life claims of everyone. The human development paradigm values human life for itself. It does not value life merely because people can produce material goods—important though that is. It values life because of its built-in assumption that all individuals must be enabled to develop their human capabilities to the fullest and to put those capabilities to the best use in all areas of their lives.

Equity in access to opportunities demands a fundamental restructuring of power in many societies.

• The distribution of productive assets may need to be changed, especially through land reform.

• The distribution of income may require a major restructuring through progressive fiscal policy, aimed at transferring income from the rich to the poor.

• Credit systems may need an overhaul so that poor people's potential enterprise is regarded as sound collateral and the allocation of bank credit is not guided only by the existing wealth of the affluent.

• Political opportunities may need to be equalized through voting rights reform, campaign finance reform, and other actions aimed at limiting the excessive political power of a feudal minority.

• Social and legal barriers that limit the access of women or of certain minorities or ethnic groups to some of the key economic and political opportunities may have to fall.

Equity is thus a powerful concept that lies at the heart of the human development paradigm. While traditional growth models have sometimes ignored this truth in the past few decades, the basic premise has been valid throughout the ages, and it is firmly enshrined as a central tenet of the human development paradigm.

Sustainability

The next generation deserves the opportunity to enjoy the same well-being that we now enjoy, a right that makes sustainability another essential component of the human development paradigm.

The concept of sustainability is sometimes confused with the renewal of natural resources, which is just one aspect of sustainable development. It is the sustainability of human opportunities that must lie at the centre of our concerns. And that, in essence, means sustaining all forms of capital—physical, human, financial and environmental. Depleting any capital mortgages the chances for sustainable development: it robs future generations of their options. So, the only viable strategy for sustainable development is to replenish and regenerate all forms of capital. In the last analysis, it is human life that must be sustained.

This concept of sustainability does not require preserving every natural resource, species, or environment in its current form. That is environmental Puritanism, and it has little to do with true sustainable development. Technological progress will always create substitutes for natural resources. And if efficient and cost-effective substitutes are available, they must be used to sustain future human choices.

What must be preserved is the capacity to produce a similar level of human well-being—even with a stock of physical, human and natural capital different from that we may have inherited. We do not have to leave the natural world in exactly the shape in which we found it. That challenge, besides being impossible, is not what sustainability means. Sustainability is a dynamic concept that fits our changing world—not a static picture with the world frozen at predetermined states. And it is a matter of distributional equity—of sharing development opportunities between present and future generations and ensuring intragenerational and intergenerational equity in access to opportunities.

The policy implications of such a concept are profound. To begin, sustainability does not mean sustaining present levels of poverty and human deprivation. If the present is miserable and unacceptable to the majority of the world's people, it must be changed before it is sustained. In other words, what must be sustained are worthwhile life opportunities, not human deprivation.

This also means that wide disparities in life styles within and between nations must be re-examined. An unjust world is inherently unsustainable—both politically and economically. We now find that it may be environmentally unsustainable as well. There is no way to stretch the world's natural limits so that all poor nations can enjoy precisely the same energy-intensive consumption life styles that prevail in the rich nations today. Nor is it conceivable that widely different consumption patterns and life styles will continue to prevail in a world that is increasingly drawn together. An adjustment in the consumption and life styles of the rich nations and a major redistribution of the world's income and resources are therefore inevitable—if the requirements of sustainability are to be fully met.

Sustainability is an essential feature of the human development paradigm. It matters little whether the paradigm is labelled "sustainable human development" or "sustainable development" or simply "human development". What is important is to understand that the essence of the human development paradigm is that everyone should have equal access to development opportunities—now and in the future. (Many central issues of sustainable development are discussed further in chapter 6.)

Productivity

An essential part of the human development paradigm is productivity, which requires investments in people and an enabling macroeconomic environment for them to achieve their maximum potential. Economic growth is therefore a subset of human development models—an essential part but not the entire structure.

Many East Asian societies have accelerated their growth through tremendous investments in human capital. In fact, it is difficult to understand how Japan and the Republic of Korea could emerge as the most efficient exporters of steel and steel products, without possessing any iron ore or coal—except in terms of their human productivity.

Most of the development literature has focused on the productivity of human endeavour. Some recent models of development are based primarily on human capital—but this unfortunately treats people only as a means of development. While valid to some extent, it obscures the centrality of people as the ultimate end of development. That is why productivity should be treated only as one part of the human development paradigm—with equal importance given to equity, sustainability and empowerment.

Empowerment

The human development paradigm is neither paternalistic nor based on charity or welfare concepts. Its focus is on development by the people, who must participate in the activities, events and processes that shape their lives.

The worst policy prescription for poor people and poor nations is to place them on permanent charity. Such a strategy is neither consistent with human dignity nor sustainable over time. That is why the human development paradigm envisages full empowerment of the people.

A comprehensive concept, empowerment means that people are in a position to exercise choices of their own free will. It implies a political democracy in which people can influence decisions about their lives. It requires economic liberalism so that people are free from excessive economic controls and regulations. It means decentralization of power so that real governance is brought to the doorstep of every person. It means that all members of civil society, particularly non-governmental organizations, participate fully in making and implementing decisions.

The empowerment of people requires action on several fronts. It requires investing in the education and health of people so that they can take advantage of market opportunities. It requires ensuring an enabling environment that gives everyone access to credit and productive assets so that the playing fields of life are more even. It implies empowering both women and men so that they can compete on an equal footing.

The empowerment of people distinguishes the human development paradigm from other development concepts with which it is normally confused. Requiring investment in people as a prelude to equal access to market opportunities, human development models are not basic needs models, which require only the provision of basic social services, normally by the state. Moreover, the human development paradigm embraces all choices—particularly political, social and cultural—while the basic needs concept is generally limited to economic choices.

A holistic concept

Nor should human welfare concepts or social safety nets or investment in education and health be equated with the human development paradigm, which includes these aspects, but only as parts of the whole. The human development paradigm covers all aspects of development—whether economic growth or international trade, budget deficits or fiscal policy, saving or investment or technology, basic social services or safety nets for the poor. No aspect of the development model falls outside its scope, but the vantage point is the widening of people's choices and the enrichment of their lives. All aspects of life—economic, political or cultural—are viewed from that perspective. Economic growth, as such, becomes only a subset of the human development paradigm.

On some aspects of the human development paradigm, there is fairly broad agreement:

- Development must put people at the centre of its concerns.
- The purpose of development is to enlarge all human choices, not just income.
- The human development paradigm is concerned both with building up human capabilities (through investment in people) and with using those human capabilities fully (through an enabling framework for growth and employment).
- Human development has four essential pillars: equity, sustainability, productivity and empowerment. It regards economic growth as essential but emphasizes the need to pay attention to its quality and distribution, analyses at length its link with human lives and questions its long-term sustainability.
- The human development paradigm defines the ends of development and analyses sensible options for achieving them.

Despite the broad agreement on many of these features, there are several controversies about the human development concept—often stemming from some misunderstanding about the concept itself. Fairly widespread is the mistaken view that human development is antigrowth and that it encompasses only social development.

The human development paradigm consistently takes the view that growth is not the end of economic development—but that the absence of growth often is. Economic growth is essential for human development, but to fully exploit the opportunities for improved well-being that growth offers, it needs to be properly managed. Some countries have been extremely successful in managing their economic growth to improve the human condition, others less so. So, there is no automatic link between economic growth and human progress. And one of the most pertinent policy issues concerns the exact process through which growth translates, or fails to translate, into human development under different development conditions.

There are four ways to create the desirable links between economic growth and human development.

First, emphasis on investment in the education, health and skills of the people can enable them to participate in the growth process as well as to share its benefits, principally through remunerative employment. This is the growth model adopted by China, Hong Kong, Japan, Malaysia, the Republic of Korea, Singapore, Thailand and many other newly industrializing countries.

Second, more equitable distribution of income and assets is critical for creating a close link between economic growth and human development. Wherever the distribution of income and assets is very uneven (as in Brazil, Nigeria and Pakistan), high GNP growth rates have failed to translate into people's lives. The link between distribution of assets and the nature of growth can be:

• Growth-led, with favourable initial conditions in asset distribution and mass education, including the participation of people in economic activities (China, the Republic of Korea).

• Unfavourable initial conditions but high growth with corrective public policy action, including people's participation (Chile, Malaysia).

• Low growth with public policy action to provide basic social services, but normally unsustainable over the long term (Jamaica, Sri Lanka).

Third, some countries have managed to make significant improvements in human development even in the absence of good growth or good distribution. They have achieved this result through well-structured social expenditures by the government. Cuba, Jamaica, Sri Lanka and Zimbabwe, among others, achieved fairly impressive results through the generous state provision of social services. So did many countries in Eastern Europe and the Commonwealth of Independent States (CIS). But such experiments generally are not sustainable unless the economic base expands enough to support the social base.

Fourth, the empowerment of people—particularly women—is a sure way to link growth and human development. In fact, empowerment should accompany all aspects of life. If people can exercise their choices in the political, social and economic spheres, there is a good prospect that growth will be strong, democratic, participatory and durable.

Another misconception—closely related to the alleged antigrowth bias of human development models—is that human development strategies have only social content, no hard economic analysis. The impression has grown that human development strategies are concerned mainly with social development expenditures (particularly in education and health). Some analysts have gone further and confused human development with development only of human resources—that is, social development expenditure aimed at strengthening human capabilities. Others have insisted that human development strategies are concerned only with human welfare aspects—or, even more narrowly, only with basic human needs—and that they have little to say about economic growth, production and consumption, saving and investment, trade and technology, or any other aspect of a macroeconomic framework.

These analysts do scant justice to the basic concept of human development as a holistic development paradigm embracing both ends and means, both productivity and equity, both economic and social development, both material goods and human welfare. At best, their critiques are based on a misunderstanding of the human development paradigm. At worst, they are the products of feeble minds.

The real point of departure of human development strategies is to approach every issue in the traditional growth models from the vantage point of people. Do they participate in economic growth as well as benefit from it? Do they have full access to the opportunities of expanded trade? Are their choices enlarged or narrowed by new technologies? Is economic expansion leading to job-led growth or jobless growth? Are budgets being balanced without unbalancing the lives of future generations? Are "free" markets open to all people? Are we increasing the options only of the present generation or also of the future generations?

None of the economic issues is ignored, but they all are related to the ultimate objective of development: people. And people are analysed not merely as the beneficiaries of economic growth but as the real agents of every change in society—whether economic, political, social or cultural. To establish the supremacy of people in the process of development—as the classical writers always did—is not to denigrate economic growth but to rediscover its real purpose.

It is fair to say that the human development paradigm is the most holistic development model that exists today. It embraces every development issue, including economic growth, social investment, people's empowerment, provision of basic needs and social safety nets, political and cultural freedoms and all other aspects of people's lives. It is neither narrowly technocratic nor overly philosophical. It is a practical reflection of life itself.

Most of the recent elaboration of the human development paradigm has been carried out by the annual *Human Development Report,* which since 1990 has been commissioned by United Nations Development Programme (UNDP) and prepared by an independent team of eminent economists and distinguished social scientists under the guidance of this author. The next chapter describes the advent of this annual report and the gradual evolution of thinking on human development issues.

Chapter 3

The Advent of the Human Development Report

> *"Would you tell me, please, which way I ought to go from here?" said Alice.*
>
> *"That depends a great deal on where you want to get to," said the Cat.*
>
> *"I don't much care where—" said Alice.*
>
> *"Then it doesn't matter which way you go," said the Cat.*
>
> *"—so long as I get somewhere," Alice added as an explanation.*
>
> *"Oh, you're sure to do that," said the Cat, "if you only walk long enough."*
>
> — Alice in Wonderland

*I*n economic science, nothing is ever new, and nothing permanent. Ideas emerge, flourish, wither and die, to be born again a few decades later. Such is the case for ideas about human development.

The founders of economic thought never forgot that the real objective of development was to benefit people—creating wealth was only a means. That is why, in classical economic literature, the preoccupation is with all of society, not just with the economy. Fascination with industrial chimneys and technology did not replace early economists' concern with real people.

After the Second World War, however, an obsession grew with economic growth models and national income accounts. What was important was what could be measured and priced. People as the agents of change and beneficiaries of development were often forgotten. Learned treatises appeared on how to increase production, but little was written on how to enhance human lives. The delinking of ends and means began, with economic science often obsessed with means.

The late 1980s were ripe for a counter-offensive. It was becoming obvious in several countries that human lives were shrivelling even as economic production was expanding. Some societies were achieving fairly satisfactory levels of human welfare even at fairly modest incomes. But no one could miss the signs of considerable human distress in the richest societies—rising crime rates, growing pollution, spreading HIV/AIDS, a weakening social fabric. A high income, by itself, was no defence against human deprivation. Nor did high rates of economic growth automatically translate into improved lives. New questions were being raised about the character, distribution and quality of economic growth.

Other events hastened such questioning. The human costs of structural adjustment programmes in the 1980s, undertaken in many developing countries under the aegis of the IMF and the World Bank, had been extremely harsh. That prompted questions about the human face of adjustment and about whether alternative policy options were available to balance financial budgets while protecting the interests of the weakest and most vulnerable sections of society. Fast-spreading pollution started reminding policy-makers about the external diseconomies of conventional economic growth models. At the same time, the strong forces of democracy started sweeping across many lands—from the communist countries to the developing world—raising new aspirations for people-centred development models.

In this favourable climate, I presented the idea of preparing an annual human development report to the Administrator of the United Nations Development Programme, William Draper III, in the spring of 1989. He readily accepted the basic idea as well as its essential corollary—that such a report should be independent of any formal clearance through the United Nations. We both recognized that only a candid, uninhibited development policy dialogue would serve the interests of the global community.

The first *Human Development Report,* published by Oxford University Press, emerged in May of 1990. Since then, reports have been produced annually. While each report monitored the progress of humanity—particularly through the country rankings in a new Human Development Index (chapter 4)—each also took up a new policy issue and explored it in depth. This chapter recapitulates the main messages of each report, and then analyses their policy impact and the healthy controversies they have generated in many fields.

1990: Concept and measurement

Concern with human development seems to be moving to centre stage in the 1990s. For too long, the recurrent question was, how much is a nation producing? Increasingly, the question now being asked is, how are its people faring? The main reason for this shift is the growing recognition that the real objective of development is to enlarge people's options. Income is only one of those options—and an extremely important one—but it is not the sum-total of human life. Health, education, physical environment and freedom—to name a few other human choices—may be just as important as income.

Human Development Report 1990, launched in London on 24 May 1990, addressed some of these concerns and explored the relationship between economic growth and human development. It challenged some of the conventional wisdom, exploded some of the old myths and reached some important policy conclusions that have significant implications for development strategies for the next decade.

First, it is wrong to suggest that the development process has failed in most developing countries in the past three decades. Judged by real indicators of human development, it has succeeded spectacularly. Average life expectancy has increased by 16 years, adult literacy by 40% and per capita nutritional levels by more than 20%, and child mortality rates have been halved. In fact, developing countries have achieved in the past 30 years the kind of real human progress that industrial countries took nearly a century to accomplish. While the income gap between North and South is still very large—with the average income of the South 6% of that in the North—the human gaps have been closing fast. Average life expectancy in the South is 80% of the northern average, adult literacy 66% and nutrition 85%.

True, the record of the developing world is uneven, with disparities between regions and countries and even within countries. And true, there is still a large unfinished agenda of human development—with one-fourth of the people in developing countries still deprived of basic human necessities, minimum incomes and decent social services. But the overall policy conclusion is that the development process does work, that international development cooperation has made a difference, that the remaining agenda of human development is manageable in the 1990s if development priorities are properly chosen. This certainly is a message of hope, though not of complacency.

Second, it is wrong to suggest that economic growth is unnecessary for human development. No sustained improvement in human well-being is possible without growth. But it is also wrong to suggest that high economic growth rates will automatically translate into higher levels of human development. They may or they may not. It all depends on the policy choices that countries make. And the real world offers too many uncomfortable examples of a wide divergence between income and human development levels. Adult literacy in Saudi Arabia is lower than that in Sri Lanka despite a per capita income that is 16 times higher. Infant mortality in Jamaica is one-fourth that in Brazil, despite Jamaica's per capita income being half that of Brazil. Life expectancy is 76 years in Costa Rica, with a per capita income of $1,870, but only 69 years in Oman, with a per capita income of $6,140.

Why such wide divergences between income and human development? The explanation lies in how equitably—or inequitably—income, physical assets, financial credit, social services and job opportunities are distributed. If income and human development are to be linked more closely, countries must adopt policies that distribute these economic assets and opportunities more equitably.

Third, it is conceptually and practically wrong to regard poverty alleviation as a goal distinct from human development. Most poverty can be explained by inadequate access to income, assets, credit, social services and job opportunities. The only long-term remedy is to invest in poor people, particularly in their education and training, and to bring them back into the mainstream of development. Poverty should not be regarded as a residual of economic growth, treated separately without modifying the growth strategies. Such an approach is inconsistent with human development strategies—which are focused on investment in all the people and on their full participation in human well-being.

Fourth, it is wrong to suggest that developing countries lack enough resources to address their human development goals. In reality, considerable potential exists for restructuring present priorities in their national budgets and in foreign assistance allocations. Many poor countries spend two to three times more on their military than on the education and health of their people. Overall, Third World military spending increased by $10 billion to $15 billion a year during the 1980s, showing the scope for diversion of resources if new concepts of security evolve in the 1990s. There also is considerable scope for saving by reducing inefficient spending on parastatals, subsidies to the richer sections of society and inappropriate priorities in the development budgets.

In bilateral foreign assistance, the share for education and health has declined from 17% to 10% over the past decade, suggesting room for improving aid allocation. Considerable scope also exists for restructuring internal and external debt. So, the potential for restructuring existing priorities is enormous. The scope for reallocating budgetary expenditure opens to serious question the human and social costs of structural adjustment programmes. Most budgets can be balanced without unbalancing the lives of future generations. And that is why aid donors must re-examine policy conditionality: they must insist that human investment will be the last item to be touched in a budget, and only when all other options have been explored and exhausted.

Fifth, it is wrong to pretend that markets alone can deliver balanced patterns of economic growth and human development. Instead, there must be a judicious mix of market efficiency and social compassion. The present situation in many developing countries is topsy-turvy. Governments are intervening inefficiently in productive processes in agriculture and industry, where they hardly belong, but spending inadequately (3–4% of GNP) on social services, which should be their primary responsibility. This situation needs to be reversed. Also necessary is to ensure that social safety nets are not seriously eroded in periods of rapid growth or social transformation. Otherwise, serious political upheavals may disrupt the development process.

The challenge now is to ensure that human development is at the forefront of growth strategies in the decade ahead. The suggested agenda for the 1990s:

- Persuading the developing countries to prepare their own human development goals for the 1990s and to integrate these goals in their overall growth models and investment budgets.
- Assisting developing countries in collecting better data on human development indicators and in undertaking more professional analysis of the link between their economic growth and human development.
- Analysing the impact of specific projects and programmes on people, not only on production.
- Incorporating human development concerns in aid allocations and policy conditionality.

The 1990s offer an exciting challenge to move from new ideas to concrete action and to treat human beings, once again, as both the means and the end of development.

1991: Financing human development

Human Development Report 1991, launched in Washington, D.C., on 23 May 1991, reached the conclusion that restructuring existing budgets can provide enough resources to finance basic social services for all the people. It is the lack of political courage to make tough decisions, rather than the paucity of financial resources, that is responsible for the current state of human neglect. There are far too many examples of wasted resources and wasted opportunities: rising military expenditures, inefficient public enterprises, numerous prestige projects, growing capital flight and extensive corruption. If priorities are recast, most budgets can accommodate more spending for human development. As much as $50 billion a year can be found in developing countries for urgent human concerns, just by changing government spending patterns.

More funds for human development can be found by taking four actions:

• *Halting capital flight*—Capital flight from the Philippines was equal to 80% of its outstanding debt between 1962 and 1986.

• *Combating corruption*—In Pakistan, public officials' illegitimate private gain from their positions is unofficially estimated at 4% of GNP.

• *Reforming public enterprises*—The losses public enterprises suffer in Cameroon, for example, exceed the country's total oil revenue.

• *Restructuring debt payments*—Debt repayments take a large share of government budgets. Jordan devotes 39% of its budget to external debt service and 18% to social services. Internal debt now exceeds external debt for many countries—including India, Malaysia, Pakistan, the Philippines and Singapore.

Four ratios could serve as the principal guide to public spending policy: the public expenditure ratio (the percentage of national income that goes into public expenditure earmarked for social services); the social allocation ratio (the percentage of public expenditure earmarked for social services); the social priority ratio (the percentage of social expenditure devoted to human priority concerns); and the human expenditure ratio (the percentage of national income devoted to human priority concerns, obtained by multiplying the first three ratios).

These ratios tell volumes about a country's priorities. Argentina spent 41% of its GNP through its government budget in 1988, yet its human expenditure ratio was only 2.3%. So Argentina realized that it could reduce public spending, release more resources for private investment and economic growth and yet substantially increase spending on human priority concerns—a course it is currently embarked on.

The report came to these conclusions:

• The human expenditure ratio may need to be at least 5% of GNP if a country wishes to do well on human development.

• An efficient way to achieve this result is to keep the public expenditure ratio moderate (around 25%), to allocate much of this expenditure to the social sectors (more than 40%) and to focus on the social priority areas (giving them more than 50%).

• Government spending need not be high if GNP growth is high and rather equitable—or if private and non-governmental organizations (NGOs) are extremely active in the social sectors.

- High government spending with low social priorities is the worst case. If more than 25–35% of national income is channelled through the government budget, and yet less than 2% of GNP goes to human priority concerns (as in Brazil, Sierra Leone and Thailand in 1988), this is the worst of all possible worlds. The public sector is huge, yet the majority of the people do not gain.

- Most countries could use existing resources more efficiently— by adopting more decentralized, participatory approaches to development, by making prudent economies and reducing unit costs, by charging many users for the benefits they receive and by encouraging private initiative in the financing and delivery of social services.

Many developing countries spend more than 25% of their GNP through their government budgets. But their expenditure on human priority goals—basic education, primary health care, rural water supply, family planning, food subsidies, social security—is generally less than one-tenth of their total public spending. And only a twelfth of total aid is earmarked for human priority goals, showing the potential for releasing more resources for human development by restructuring priorities in aid budgets. If only one-third of today's aid were committed to human priority areas, the aid allocation to these areas would increase fourfold.

The plea for greater efficiency should not be confused with indifference to economic growth or to the mobilization of additional resources. In fact, additional resources are needed, because all the essential human goals for the 1990s cannot be financed without more money. But the best argument for mobilizing more resources is to spend existing resources well. Because today's distribution of resources usually suits those in power and their influential supporters, a workable political strategy is needed to restructure resource allocation priorities. The elements of such a strategy: empowering weaker groups, channelling credit to the poor, building coalitions based on common interests, compensating powerful groups and coordinating external pressures.

1992: International dimensions of human development

The central thesis of *Human Development Report 1992,* launched in Stockholm on 23 April 1992, is that the search for equitable access to market opportunities must extend beyond national borders to the global system. Otherwise, economic disparities between the richest and the poorest people, having doubled over the past three decades, are likely to explode. The income of the richest billion people is 150 times that of the poorest billion, a dangerously large gap. To put this in perspective, the income disparity between the richest 20% and the poorest 20% of people within nations is far smaller—the income of the richest fifth is five times higher in Sweden, six times higher in Germany, nine times higher in the United States and 32 times higher (the highest) in Brazil. What would be considered politically and socially unacceptable within nations is being quietly tolerated at the global level.

No end appears to be in sight for these widening gaps—since the gaps are not only in current levels of income but also in future market opportunities and in human development. The bottom 20% of the world's population receives only 1.4% of global GNP—and has a share of only 1% in global trade, 0.2% in global commercial lending and 1.3% in global investment. Because of the barriers to the movement of goods and people and because poor nations pay four times higher real interest rates than do the rich, global markets deny as much as $500 billion of market opportunities to poor nations and poor people every year—which is ten times the foreign assistance that poor nations receive. Precision in these numbers is not important. What is important is that the cost of denied market opportunities far exceeds foreign assistance. It is certainly better for the poor to earn their living than to receive indefinite and uncertain international charity. But unless their access to market opportunities is increased, there is little chance for poor people or poor nations to break out of their poverty trap.

The situation looks even more difficult after adding the widening disparities in higher education, technology and information systems to the picture. The tertiary enrolment rate in the South is only a fifth that in the North, research and development expenditure only 4% and scientific and technical personnel only a ninth. These widening human gaps have a telling impact in a world where technological progress accounts for one-third to one-half of the increases in national output. The combination of technological disparities and limited market opportunities can be devastating.

What can be done? The primary responsibility lies with the developing countries, for global reforms can never substitute for national reforms. The developing countries must improve their economic management, liberate their private initiative and invest in the education of their people and in the technological progress of their societies. The basis for such a further advance has already been laid by the rapid strides in basic education and primary health care in most developing countries. Japan, the Republic of Korea, Singapore and, more recently, China, Malaysia and Thailand have followed this human investment path to development. They made spectacular increases in their share of global markets. East and South-East Asia doubled their share of world trade between 1970 and 1990, as did China. But Sub-Saharan Africa, with minimal investments in human development, had its share in world trade plummet to a fourth of the 1970 level.

A fatal contradiction afflicts the global economic system. As national markets open up—from New Delhi to Rio, from Moscow to Warsaw—can global markets close down further? That is precisely what is happening. The OECD nations have become more protectionist in the past decade, just when additional export surpluses are likely to emerge from the liberalizing markets of developing countries and the former socialist bloc. For example, if India follows the path of the Republic of Korea, it will have at least $60 billion of additional exports to offer the world markets each year.

It does not take a genius to figure out that the ongoing, rapid structural adjustment in the South and in the former socialist bloc has a logical corollary—a structural change in the North. Yet this simple truth is being largely ignored—sometimes even bitterly contested. Buffeted by recession and unemployment, many northern economies are unprepared to invest in changing their production and job structures, not recognizing that their lack of adjustment will greatly frustrate the liberal market experiments they are so actively encouraging all over the world.

Many of the poorest nations, particularly in Africa, cannot even begin to fully make use of market opportunities without additional financial help. Market efficiency must be balanced by social equity. Even in the market economies of the United States and the United Kingdom, about 15% of GNP is recycled in medicare, food stamps, unemployment benefits and social security payments. In the Nordic countries, the social safety nets consume roughly a third of GNP. But what about the developing world, where 1.2 billion people barely survive below an absolute poverty line of about $400? The rich nations can spare only 0.3% of GNP for official development assistance, the closest approximation to an international social safety net. This, with about 100 million people below the official poverty line of around $5,000 in income a year.

Even more relevant than the inadequacy and unpredictability of such a social safety net is whether it catches the most deserving people. Twice as much aid per capita goes to high military spenders in the developing world than to more moderate military spenders. Only a quarter of official development assistance is earmarked for the ten countries containing three-fourths of the world's absolute poor. India, Pakistan and Bangladesh have nearly one-half of the world's poor but get only one-

REFLECTIONS ON HUMAN DEVELOPMENT

tenth of total aid. Less than 7% of global aid is spent on human priority concerns of basic education, primary health care, family planning, safe drinking water and nutritional programmes. Even mighty international institutions like the World Bank and the IMF now take more money from the developing world than they put in, adding to the reverse transfer of around $50 billion a year to the commercial banks.

Much of today's pattern of development cooperation was shaped by the anxieties of the cold war, and the link with global poverty or human development is far from clear. A new framework of development cooperation is needed, one focused more directly on people.

Who can persuade the rich nations that it is in their interest to open their markets, to design a people-centred framework for development cooperation and to prepare their economic systems for a structural change? International institutions of global governance—supposedly with an international reach—are often confined to influence only in poor nations. The IMF's structural adjustment programmes are enforced only in the developing world—which accounts for less than 10% of global liquidity. And as little as 7% of global trade conforms to the GATT rules— since textiles, agriculture, tropical products, services, intellectual property and trade-related investment flows are all outside the GATT's purview and awaiting the ratification of the Uruguay Round of Multilateral Trade Negotiations. The global institutions, so charitably described as the international economic system, are hardly global. To make these institutions truly global in their reach, in their policy frameworks and in their management structures, an Economic Security Council within the United Nations is proposed as a manageable forum for global economic policy coordination.

For the global institutions to become truly global will take time. What about now? What pressures are there for both North and South to move toward equitable access to global markets, to people-centred development cooperation and to structural changes in their economies? For the North, pressure could derive from a combination of hope and fear—a mixture of self-interest and leadership. The high cost of protectionism must be explained to the people. Consumers in the United States pay $70 billion a year more in higher prices for protected goods. There is one hopeful sign: global military spending has been declining since 1987. Still missing, however, is a clear link between reduced military spending and greater attention to the neglected national and global human agendas. A part of the peace dividend could be invested in worker training and in technological development to prepare the northern societies for the future.

Fear may prove to be an even greater motivating force than hope. Fear of international migration of people—as people begin to travel towards opportunities when opportunities fail to travel towards them. Or fear of the migration of poverty—since poverty respects no international frontiers. Or fear of global pollution and the growing threats to common survival. It may not be possible to make the world environmentally safe for anyone unless it is made safe for everyone. The global environment is closely linked to global poverty.

For the South, the sterile dialogue of the 1970s must give way to a more enlightened dialogue on new patterns of development cooperation in a changing world—mutual interests, not unilateral concessions; two-sided responsibility, not one-sided accusations; more equitable access to global opportunities, not massive transfers of financial resources; more open markets, not more managed markets. Yes, there should be pressure for developing countries to reduce their military expenditures. But there should be a similar pressure at the global level to replace military assistance by economic assistance, phase out military bases, restrain arms shipments and eliminate export subsidies for defence industries. And yes, more attention should go to reducing corruption in developing countries. But there should be as much accountability for the multinational corporations that bribe officials and for the banks that park the illegal gains of corruption—accountability tracked by a new NGO, perhaps an Honesty International.

1993: People's participation

Across the globe, people are uniting in a common struggle: to participate freely in the events and processes that shape their lives. From Russia to Poland, from the Republic of Korea to Brazil, from the turbulent slums of Los Angeles to the restless ghettos of Johannesburg, the forces of people's participation are gathering momentum. These forces, constrained neither by time nor by tradition, respect no geographical boundaries or ideological frontiers. They are the messengers of a new age—an age of people's participation—and the central theme of *Human Development Report 1993,* launched in New Delhi on 25 May 1993.

Despite the impatient urge for people's participation, too many barriers still block the way. Our world is still a world of difference.

• It is a world where more than a billion people still languish in absolute poverty—surviving at the bare margins of existence, below any common concept of human dignity.

• It is a world that calmly tolerates a huge global income disparity, with the top one billion people receiving 150 times more income than the bottom one billion, even as disparities only a tenth as large within nations are leading to convulsions in many countries.

• It is a world where women still earn only half as much as men—and despite casting about half the votes, secure less than 10% of the representation in parliaments.

• It is a world where many ethnic minorities still live like a separate nation within their countries, creating tremendous potential for ethnic explosions. Despite commendable efforts at national integration in the United States, the country's whites rank number 1 in the world in the Human Development Index—ahead of all nations—while its blacks rank only number 31, behind Trinidad and Tobago.

Few people have the opportunity to participate fully in the economic and political lives of their nations. And the dangerous potential for human strife that often emerges from the irresistible urge for people's participation clashing with inflexible systems must be recognized.

Needed today is a fundamental change in the management of economic and political systems—from markets to governance to institutions of civil society.

Today's markets are marvels of technology, and open markets are often the best guarantee for unleashing human creativity. But not enough people benefit from the opportunities that markets normally create. Insufficient human investment may mean that many people enter the market at a considerable disadvantage. With literacy rates below 50% in South Asia and Sub-Saharan Africa, about a billion people lack even the basic education and skills to take advantage of market opportunities. The very poverty of many people makes them uncreditworthy—and the same goes for nations. Paradoxically, where the need for credit is the greatest, the market creditworthiness may be the lowest. In Kenya, less than 5% of institutional credit goes to the informal sector. And the bottom 20% of the world's population receives only 0.2% of global commercial credit. People enter the markets with unequal endowments and naturally leave the markets with unequal rewards. It should come as no surprise that the playing fields of life are uneven.

Policy actions must be taken to ensure that people participate fully in the operations of markets and share equitably in their benefits. Markets must be made people-friendly. This is where the state comes in—not to replace markets but to enable more people to share market opportunities. The state has a major role in levelling the playing field—by improving the access of all people to human resource investments, productive assets, credit facilities, information flows and physical infrastructure. The state also has to serve as a referee—correcting the price signals and the incentive system, disallowing the exploitation of future generations for present gains (as in the case of the environment) and protecting the legitimate interests of producers, consumers, workers and vulnerable groups in society. In addition, the state must extend a social safety net to the victims of the market-place for temporary periods—to enable them to get back into the market to take advantage of its full opportunities.

The presumption of a conflict between the state and the market is thus false—and dangerous. People must be empowered to guide both the state and the market—to serve the interests of the people.

That is all the more necessary in a period in which markets fail to create enough jobs and not all people are participating in productive market opportunities, even in industrial nations. Witness the new and disturbing phenomenon: jobless growth. Output is increasing, but jobs are lagging way behind. In Germany, the output index increased from 100 in 1960 to 268 in 1987, but the employment index fell from 100 to 91. In developing countries, the increase in employment has been proceeding at about half the rate of increase in output in the past three decades. The great strides in human productivity—thanks to automation and new technological innovations—are to be cheered. But not enough people are participating in this productivity growth. Rising unemployment not only denies income opportunities—it strips away human dignity. And merely expanding unemployment benefits is not the solution to this disturbing phenomenon of jobless growth.

Developing countries are experiencing double-digit unemployment rates. They need to create one billion new jobs in the 1990s to stay abreast of increases in the labour force and to absorb the reservoir of unemployed workers. They need to learn from the experience of Japan and the industrializing tigers of East Asia and to experiment with new employment strategies. These strategies should stress massive investment in education, skills and training. They should also stress the restructuring of the credit system to make it accessible to the majority of the people and the establishment of more open, people-friendly markets. And they should stress government support to small-scale enterprises and the informal sector, greater fiscal incentives for labour-intensive technologies, and employment safety nets in areas and periods of severe unemployment. It would be folly for the state to displace markets in the name of fancy employment generation schemes. But it would also be a folly to fail to take the policy actions necessary to open market opportunities to increasing numbers of people—particularly investing vigorously in education, skills and infrastructure and opening the credit system to more people.

The industrial nations face even more fundamental dilemmas. Reduced working hours, innovative proposals for work-sharing and redefined concepts of work are all on the policy agenda. These nations may have to consider whether it is better for most people to work five days a week—to support some people on unemployment benefits—or for all people to work, say, four days a week. People's participation in these decisions may create new norms of work and employment.

At the same time, new patterns of national and global governance are needed to accommodate the rising aspirations of the people. The nation-state is already under pressure. It is too small for the big things, and too big for the small. Only meaningful decentralization can take decision-making closer to the people. But new patterns of global governance must be designed for an increasingly interdependent world.

Most developing countries are overcentralized. On average, less than 10% of their budgetary spending is delegated to local levels, compared with more than 25% in industrial nations. Even foreign aid has a centralizing influence. Most decision-making is kept in the hands of a small, central elite. These patterns of governance are inappropriate in societies that have considerable ethnic and cultural diversity and where people increasingly resist dictates from above. What may save these societies from internal explosions is a sweeping decentralization of decision-making powers and faster movement towards economic and political democracy. Unless this is done before people begin to agitate for their rights, the change may come too late and prove too disruptive.

Democracy is rarely so obliging as to stop at national borders. The gathering forces of participation are likely to affect all institutions of global governance. They may lead to more democratic decision-making in the World Bank and the IMF and to a strengthened socio-economic role for the UN system. The new demands are for the security of people, not just for the security of nation-states. And the new conflicts are increasingly between people, rather than between nations—as in Somalia, Bosnia, Cambodia, Angola and Sri Lanka. Soldiers in uniform—even when in blue berets—are only a poor short-term response to these emerging crises. Needed instead are new participatory socio-economic processes. To play a greater role in this area, the UN system needs a new socio-economic mandate, vastly increased financial resources, and a manageable decision-making forum—maybe an

Economic Security Council—to meet the new demands of preventive diplomacy and human security.

Although the forces of people's participation demand new structures for markets and the state, they can find their ultimate fulfilment only in the institutions of a civil society that enable people to take control of their own lives. Rule of law, freedom of expression, non-governmental organizations and other community associations are an integral part of such a civil society. NGOs in particular have become very important in recent years, especially in their advocacy of such emerging policy concerns as the environment, women's development, ethnic protection and human rights. Often, people are ahead of their governments—and by organizing themselves, they can bend their governments to the popular will, particularly in a democratic framework in which politicians are sensitive to every shift in public opinion.

There has been an explosion in the number of NGOs in the past decade, with more than 50,000 major NGOs reaching more than 250 million people and channelling more than $5 billion of aid funds a year to the developing countries. But the role of NGOs must be put in its proper perspective. Although they create the necessary pressure for new policy directions and often supplement government action, they can never replace it. The scale and impact of even the most successful of NGOs are surprisingly limited. For instance, the Grameen Bank in Bangladesh—one of the internationally renowned NGOs providing credit to the poor—accounts for only 0.1% of total national credit. The major achievements of NGOs lie in generating new policy pressure for change, in organizing the weak and the vulnerable and in designing innovative ways of reaching the people in a cost-effective manner.

In sum: people's participation is a powerful and overarching concept. It must inspire a search for a people-centred world order built on five new pillars:

• New concepts of human security that stress the security of people, not only of nations.

• New strategies of sustainable human development that weave development around people, not people around development.

• New partnerships between the state and the market, to combine market efficiency with social compassion.

• New patterns of national and global governance, to accommodate the rising tide of democracy and the steady decline of the nation-state.

- New forms of international cooperation, to focus assistance directly on the needs of the people rather than only on the preferences of governments.

The rising tide of people's participation must be channelled into the foundation for a new human society—where people finally take charge of their own destiny.

1994: Human security

Human Development Report 1994, launched in Copenhagen on 1 June 1994, underscored the new imperatives of human security in the post–cold war era. Security is now increasingly interpreted as the security of people in their daily lives—in their homes, in their jobs, in their streets, in their communities and in their environment.

Many perceptions have to change. Human security must be regarded as universal, global and indivisible. Just imagine for a moment that every drug that quietly kills, every disease that silently travels, every form of pollution that roams the globe and every act of senseless terrorism all carried a national label of origin, much as traded goods do. That would bring sudden realization that human security concerns today are more global than even global trade.

A second perception must change: it must be recognized that poverty cannot be stopped at national borders. Poor people may be stopped. But not the tragic consequences of their poverty: drugs, AIDS, pollution and terrorism. When people travel, they bring much dynamism and creativity with them. But when only their poverty travels, it brings nothing but human misery.

One more perception must change: it must be seen that it is easier, more humane, and less costly to deal with the new issues of human security upstream rather than downstream. Did it make sense in the past decade to incur the staggering cost of $240 billion for HIV/AIDS treatment when investing even a small fraction of that amount in primary health care and family planning education might have prevented such a fast spread of this deadly disease? Is it a great tribute to international diplomacy to spend $2 billion in a single year on soldiers in Somalia to deliver humanitarian assistance when investing the same amount much earlier in increased domestic food production and social development might have averted the final human tragedy—not just for one year, but for a long time to come? Is it a reflection of human ingenuity to spend hundreds of billions of dollars on administrative control of drug trafficking and on the rehabilitation of drug addicts but not even a small part

of that amount for drug education of consumers or alternative livelihoods for producers?

It is time to fashion a new concept of human security that is reflected
not in better weapons for countries but in better lives for people.
Countries that have ignored the security of their people could not protect even the security of their nations. In 1980, Iraq, Somalia and
Nicaragua had the highest ratios of military to social spending. By the
1990s, these countries were beginning to disintegrate. By contrast,
Costa Rica invested one-third of its national income in the education,
health and nutrition of its people and nothing in the army that it had abolished in 1948. Any wonder that Costa Rica survived as the only pros-
pering democracy in the inflamed Central America of the past few
decades?

The emerging concept of human security will lead to many fundamental changes in thinking.

First, new models of human development will treat GNP growth as
a means, not as an end; enhance human life, not marginalize it; replenish natural resources, not run them down; and encourage grass-roots
participation of people in the events and processes that shape their lives.
The real issue is not just the level of economic growth, but its character
and distribution. Those who postulate a fundamental conflict between
economic growth and human development do no service to the poor
nations. To address poverty, economic growth is not an option, it is an
imperative. But what type of growth? Who participates in it? And who
derives the benefits? These are the real issues.

For a long time, it was quietly assumed that high levels of economic
growth would automatically translate into high levels of human development. But that does not neccessarily happen, so there is no automatic
link between economic growth and human lives. The practical experience of many nations demonstrates this reality. Sri Lanka and Guinea
show exactly the same GNP per capita: $500. But they display stark con-
trasts in the quality of life in their societies. Life expectancy is 71 years
in Sri Lanka, only 44 years in Guinea. Adult literacy is 89% in Sri Lanka,
only 27% in Guinea. Infant mortality is 24 per thousand in Sri Lanka and
135 in Guinea. It is not just the level of income that matters. It is how
society spends that income. Also important are the many choices that
human beings make—particularly in social, cultural and political
areas—that may be largely independent of their income. The quality of
growth is more important than quantity.

The emerging concept of sustainable human development is based
on equal access to development opportunities, for present and for future

generations. The heart of this concept is equity—in access to opportunities, not necessarily in results. What people do with their opportunities is their concern. But they should not be denied an equal opportunity to develop and to use their human capabilities. We must acknowledge the universalism of life claims for every individual.

The concept of sustainable human development focuses attention not only on the future generations but also on the present ones. It would be immoral to sustain the present levels of poverty. Development patterns that perpetuate today's inequities are neither sustainable nor worth sustaining. Indeed, an unjust world is inherently unsustainable. A major restructuring of the world's income and consumption patterns—especially a fundamental change in the current life styles of the rich nations—may be a necessary precondition for any viable strategy of sustainable human development.

Second, a new framework of development cooperation must be based on global compacts among nations, not on charity. Foreign assistance must emerge from the shadows of the cold war. Even today, foreign aid is more often linked to strategic alliances from the past than to any specific global objectives for the future—from poverty reduction to human development, from slowing population growth to improving the physical environment. Only one-third of official development assistance is earmarked for the ten countries containing two-thirds of the world's absolute poor. Twice as much ODA per capita goes to the richest 40% in the developing world as to the poorest 40%. Less than 7% of bilateral ODA goes to the human priority concerns of primary health care, basic education, safe drinking water, nutrition programmes and family planning services. So, enormous scope still exists to get much more policy mileage and much better allocations from existing aid funds.

At the same time, the concept of development cooperation must be broadened to include all development flows—including trade, investment, technology and labour. It is simply unacceptable that while aid transfers so few resources to the developing world, several times more is taken away through trade protection, immigration barriers and an increasing debt burden. In such a situation, it is critical for poor nations to bargain for more equitable access to global market opportunities.

The 1994 report outlined a new design for development cooperation in the coming decades:

- Aid is regarded as an essential investment by the rich nations in their own human security.
- Developing countries are compensated for trade and immigration barriers imposed by the rich nations.

- Polluting nations are made to pay for their overuse of the global commons.

- The potential peace dividend of nearly $500 billion between 1995 and 2000 is earmarked primarily for the priority human development agenda.

- Global compacts are negotiated in specific areas—population, environment, drug control—between rich and poor nations based on two-way cooperation, not on one-way conditionality or coercion.

Third, the new imperatives of global human security demand an entirely new system of global governance—particularly a greatly strengthened role of the United Nations in development. The nature of conflicts has changed dramatically. Of the 82 conflicts in the early 1990s causing more than a thousand deaths, 79 were within—not between—nations. Many developing countries are already heading towards social disintegration, and behind every failed state, there lies a long trail of failed development or unacceptably high socio-economic disparities. These countries require preventive development, not more weapons of war. The United Nations should be enabled to play a more significant role in social and human development of these poor nations. Only by designing an early warning system and by undertaking upstream preventive development can the United Nations help these nations avert a national collapse. It can no longer fight the battles of tomorrow with the weapons of yesterday.

In this context, the 1994 report offered at least six concrete proposals for consideration by the global community:

- A world social charter, to arrive at a new social contract among all nations and all people.

- A 3% annual reduction in global military spending, with 20% of the savings by rich nations and 10% of those by poor nations earmarked for global human security.

- A 20:20 compact for human development—to provide basic education, primary health care, safe drinking water and essential family planning services to all people over the next decade, by earmarking 20% of existing developing country budgets and 20% of existing aid allocations to these basic human priority concerns.

- A global human security fund—financed from such global taxes as the "Tobin tax" on speculative movements of international funds, an international tax on the consumption of non-renewable energy, global environmental permits and a tax on arms trade.

- A new framework of development cooperation, in which developing and industrial countries would graduate from their present aid relationship to a more mature development partnership—by including trade, technology, investment and labour flows in a broader design to be negotiated among nations.

• An Economic Security Council in the United Nations, as the highest decision-making forum to consider basic issues of human security—such as global poverty, unemployment, food security, drug trafficking, global pollution, international migration and a new framework of sustainable human development.

These proposals demand much from the international community—but they are feasible. What is more, they are urgently needed if we are to design a new architecture of peace through development in the 21st century.

A final observation. The world has seen more hopeful changes in the past decade than ever before—from the collapse of communism to the fall of the Berlin Wall, from the end of apartheid in South Africa to a dim outline of peace in occupied Palestine. This is the time to build a new edifice of human security throughout the world.

Since its birth in San Francisco 50 years ago, the United Nations has committed itself to the first pillar of global security—to freedom from fear, to territorial security, to peace between nations. Can a "second birth" of the United Nations be engineered at the time of its 50th anniversary, giving rise to a United Nations committed to the second pillar of human security—to freedom from want, to socio-economic development, to peace within nations? That is the supreme challenge. And the 1994 report is a modest attempt to respond to that challenge.

Impact of the *Human Development Report*

The impact of the *Human Development Report* on the global policy dialogue has exceeded expectations. More than 100,000 copies of the report now circulate in 13 languages. The report has been prescribed as a text in most leading universities—a tribute to its professional quality. In five years, it has become one of the most influential reports—not only for governments, donors and international institutions but even more so for the grass-roots movements, media and institutions of civil society. Many commentators describe it as one of the most eagerly awaited reports of the year.

This response is rather unusual for a report from the UN system. What has made the *Human Development Report* an invaluable addition to the global policy dialogue is its intellectual independence and its professional integrity—its courage more than its analysis. It has not hesitated to present unpleasant facts in a fairly blunt fashion. It has chosen to identify specific country experiences—both successes and failures—rather than to bury them in vague generalizations. It has quantified social progress—and even attempted for a brief period to rank countries by political freedom. It has ventured into many areas where international dialogue had remained somewhat muted—from the high human costs of military spending to the new imperatives of human security, from lack of a clear link between ODA allocations and global policy objectives to the corruption and waste in many societies.

Controversies have accompanied the report from its inception. This was inevitable. Most governments and their representatives abroad do not like to be criticized in international reports. What irks them even more is when NGOs and the media take up the issues in the report and generate pressure for change on their own governments. The tendency for many governments has been to go after the messengers rather than to listen to the message. It is a tribute to the *Human Development Report* that it has withstood such onslaughts year after year.

What is the real impact of the *Human Development Report*? First, the report has greatly influenced the global search for new development paradigms. It is now broadly accepted that economic growth does not automatically translate into a better quality of life. For that to happen, policies must be initiated to ensure a more equitable distribution of growth as well as to change the very pattern of growth in response to people's aspirations. It is also recognized that development opportunities must be created not only for the present generations but for the future generations, by making growth models responsive to the need to regenerate natural capital. No debate is complete today without reference to people-centred, environmentally sound development strategies—irrespective of the precise label given to such strategies. What is more, one can detect some accommodating gestures coming out of the citadels of economic growth—the World Bank and the IMF—though how far this conversion to human development is real rather than rhetorical has yet to be seen.

Second, the *Human Development Report* has helped launch many new policy proposals. For instance, the report has focused on the human costs of military spending, especially in poor nations, and made concrete proposals for reaping a peace dividend by investing in people rather than in arms. The report has also documented the great potential for restructuring existing budgets, the basis of the 20:20 global compact (chapter 15). The report has suggested several innovations in global governance—including the setting up of an Economic Security Council within the United Nations to deal with global socio-economic issues (chapter 16) and an international NGO, Honesty International, to monitor corruption. *Human Development Report 1994* was the first attempt to identify a concrete agenda for the World Summit on Social Development.

Third, the real impact of the report can be seen in the human development strategies that many developing countries have begun to formulate. Several countries have taken major steps on the road to formulating and implementing their own long-term human development plans: for example, Bangladesh, Bhutan, Bolivia, Botswana, Cameroon, Colombia, Egypt, Ghana, Malawi, Nepal, Pakistan, the Philippines, Tunisia and Turkey. Many others are beginning to take concrete action to move towards human development programmes. UNDP technical assistance has supported these exercises, but real leadership has emerged within the developing countries—and the new strategies are fully owned by the implementing nations themselves.

Fourth, one of the most influential devices—though also one of the most controversial—has been the Human Development Index and the ranking of countries by this index. The index—particularly in its disaggregated form—holds a mirror up to all societies so that policy-makers can see how the people in their societies live and breathe and where the key tension points are for urgent attention. In order to better understand the index, we need to trace its birth and its influence in international policy dialogue, the subject of the next chapter.

Chapter 4

The Birth of the Human Development Index

After a while [Alice] remembered that she still held the pieces of mushroom in her hands, and she set to work very carefully, nibbling first at one and then at the other, and growing sometimes taller and sometimes shorter, until she had succeeded in bringing herself down to her usual height.

—Alice in Wonderland

*A*ny measure that values a gun several hundred times more than a bottle of milk is bound to raise serious questions about its relevance for human progress. It is no surprise, then, that since the emergence of national income accounts, there has been considerable dissatisfaction with gross national product as a measure of human welfare. GNP reflects market prices in monetary terms. Those prices quietly register the prevailing economic and purchasing power in the system—but they are silent about the distribution, character or quality of economic growth. GNP also leaves out all activities that are not monetized—household work, subsistence agriculture, unpaid services. And what is more serious, GNP is one-dimensional: it fails to capture the cultural, social, political and many other choices that people make.

There has been a long search for a more comprehensive measure of development that could capture all, or many more, of the choices people make—a measure that would serve as a better yardstick of the socio-economic progress of nations. Several difficulties have marked this search. First, some analysts came out with scores of economic and social indicators but did not aggregate them into a composite index—so policymakers found such measures hard to digest. Second, several composite measures lacked a sound methodological base and were abandoned after brief trials. Third, not enough investment was made in constructing measures that were alternatives to GNP—nor was the effort sustained long enough to develop, refine and test such socio-economic indices.

Emergence of the HDI

The search for a new composite index of socio-economic progress began in earnest in preparing the *Human Development Report* under the sponsorship of UNDP in 1989 (chapter 3).[1] Several principles guided this search. First, the new index would measure the basic concept of human development to enlarge people's choices. These choices covered the desire to live long, to acquire knowledge, to have a comfortable standard of living, to be gainfully employed, to breathe clean air, to be free, to live in a community. Obviously, not all these choices could be quantified or measured. The basic idea was to measure at least a few more choices besides income and to reflect them in a methodologically sound composite index.

Second, the new index would include only a limited number of variables to keep it simple and manageable. Initially, life expectancy was chosen as an index of longevity, adult literacy as an index of knowledge, and GNP per capita adjusted for purchasing power parity (PPP) as an index of access to a multiplicity of economic choices. Several other variables were considered and discarded. They showed a significant correlation with the variables already chosen—infant and child mortality, for instance, has almost perfect correlation with life expectancy. Or they inadequately reflected real situations—for example, average calorie supply data failed to show how food was actually distributed among the population so that considerable hunger could coexist with "satisfactory" national averages.

Third, a composite index would be constructed rather than a plethora of separate indices. This posed several problems. Unlike GNP, for which money serves as a "common measuring rod", there is no such common currency for measuring socio-economic progress. Life expectancy is measured in years, adult literacy in percentages of adults, and real income in PPP-adjusted dollars. How to reduce these indicators to a common denominator? The methodological breakthrough was to measure actual progress in each indicator as relative distance from a desirable goal. The maximum and minimum observed values for each variable were reduced to a scale between 0 and 1: each country was at some point on this scale. The advantage of this methodology: every nation's actual progress was measured in relation to a goal. The disadvantage, of course, was that all values became relative to each other, a disadvantage later removed by agreeing on certain fixed goal posts—an aspect that is discussed later. Another problem in the composite index was that of weighting. Equal weights were decided for the three variables on the simple premise that all these choices were very important and that there was no *a priori* rationale for giving a higher weight to one choice than to another. Besides, experimentation with different weights yielded no significantly different results.

Fourth, the HDI would cover both social and economic choices. A mistake in the past had been to construct separate measures for economic progress (GNP) and for social progress (such as the physical quality of life index, or PQLI). Such a formulation misses the synergy between social and economic progress. Economic growth increases the resources and options available for social progress. And social progress creates a conducive environment for economic growth. Progress of nations and individuals must be measured on both fronts, not separately, in any comprehensive index of development. This reasoning led to the inclusion of real income (PPP dollars) as well as life expectancy and educational attainment in the HDI. Some critics have regarded it as a weakness of HDI that income, essentially a means, is aggregated with variables that represent the real ends of development. This is not a valid criticism, as discussed later, because it is based on a misunderstanding of the manner in which income is treated in the index. The merging of economic and social indicators is one of the distinctive features and chief strengths of the HDI.

Fifth, one of the most important decisions was to keep the coverage and methodology of HDI quite flexible—subject to gradual refinements as analytical critiques emerged and better data became available. National income accounts had taken five decades of investment and research, and yet many aspects of these accounts were still being investigated. If a worthwhile socio-economic index were to emerge, it would also require patient, long-term investigation, research and investment.

Sixth, even though an index can be only as good as the data fed into it, a lack of reliable and up-to-date data series was not allowed to inhibit the emergence of the HDI. Instead, HDI country rankings would be used as a pressure point to persuade policy-makers to invest adequate amounts in producing relevant data and to encourage international institutions to prepare comparable statistical data systems. The HDI calculations still suffer from some inadequate and unreliable data, but the production of the index has already put considerable pressure on the global community to improve the quality of underlying social and human statistics.

48

Method for constructing the HDI

The HDI has three key components: longevity, knowledge and income.[2] Longevity is measured by life expectancy at birth as the sole unadjusted indicator. Knowledge is measured by two education variables: adult literacy and mean years of schooling, with a weight of two-thirds to literacy and one-third to mean years of schooling. Initially, only adult literacy was in the index. Mean years of schooling were added later because, unlike developing countries, few industrial countries maintain separate figures for adult literacy, and there was a need to differentiate the performance of countries already close to 100% literacy.

The third variable, income, has proved more troublesome. Some critics even contend that it does not belong in the index because the HDI is concerned with ends, not means, and income is a means. Moreover, the HDI is a stock figure, while income is a flow figure. But this perception is based on a misunderstanding, for income in the HDI is merely a proxy for a bundle of goods and services needed for the best use of human capabilities. It is thus important to understand the treatment of income in the HDI.

The HDI is based on a cut-off point defined by a level of income regarded as adequate for a reasonable standard of living and for a reasonable fulfilment of human capabilities. Initially, this cut-off point was derived from the poverty-level income of the industrial countries, as reflected in the Luxembourg Income Study, with values updated and translated into purchasing power parity dollars. Later, it was taken as the current global average real GDP per capita in PPP dollars. In both cases, the threshold income is around $5,000. The difference in methodology is analytical rather than statistical and is based on certain pragmatic considerations of political acceptability.

The HDI treats income up to the cut-off point as having full value. But beyond the cut-off point, income has a sharply diminishing return—for which a specific formulation is used. The premise is that people do not need an infinite amount of income for a decent life. Wherever the upper line is drawn will always remain somewhat controversial—as will the rate of discount applied to income beyond the cut-off point.

The HDI method thus emphasizes sufficiency rather than satiety. It does not treat income as a means but reinterprets it in terms of the ends it serves. That is why, for example, the high income of the industrial countries is de-emphasized in the HDI and an overwhelming weight is given to the social progress they have achieved with this income.

With these basic variables—longevity, knowledge and income—the HDI is constructed in three simple steps (annex 4.1).

The first step is to define a country's measure of deprivation for each of the three basic variables. Minimum and maximum values are defined for the actual observed values of each of the three variables in all countries. The deprivation measure then places the country in the 0–1 range, where 0 is the minimum observed value and 1 the maximum. So, if the minimum observed life expectancy is 40 years and the maximum 80 years, and a country's life expectancy is 50 years, its index value for life expectancy is 0.25. Similarly for the other variables.

The second step is to compile an average indicator by taking a simple average of the three indicators. As mentioned earlier, it is difficult to argue for giving different weights to the different choices that people make. The third step is to measure the HDI as one minus the average deprivation index. The value of the HDI shows where a country is placed relative to other countries.

For the first few years, this relative nature of the index created several problems of comparison. The minimum value of each dimension—longevity, knowledge and income—was set at the level of the poorest-performing country and the maximum at that of the best-performing country. But maximums and minimums changed each year—following the performance of the countries at the ends of the scale. A country could thus improve its performance and yet see its HDI fall because the countries at the top or bottom had done even better. The shifting goal posts also meant that the progress of each nation could not be measured by the rate of change in the absolute value of its HDI over time.

Recently, the HDI methodology was changed to solve this problem. Rather than constantly shifting goal posts, fixed goal posts have been adopted. Now, the maximum and minimum values are not actually observed values in the best- and worst-performing countries but the most extreme values observed over the previous three decades or expected over the next three decades. These fixed goal posts permit meaningful comparisons of countries' performance over 60 years.

The HDI versus GNP

The HDI does not replace GNP, but it adds considerably to an understanding of the real position of a society in several respects:[3]

• Besides income, the HDI measures education and health and is thus multidimensional, rather than one-dimensional.

• It focuses the attention of the policy-makers on the ultimate objectives of development, not just the means.

• It is more meaningful as a national average than GNP because there are much greater extremes in income distribution than in the distribution of life expectancy and literacy.

• It shows that the human development gaps between nations are more manageable than the ever-widening disparities in income. The average income of the South may be only 6% of the North's—but its life expectancy is 80%, its nutrition level 85% and its adult literacy rate 66% of the North's.

• The HDI can be disaggregated by gender, ethnic group or geographical region and in many other ways—to present relevant policy inputs as well as to forecast impending trouble. Indeed, one of the HDI's greatest strengths is that it can be disaggregated in ways that hold a mirror up to society.

Some argue that the income of a society reflects all its other achievements, so a separate index for those achievements is unnecessary. This is patently false. As chapters 2 and 3 point out, there is no automatic translation of the income of a society into the lives of its people. Several telling examples:

• Saudi Arabia has a per capita income 16 times that of Sri Lanka but a much lower literacy rate.

• The infant mortality rate in Brazil is four times higher than that in Jamaica even though Brazil enjoys twice the per capita income.

• Oman has three times the per capita income of Costa Rica but about one-third its literacy rate and seven fewer years of life expectancy, and it lacks most political and economic freedoms.

• The life expectancy of black males in Harlem, in New York City, is lower than that in Bangladesh or Sudan.

These examples can be multiplied. The point is that GNP, by itself, reveals little about how the people in a society live and breathe. Ideally, a high income brings within reach many social services and improvements in human life. But whether this happens depends on many other factors: What is the composition of this income? What is being produced and consumed? How is the income distributed?

It is the actual distribution and use of the income that is decisive, not just its level—an obvious fact that is often forgotten. For this reason, if for no other, the HDI is a useful supplement to GNP in understanding and analysing a society. Compare the HDI and GNP rankings of countries. Of 173 countries included in these rankings, there is no difference in the ranks for four countries and less than a five-rank difference for 29 countries. But for most other countries, the differences are substantial.

The HDI and GNP ranks of more than a third (60) of the countries differ by more than 20 places (table 4.1). There are differences of more than 40 ranks for 10 countries and more than 30 ranks for 26 countries. These comparisons of HDI and GNP ranks raise serious doubts about the notion that there is a perfect trickle-down of income growth to all mem-

Table 4.1 GNP and HDI rankings of selected countries
(GNP per capita rank minus HDI rank)

More favourable HDI rank		Less favourable HDI rank	
More favourable by more than 40 ranks		*Less favourable by more than 40 ranks*	
China	+49	Gabon	−72
Guyana	+44	Oman	−54
Colombia	+41	United Arab Emirates	−52
		Guinea	−44
		Seychelles	−44
		Namibia	−43
		Iraq	−41
More favourable by more than 30 ranks		*Less favourable by more than 30 ranks*	
Sri Lanka	+38	Djibouti	−38
Costa Rica	+36	Libyan Arab Jamahiriya	−38
Lithuania	+35	Algeria	−37
Viet Nam	+34	Suriname	−37
Nicaragua	+33	Qatar	−36
Madagascar	+31	Saudi Arabia	−36
Poland	+30	Angola	−35
		South Africa	−33
		Mauritania	−31
More favourable by more than 20 ranks		*Less favourable by more than 20 ranks*	
Czechoslovakia	+29	Botswana	−29
Bulgaria	+28	Senegal	−29
Chile	+28	Vanuatu	−26
Ecuador	+28	Bahrain	−25
Thailand	+28	Central African Rep.	−25
Lao People's Dem. Rep.	+24	Congo	−23
Hungary	+23	Kuwait	−23
Panama	+23	Saint Kitts and Nevis	−23
Ukraine	+23	Gambia	−22
Jamaica	+22	Iran, Islamic Rep. of	−22
Tanzania	+22	Singapore	−22
Azerbaijan	+21	Niger	−21
Cuba	+21	Papua New Guinea	−21
Kenya	+21	Swaziland	−21
Syrian Arab Rep.	+21	Lebanon	−20
Armenia	+20	Saint Lucia	−20
Uruguay	+20		
Zaire	+20		

Source: UNDP, *Human Development Report 1994*, New York: Oxford University Press, 1994.

REFLECTIONS ON HUMAN DEVELOPMENT

bers of society or that the quality of human lives in each country is correlated with its per capita income.

These comparisons also bring out different development strategies. Some countries give a high priority to the provision of basic social services to all their people as a matter of deliberate public policy: notable examples are China, Colombia, Costa Rica, Cuba, Jamaica and Sri Lanka. The results are fairly high indicators of education and health at fairly modest incomes. For other countries, income distribution has been very uneven, and government policy has not focused on provision of social services. Their HDI ranks are significantly below their per capita GNP ranks, as for Papua New Guinea, Gabon and several other countries in Sub-Saharan Africa.

Several Arab nations also show an HDI rank less favourable than their GNP per capita rank: Oman, United Arab Emirates, Iraq, Libya, Algeria, Qatar, Saudi Arabia, Bahrain, Kuwait and Lebanon. Many of them acquired their new wealth only after the rise in the price of oil in the mid-1970s. It is taking them some time to translate this financial wealth into the well-being of their people. But the process has accelerated considerably in the past two decades. The Gulf states have made much faster progress than the average developing country in the past 20 years (chapter 8). Saudi Arabia increased its HDI from 0.386 in 1970 to 0.688 in 1990—among the largest increases in HDI during that period. Thus, while there is a link between income and human development, the nature of that link depends on the development priorities that countries choose.

Several countries have similar levels of per capita GNP but vastly different social progress (table 4.2). Malaysia and Iraq have the same per capita GNP (around $2,500). But life expectancy in Malaysia is five years longer, adult literacy about 17 percentage points higher and infant mortality less than one-fourth that in Iraq. In such cases, GNP per capita is totally misleading as an indicator of human development.

But an HDI rank higher than a GNP per capita rank is not always a cause for celebration. East European countries and the former Soviet Union enjoyed such a status for a long time. But because their social progress was not supported by economic growth, the long-term sustainability of their human development levels became dubious.

To summarize, to examine the link between economic and social progress, we must see how income is distributed and used in a society and how far it has been translated into the lives of people. If a country's HDI rank is more favourable than its GNP per capita rank, this should reassure policy-makers that their social priorities are headed in the right direction and that the country is building up an adequate base of human capital for accelerated growth. It should also remind them that social progress cannot be sustained for long without an adequate economic base—so they should also correct the imbalance on the economic growth side.

But if the HDI rank is far less favourable than the GNP per capita rank, this should signal to policy-makers that the benefits of national income are not being distributed to the people. It should prompt them to examine whether the problem lies in maldistribution of income or assets, or in wrong development priorities or in lack of public policy attention to social services. Comparison with other countries with similar incomes should reassure them that it is possible to generate greater human welfare at that level of income. So, there should be no tension between the HDI and GNP measures. Both can inform public policy.

What the HDI reveals

The HDI captures far more reality than GNP does. It can also be disaggregated by income class, gender, geographical region, ethnic group or other classifications to bring out a graphic profile of society—and this is one of its chief virtues.

It captures many aspects of the human condition:

National priorities. Even a quick glance at HDI rankings shows which countries are combining economic progress with social development and which lag behind. Such rankings are particularly effective in

Table 4.2 Similar incomes, different HDIs, 1991/92

Country	GNP per capita (US$)	HDI value	HDI rank	Life expectancy (years)	Adult literacy rate (%)	Infant mortality (per 1,000 live births)
	GNP per capita around $500					
Sri Lanka	500	0.665	90	71.2	89	24
Guinea	500	0.191	173	43.9	27	135
	GNP per capita around $1,000 to $1,100					
El Salvador	1,090	0.543	112	65.2	75	46
Congo	1,040	0.461	123	51.7	59	83
	GNP per capita around $2,500 to $2,600					
Malaysia	2,520	0.794	57	70.4	80	14
Iraq	2,550	0.614	100	65.7	63	59

Source: UNDP, *Human Development Report 1994,* New York: Oxford University Press, 1994, p. 15.

putting pressure on policy-makers to improve their performance. The HDI measure also reveals the area—whether education, health or income—in which their country's performance lags behind other comparable countries.The publication of HDI rankings each year has generated an enormous amount of attention, controversy and followup.

Potential growth. The HDI can reveal the future potential for economic growth in a country. If a country has built up considerable human capital, it can accelerate its GNP growth by choosing the right macroeconomic policies—as is true for many formerly socialist countries now in transition to a market economy. But if human capital is largely missing, it would take a country considerable time to create the human infrastructure needed for sustainable growth—which is true for much of Sub-Saharan Africa today. Moreover, if there has been a significant investment in education and health, there is a reasonable prospect that people will be able to gain access to market opportunities so that economic growth will be more equitable.

Disparities between people. The HDI can be disaggregated to bring out disparities between various sections of society. The *Human Development Report* has disaggregated the HDI by income class, gender, ethnic group and geographical region. These exercises have led to some important conclusions.

For instance, gender-adjusted HDI comparisons have revealed the shocking reality that no country treats women as well as men. And when countries see their HDI ranking decline or improve significantly as a result of adjustment for gender disparities, it evokes controversy and helps galvanize policy action (table 4.3).

The policy impact is even greater for disaggregations by ethnic group. *Human Development Report 1993* brought out the HDI disparity among whites, blacks and hispanics in the United States. It pointed out that, if considered as separate nations, whites would outrank all other countries, blacks would rank number 31 (after Trinidad and Tobago), and hispanics would rank number 35 (next to Estonia). So, ethnic disparities persist in the United States despite many legal battles, considerable mobility of labour and fast-opening market opportunities. Naturally, the comparison led to much excited debate.

Early warning system. Ideally, it should be possible to disaggregate the HDI measure so that a society can see all its strengths, blemishes and tension points. Such an exercise depends on the availability of relevant data, which countries sometimes are reluctant to collect. Many countries have already started preparing detailed HDI estimates in a fairly disaggregated form—among them, Bangladesh, Bolivia, Egypt,

India, the Philippines, South Africa and Turkey. This is politically courageous and timely, since one of the key uses of the HDI can be to provide an early warning about impending trouble.

Widening disparities in the HDI among regions or ethnic groups suggests a possibility of open conflict or violence. For instance, *Human Development Report 1993* documented disparities between components of the HDI for Mexico's Chiapas region and the Mexican national average—a year before Chiapas erupted in open revolt. The 1994 report documents even wider disparities in Brazil, China, Egypt and Nigeria (table 4.4). Such gaps should be treated as a timely warning, not a source of national embarrassment. In fact, an obligatory part of preparing national development plans should be to draw up a disaggregated profile of society over time to see which sections of society are gaining or losing in the development race and where the future tension points are likely to be.

Change over time. With the adoption of fixed goal posts, it has become possible to make meaningful comparisons of countries by their HDI values over time (table 4.5). The main conclusions:

• In 1960, the majority of the world's people, 73%, were in the low human development category, but in 1992, only 35% were in that category. So, nearly two-thirds had shifted to the medium or high human development category.

Table 4.3 Gender-disparity-adjusted HDI

Country	HDI rank	Gender-disparity-adjusted HDI rank	Difference between HDI rank and gender-disparity-adjusted HDI rank
Improved rank			
Finland	16	3	+13
Denmark	15	4	+11
New Zealand	18	8	+10
Czechoslovakia	25	15	+10
Iceland	14	6	+ 8
Fallen rank			
Japan	3	19	−16
Switzerland	2	17	−15
Canada	1	9	−8
Hong Kong	22	30	−8

Note: Only 43 countries are included in the exercise to calculate gender-disparity-adjusted HDI because of limited availability of data. HDI ranks are therefore recalculated for this exercise, taking as the total universe 43 countries rather than the 173 countries included in the total exercise. The differences in ranks in the last column are extremely significant in the context of this limited universe.

Source: UNDP, *Human Development Report 1994,* New York: Oxford University Press, 1994.

• Developing countries more than doubled their average HDI between 1960 and 1992, while industrial countries, starting from a much higher level, increased theirs by only 15%. This rapidly closed the HDI gaps between North and South—from nearly 70% in 1960 to around 40% in 1992.

• The fastest progress in accelerating human development between 1960 and 1992 was in East Asia and the Arab States.

• Many countries with modest incomes—such as Botswana, China, Costa Rica, Malaysia and the Republic of Korea—increased their education and health investments rapidly during 1960–92, which enabled them to accelerate their economic growth as well.

• Among the industrial countries, Japan made the most extraordinary progress, jumping from an HDI rank of 23 in 1960 to 3 in 1992.

Current criticisms and possible refinements

The HDI is still evolving. It must continue to respond to constructive criticism so that a more useful measure emerges. In that spirit, it is worthwhile to summarize some of the key suggestions made in recent years and to explore how the index can be further refined.

More variables. Several critics have pointed out that the variables included in the HDI are very limited. Several additional indices of socio-

Table 4.4 Disaggregated HDIs

Reflecting regional disparities

Country	Region with highest HDI value		Region with lowest HDI value		Index [a]
Mexico	Nuevo Leon	0.868	Chiapas	0.619	140
Brazil	Southern region	0.839	North-East region	0.544	154
China	Shanghai (Beijing)	0.860	Tibet	0.400	215
Egypt	Cairo	0.738	Rural Upper Egypt	0.444	362
Nigeria	Bendel	0.666	Borno	0.156	427

Reflecting ethnic disparities

Country	Ethnic group with highest HDI value		Ethnic group with lowest HDI value		Percentage difference [b]
United States	Whites	0.990	Blacks	0.890	11
South Africa	Whites	0.878	Blacks	0.462	90
Malaysia (1970)	Chinese	0.580	Malays	0.400	45
Malaysia (1991)	Chinese	0.900	Malays	0.730	23

a. Index of highest regional HDI value with lowest regional HDI value = 100.
b. Percentage difference calculated by taking lowest HDI value as the denominator.
Source: UNDP, *Human Development Report 1993*, New York: Oxford University Press, 1993, and *Human Development Report 1994*, New York: Oxford University Press, 1994.

economic progress have been advanced with varying intensity—food security, housing, environment. These deserve serious consideration and should be added when adequate and reliable data become available. Some critics believe that a Human Development Index that does not include political freedoms is incomplete. This criticism is justified, and the next chapter discusses how a political freedom index can be constructed and integrated with the HDI. But some suggestions are more difficult to pursue—such as including cultural and spiritual values, since any attempt at quantification will raise more issues than it settles.

More variables will not necessarily improve the HDI. They may confuse the picture and blur the main trends. It is best to recognize that the HDI will remain a partial reflection of reality. And there is some virtue in keeping the index sharp and simple, studying other legitimate concerns alongside the HDI rather than trying to integrate everything into the HDI.

No composite index. Several critics have suggested that it is better to produce a series of separate indicators to document different aspects of social progress rather than a composite index—which raises serious

Table 4.5 Changes in HDI over time

	1960	1992	Change 1960–92 (%)
Distribution of people (%)			
High human development group	16	23	+44
Medium human development group	11	42	+282
Low human development group	73	35	−47
HDI value by country group			
Developing countries	0.260	0.541	+108
Industrial countries	0.799	0.918	+15
World	0.392	0.605	+54
HDI value by region			
East Asia	0.255	0.653	+156
Arab States	0.277	0.631	+128
South Asia	0.202	0.376	+86
Sub-Saharan Africa	0.200	0.357	+78
Latin America and the Caribbean	0.467	0.757	+62
Notable performers (HDI value)			
Botswana	0.207	0.670	+224
China	0.248	0.644	+160
Korea, Rep. of	0.398	0.859	+159
Malaysia	0.330	0.794	+141
Costa Rica	0.550	0.848	+54
Japan	0.686	0.929	+54

Source: UNDP, *Human Development Report 1994,* New York: Oxford University Press, 1994.

issues about the weights chosen or the methods used for compiling the index. This is academic puritanism taken too far, for the same criticism can apply to all composite indices—particularly GNP. Moreover, practical considerations dictate the evolution of a composite index: busy policy-makers cannot absorb a host of separate social indicators pointing in all directions. For any useful policy index, some compromises must be made. But such compromises must not sacrifice the professional integrity of the broad picture that the composite index intends to convey.

It helps to keep reminding ourselves that human development is a much richer concept than the HDI can ever hope to capture. The HDI is not intended to replace the other detailed socio-economic indicators essential for understanding the real situation in any country. It should be regarded as a useful measure for some policy purposes, supplemented by other, more detailed socio-economic indicators.

Different HDIs for different country groups. The HDI measures only the most elementary human achievements: life expectancy at birth, basic education and literacy, and income up to only a low cut-off point (normally around $5,000). So, some have argued that, although the HDI may capture the priorities of the poorest nations of Sub-Saharan Africa and South Asia, it does not do full justice to regions where human development priorities have already moved beyond these basic levels, such as East Asia and Latin America. The criticism is even more valid for industrial countries: they already have high levels of adult literacy, and their incomes have little impact on their HDI values because of the sharply diminishing returns assumed for income beyond the cut-off point. The ranking of industrial countries then corresponds more to the differences in their life expectancy than to any other variable—and fails to capture the full range of their socio-economic progress.

The argument is valid, but it raises a dilemma. Comparisons across all countries require a simple index for which data are available for most countries. Yet there is a need to differentiate among groups of countries at different stages of development. The *Human Development Report* has resolved this dilemma by keeping the HDI estimates focused on the three basic variables—but supplementing them by detailed human development indicator tables, particularly for industrial countries, which bring out the full profile of their socio-economic progress. Another way of dealing with this issue, proposed by Anand and Sen, is to supplement the HDI with three separate indices for low, medium and high human development categories that better reflect their stage of human progress (table 4.6).[4] Supplementary tables on these lines can be compiled to illustrate the additional light they throw on the human development achievements in different groups of countries.

Inadequate and unreliable data. Some critics have pointed out that the underlying data for HDI estimates are weak and unreliable.[5] While this concern is valid, it should be used to improve the quality of data rather than to abandon the exercise. To stop the production of the HDI on this reasoning would be to throw out the baby rather than change the bath water. In fact, the preparation of HDI estimates and rankings have persuaded many countries to invest more resources and effort in preparing better statistical series. Several countries have noticed the poor quality of their data only after it has embarrassed them in the country rankings. The only sensible solution, therefore, is to earmark more resources to improve statistics. Meanwhile, HDI values should be treated as indicating a sense of direction rather than precise magnitudes.

Allocation criteria and aid conditionality. There has been considerable nervousness among policy-makers in the developing world that aid donors will adopt the HDI for allocating their funds and base their policy conditionality on it. This concern is difficult to understand since the availability of statistical measures does not by itself dictate whether there will be aid conditionality. The donors first decide on their aid conditionality and then look for relevant statistical measures to judge the performance of the recipient countries. Today, country performance is

Table 4.6 Supplementary human development indices

Low human development	Medium human development	High human development
1.1 Life expectancy	1.1 Life expectancy 1.2 Under-five mortality	1.1 Life expectancy 1.2 Under-5 mortality 1.3 Maternal mortality
2.1 Adult literacy	2.1 Adult literacy 2.2 Secondary school enrolment	2.1. Adult literacy 2.2 Secondary school enrolment 2.3 Tertiary enrolment
3.1 Log per capita GDP (up to international poverty line)	3.1 Log per capita GDP (up to international poverty line) 3.2 Incidence of poverty	3.1 Log per capita GDP (up to international poverty line) 3.2 Incidence of poverty 3.3 Gini-corrected mean national income

Source: Sudhir Anand and Amartya Sen, "Human Development Index: Methodology and Measurement," background paper for *Human Development Report 1993*, UNDP, New York, 1992.

REFLECTIONS ON HUMAN DEVELOPMENT

measured largely by GNP growth and other macroeconomic indicators. Why should it hurt the developing countries if their progress is judged not only on economic criteria but also on human development criteria, where they have made far more rapid progress in the past three decades than in GNP?

Should the HDI be used as the basis for aid allocations? This is a difficult issue. Should aid go to countries with low HDIs—to the needy? Or should it go to countries with the fastest improvement over time—to the speedy? A case can be made for both options. Perhaps the best option is to focus aid on countries that have a low HDI but are making a determined effort to raise it. The point is that the HDI reveals much more about the socio-economic progress of a country than GNP does, and there is no reason not to use it increasingly in the development policy dialogue.

To conclude, the HDI is neither perfect nor fully developed. It requires continuous analysis and further refinement. And one of the key questions is whether the HDI should incorporate some measure of political freedom, discussed in the next chapter.

Notes

1. A small group was assembled under the direction of the author to prepare the new index. Those who made significant contributions at an initial stage to the evolution of the Human Development Index include Amartya Sen and Meghnad Desai, later joined by Gustav Ranis, Frances Stewart, Paul Streeten, Inge Kaul and Sudhir Anand. Many more from among the consultants and staff of the UNDP Human Development Report Office contributed to this collective exercise.

2. For a fuller treatment of the HDI methodology, see the technical notes in the 1991, 1992 and 1993 *Human Development Reports* (New York: Oxford University Press). See also chapter 5 in *Human Development Report 1994* (New York: Oxford University Press). A detailed analysis is given in Sudhir Anand and Amartya Sen, "Human Development Index: Methodology and Measurement," Human Development Report Office Occasional Paper 12, UNDP, New York, 1994.

3. I am grateful to Paul Streeten for pointing out some of these characteristics of the HDI.

4. See Sudhir Anand and Amartya Sen, "Human Development Index: Methodology and Measurement," Human Development Report Office Occasional Paper 12, UNDP, New York, 1994, pages 13–14.

5. See, for example, T.N. Srinivasan, "Human Development: A Paradigm or Reinvention of the Wheel?" Paper presented at American Economic Association meeting, 3 January 1994, Boston.

Annex 4.1 Components of the Human Development Index

HDI rank	Human development index 1992	Life expectancy at birth (years) 1992	Adult literacy rate (%) 1992	Mean years of schooling 1992	Real GDP per capita (PPP$) 1991	Adjusted real GDP per capita 1991
High human development	0.886	74.1	97.3	9.8	14,000	
1 Canada	0.932	77.2	99.0	12.2	19,320	5,347
2 Switzerland	0.931	77.8	99.0	11.6	21,780	5,370
3 Japan	0.929	78.6	99.0	10.8	19,390	5,347
4 Sweden	0.928	77.7	99.0	11.4	17,490	5,342
5 Norway	0.928	76.9	99.0	12.1	17,170	5,341
6 France	0.927	76.6	99.0	12.0	18,430	5,345
7 Australia	0.926	76.7	99.0	12.0	16,680	5,339
8 USA	0.925	75.6	99.0	12.4	22,130	5,371
9 Netherlands	0.923	77.2	99.0	11.1	16,820	5,340
10 United Kingdom	0.919	75.8	99.0	11.7	16,340	5,337
11 Germany	0.918	75.6	99.0	11.6	19,770	5,347
12 Austria	0.917	75.7	99.0	11.4	17,690	5,343
13 Belgium	0.916	75.7	99.0	11.2	17,510	5,342
14 Iceland	0.914	78.1	99.0	9.2	17,480	5,342
15 Denmark	0.912	75.3	99.0	11.0	17,880	5,343
16 Finland	0.911	75.4	99.0	10.9	16,130	5,336
17 Luxembourg	0.908	75.2	99.0	10.5	20,800	5,364
18 New Zealand	0.907	75.3	99.0	10.7	13,970	5,310
19 Israel	0.900	76.2	95.0	10.2	13,460	5,307
20 Barbados	0.894	75.3	99.0	9.4	9,667	5,255
21 Ireland	0.892	75.0	99.0	8.9	11,430	5,295
22 Italy	0.891	76.9	97.4	7.5	17,040	5,340
23 Spain	0.888	77.4	98.0	6.9	12,670	5,303
24 Hong Kong	0.875	77.4	90.0	7.2	18,520	5,345
25 Greece	0.874	77.3	93.8	7.0	7,680	5,221
26 Cyprus	0.873	76.7	94.0	7.0	9,844	5,257
27 Czechoslovakia	0.872	72.1	99.0	9.2	6,570	5,196
28 Lithuania	0.868	72.6	98.4	9.0	5,410	5,154
29 Estonia	0.867	71.2	99.0	9.0	8,090	5,229
30 Latvia	0.865	71.0	99.0	9.0	7,540	5,218
31 Hungary	0.863	70.1	99.0	9.8	6,080	5,182
32 Korea, Rep. of	0.859	70.4	96.8	9.3	8,320	5,233
33 Uruguay	0.859	72.4	96.5	8.1	6,670	5,199
34 Russian Fed.	0.858	70.0	98.7	9.0	6,930	5,205
35 Trinidad and Tobago	0.855	70.9	96.0	8.4	8,380	5,234
36 Bahamas	0.854	71.9	99.0	6.2	12,000	5,299
37 Argentina	0.853	71.1	95.5	9.2	5,120	5,120
38 Chile	0.848	71.9	93.8	7.8	7,060	5,208
39 Costa Rica	0.848	76.0	93.2	5.7	5,100	5,100
40 Belarus	0.847	71.0	97.9	7.0	6,850	5,203

HDI rank	Human development index 1992	Life expectancy at birth (years) 1992	Adult literacy rate (%) 1992	Mean years of schooling 1992	Real GDP per capita (PPP$) 1991	Adjusted real GDP per capita 1991
41 Malta	0.843	75.7	87.0	6.1	7,575	5,219
42 Portugal	0.838	74.4	86.2	6.4	9,450	5,252
43 Singapore	0.836	74.2	92.0	4.0	14,734	5,313
44 Brunei Darussalam	0.829	74.0	86.0	5.0	14,000	5,310
45 Ukraine	0.823	70.0	95.0	6.0	5,180	5,135
46 Venezuela	0.820	70.1	89.0	6.5	8,120	5,230
47 Panama	0.816	72.5	89.6	6.8	4,910	4,910
48 Bulgaria	0.815	71.9	94.0	7.0	4,813	4,813
49 Poland	0.815	71.5	99.0	8.2	4,500	4,500
50 Colombia	0.813	69.0	87.4	7.5	5,460	5,157
51 Kuwait	0.809	74.6	73.9	5.5	13,126	5,306
52 Mexico	0.804	69.9	88.6	4.9	7,170	5,211
53 Armenia	0.801	72.0	98.8	5.0	4,610	4,610
Medium human development	0.649	68.0	80.4	4.8	3,420	
54 Thailand	0.798	68.7	93.8	3.9	5,270	5,144
55 Antigua and Barbuda	0.796	74.0	96.0	4.6	4,500	4,500
56 Qatar	0.795	69.6	79.0	5.8	14,000	5,310
57 Malaysia	0.794	70.4	80.0	5.6	7,400	5,215
58 Bahrain	0.791	71.0	79.0	4.3	11,536	5,296
59 Fiji	0.787	71.1	87.0	5.1	4,858	4,858
60 Mauritius	0.778	69.6	79.9	4.1	7,178	5,211
61 Kazakhstan	0.774	69.0	97.5	5.0	4,490	4,490
62 United Arab Emirates	0.771	70.8	65.0	5.6	17,000	5,340
63 Brazil	0.756	65.8	82.1	4.0	5,240	5,142
64 Dominica	0.749	72.0	97.0	4.7	3,900	3,900
65 Jamaica	0.749	73.3	98.5	5.3	3,670	3,670
66 Georgia	0.747	73.0	99.0	5.0	3,670	3,670
67 Saudi Arabia	0.742	68.7	64.1	3.9	10,850	5,289
68 Turkey	0.739	66.7	81.9	3.6	4,840	4,840
69 Saint Vincent	0.732	71.0	98.0	4.6	3,700	3,700
70 Saint Kitts and Nevis	0.730	70.0	99.0	6.0	3,550	3,550
71 Azerbaijan	0.730	71.0	96.3	5.0	3,670	3,670
72 Romania	0.729	69.9	96.9	7.1	3,500	3,500
73 Syrian Arab Rep.	0.727	66.4	66.6	4.2	5,220	5,140
74 Ecuador	0.718	66.2	87.4	5.6	4,140	4,140
75 Moldova, Rep. of	0.714	69.0	96.0	6.0	3,500	3,500
76 Albania	0.714	73.0	85.0	6.2	3,500	3,500
77 Saint Lucia	0.709	72.0	93.0	3.9	3,500	3,500
78 Grenada	0.707	70.0	98.0	4.7	3,374	3,374

HDI rank	Human development index 1992	Life expectancy at birth (years) 1992	Adult literacy rate (%) 1992	Mean years of schooling 1992	Real GDP per capita (PPP$) 1991	Adjusted real GDP per capita 1991
79 Libyan Arab Jamahiriya	0.703	62.4	66.5	3.5	7,000	5,207
80 Turkmenistan	0.697	66.0	97.7	5.0	3,540	3,540
81 Tunisia	0.690	67.1	68.1	2.1	4,690	4,690
82 Kyrgyzstan	0.689	68.0	97.0	5.0	3,280	3,280
83 Seychelles	0.685	71.0	77.0	4.6	3,683	3,683
84 Paraguay	0.679	67.2	90.8	4.9	3,420	3,420
85 Suriname	0.677	69.9	95.6	4.2	3,072	3,072
86 Iran, Islamic Rep. of	0.672	66.6	56.0	3.9	4,670	4,670
87 Botswana	0.670	60.3	75.0	2.5	4,690	4,690
88 Belize	0.666	68.0	96.0	4.6	3,000	3,000
89 Cuba	0.666	75.6	94.5	8.0	2,000	2,000
90 Sri Lanka	0.665	71.2	89.1	7.2	2,650	2,650
91 Uzbekistan	0.664	69.0	97.2	5.0	2,790	2,790
92 Oman	0.654	69.1	35.0	0.9	9,230	5,248
93 South Africa	0.650	62.2	80.0	3.9	3,885	3,885
94 China	0.644	70.5	80.0	5.0	2,946	2,946
95 Peru	0.642	63.6	86.2	6.5	3,110	3,110
96 Dominican Rep.	0.638	67.0	84.3	4.3	3,080	3,080
97 Tajikistan	0.629	70.0	96.7	5.0	2,180	2,180
98 Jordan	0.628	67.3	82.1	5.0	2,895	2,895
99 Philippines	0.621	64.6	90.4	7.6	2,440	2,440
100 Iraq	0.614	65.7	62.5	5.0	3,500	3,500
101 Korea, Dem. Rep. of	0.609	70.7	95.0	6.0	1,750	1,750
102 Mongolia	0.607	63.0	95.0	7.2	2,250	2,250
103 Lebanon	0.600	68.1	81.3	4.4	2,500	2,500
104 Samoa	0.596	66.0	98.0	5.8	1,869	1,869
105 Indonesia	0.586	62.0	84.4	4.1	2,730	2,730
106 Nicaragua	0.583	65.4	78.0	4.5	2,550	2,550
107 Guyana	0.580	64.6	96.8	5.1	1,862	1,862
108 Guatemala	0.564	64.0	56.4	4.1	3,180	3,180
109 Algeria	0.553	65.6	60.6	2.8	2,870	2,870
110 Egypt	0.551	60.9	50.0	3.0	3,600	3,600
111 Morocco	0.549	62.5	52.5	3.0	3,340	3,340
112 El Salvador	0.543	65.2	74.6	4.2	2,110	2,110
113 Bolivia	0.530	60.5	79.3	4.0	2,170	2,170
114 Gabon	0.525	52.9	62.5	2.6	3,498	3,498
115 Honduras	0.524	65.2	74.9	4.0	1,820	1,820
116 Viet Nam	0.514	63.4	88.6	4.9	1,250	1,250
117 Swaziland	0.513	57.3	71.0	3.8	2,506	2,506
118 Maldives	0.511	62.6	92.0	4.5	1,200	1,200

HDI rank	Human development index 1992	Life expectancy at birth (years) 1992	Adult literacy rate (%) 1992	Mean years of schooling 1992	Real GDP per capita (PPP$) 1991	Adjusted real GDP per capita 1991
Low human development	0.355	55.8	47.4	2.0	1,170	
119 Vanuatu	0.489	65.0	65.0	3.7	1,679	1,679
120 Lesotho	0.476	59.8	78.0	3.5	1,500	1,500
121 Zimbabwe	0.474	56.1	68.6	3.1	2,160	2,160
122 Cape Verde	0.474	67.3	66.5	2.2	1,360	1,360
123 Congo	0.461	51.7	58.5	2.1	2,800	2,800
124 Cameroon	0.447	55.3	56.5	1.6	2,400	2,400
125 Kenya	0.434	58.6	70.5	2.3	1,350	1,350
126 Solomon Islands	0.434	70.0	24.0	1.0	2,113	2,113
127 Namibia	0.425	58.0	40.0	1.7	2,381	2,381
128 São Tomé and Principe	0.409	67.0	60.0	2.3	600	600
129 Papua New Guinea	0.408	55.3	65.3	1.0	1,550	1,550
130 Myanmar	0.406	56.9	81.5	2.5	650	650
131 Madagascar	0.396	54.9	81.4	2.2	710	710
132 Pakistan	0.393	58.3	36.4	1.9	1,970	1,970
133 Lao People's Dem. Rep.	0.385	50.3	55.0	2.9	1,760	1,760
134 Ghana	0.382	55.4	63.1	3.5	930	930
135 India	0.382	59.7	49.8	2.4	1,150	1,150
136 Côte d'Ivoire	0.370	51.6	55.8	1.9	1,510	1,510
137 Haiti	0.354	56.0	55.0	1.7	925	925
138 Zambia	0.352	45.5	74.8	2.7	1,010	1,010
139 Nigeria	0.348	51.9	52.0	1.2	1,360	1,360
140 Zaire	0.341	51.6	74.0	1.6	469	469
141 Comoros	0.331	55.4	55.0	1.0	700	700
142 Yemen	0.323	51.9	41.1	0.9	1,374	1,374
143 Senegal	0.322	48.7	40.0	0.9	1,680	1,680
144 Liberia	0.317	54.7	42.5	2.1	850	850
145 Togo	0.311	54.4	45.5	1.6	738	738
146 Bangladesh	0.309	52.2	36.6	2.0	1,160	1,160
147 Cambodia	0.307	50.4	37.8	2.0	1,250	1,250
148 Tanzania, U. Rep. of	0.306	51.2	55.0	2.0	570	570
149 Nepal	0.289	52.7	27.0	2.1	1,130	1,130
150 Equatorial Guinea	0.276	47.3	51.5	0.8	700	700
151 Sudan	0.276	51.2	28.2	0.8	1,162	1,162
152 Burundi	0.276	48.2	52.0	0.4	640	640
153 Rwanda	0.274	46.5	52.1	1.1	680	680

Annex 4.1 Components of the Human Development Index (continued)

HDI rank	Human development index 1992	Life expectancy at birth (years) 1992	Adult literacy rate (%) 1992	Mean years of schooling 1992	Real GDP per capita (PPP$) 1991	Adjusted real GDP per capita 1991
154 Uganda	0.272	42.6	50.5	1.1	1,036	1,036
155 Angola	0.271	45.6	42.5	1.5	1,000	1,000
156 Benin	0.261	46.1	25.0	0.7	1,500	1,500
157 Malawi	0.260	44.6	45.0	1.7	800	800
158 Mauritania	0.254	47.4	35.0	0.4	962	962
159 Mozambique	0.252	46.5	33.5	1.6	921	921
160 Central African Rep.	0.249	47.2	40.2	1.1	641	641
161 Ethiopia	0.249	46.4	50.0	1.1	370	370
162 Bhutan	0.247	47.8	40.9	0.3	620	620
163 Djibouti	0.226	48.3	19.0	0.4	1,000	1,000
164 Guinea-Bissau	0.224	42.9	39.0	0.4	747	747
165 Somalia	0.217	46.4	27.0	0.3	759	759
166 Gambia	0.215	44.4	30.0	0.6	763	763
167 Mali	0.214	45.4	35.9	0.4	480	480
168 Chad	0.212	46.9	32.5	0.3	447	447
169 Niger	0.209	45.9	31.2	0.2	542	542
170 Sierra Leone	0.209	42.4	23.7	0.9	1,020	1,020
171 Afghanistan	0.208	42.9	31.6	0.9	700	700
172 Burkina Faso	0.203	47.9	19.9	0.2	666	666
173 Guinea	0.191	43.9	26.9	0.9	500	500

Source: UNDP, *Human Development Report 1994,* New York: Oxford University Press, 1994.

REFLECTIONS ON HUMAN DEVELOPMENT

Chapter 5

The Design of a Political Freedom Index

> *"Let the jury consider their verdict," the King said, for about the twentieth time that day.*
> *"No, no!" said the Queen. "Sentence first—verdict afterwards."*
>
> — Alice in Wonderland

here has been considerable controversy over whether political freedom is an integral part of human development. At a conceptual level, there should be no hesitation. The purpose of human development is to enlarge the range of people's choices—and the most basic choice is the freedom to make a choice, rather than have someone else make it. As Paul Streeten points out in his thoughtful foreword: "Life expectancy and literacy could be quite high in a well-managed prison. Basic physical needs are well met in a zoo." Thus, freedom cannot be separated from human development.

Opposition to a freedom index

There is considerable opposition to a political freedom index on several grounds.

First, it is suggested that freedom is difficult to measure—and that freedom is so valuable that it should not be reduced to a number, as the very act of measurement will diminish it. Rather weak, this argument can apply to any measure—to the HDI or even to GNP. But professional enquiry must go on. Literature, beauty and art are judged and ranked. Why not freedom? Besides, most of the components of political freedom—multiparty systems, fair elections, freedom of the press, rule of law, instances of discrimination, arbitrary arrests or disappearances, violations of specific human rights—can be, and have been, documented through professional analysis and investigation. True, some cultural and religious freedoms cannot be easily quantified. Nor can the quality of political life be easily summarized. So, we have to settle for incomplete indices—but all other indices are similarly incomplete.

Second, it is suggested that political rights are not as important in poor countries as economic and social rights—that the right to vote is greatly diminished in the hands of an illiterate and starving person. Such arguments have an elitist ring to them, for the starving masses have often led liberation struggles and freedom movements. And it was ordinary people who recently toppled the communist regimes in the former Soviet Union and the Eastern European countries. Political rights are as important as economic and social rights, and should be measured together.

Third, it is suggested that there has been only a tenuous link between freedom and economic growth throughout history. Industrial England, Meiji Japan, Nazi Germany, the Republic of Korea under General Park and Chile under General Pinochet were not shining examples of political democracy—though they did quite well in economic growth. This argument, while true, is largely irrelevant because the world has changed, and history offers few precedents for today. People are demanding both development and democracy. And the absence of basic human rights is no longer a national concern—it is an international concern, with global media bringing human rights violations dramatically to our doorsteps. As *Human Development Report 1992* pointed out: "Human cruelty can no longer be hidden in dark and distant corners of the planet."

Although the link between economic growth and democracy is weak at times, those who find comfort in it will do well to reflect on two propositions. One, for every country that accelerated its economic growth under authoritarian rule, there are many more instances of authoritarian regimes that sacrificed both freedom and growth. Two, while the paradigm of economic growth can be indifferent to political freedom, the paradigm of human development cannot. People are not at the centre of development if they are in a political prison.

Fourth, most opposition to a political freedom index comes from a few governments in the developing world, which is only natural. Many governments can explain away their low rankings in the human development index: poverty and a lack of resources are the usual excuses. But they find it more difficult to explain their low rankings on a political freedom index. After all, governments do not have to torture their political opponents or censor press just because they are poor. And most violations of human rights originate with governments. For the same reason, members of civil society and the media are greatly in favour of measures of political freedom even as their governments steadily oppose them.

Fifth, one surprising stumbling block to a political freedom index has been the fear that any such index will be used to impose additional conditionality for aid, and the enthusiastic support of the industrial world for a political freedom index has only fueled this fear. Although it is essential for work to proceed on the construction of a political freedom index, its use for aid conditionality would be totally inappropriate— and would inhibit serious professional enquiry in this area.

The 1991 and 1992 *Human Development Reports* tried to advance the dialogue on the construction of a political freedom index, but this effort was given up because of mounting opposition from some governments. The 1992 report concluded that "further research on the political freedom index ought now to be undertaken—in a university or other research centre—to improve its conceptual, methodological and statistical basis." This chapter explores concrete ways of doing this.

Method for a political freedom index

Because no index can capture all dimensions of political freedom, there is a need to be selective. And because only those aspects of political freedom that are more readily quantified can be included in an index, attention should go to four clusters:

- *Political participation.* Freedom to participate in, and influence, political decision-making at the national and local levels.
- *Rule of law.* Protection of individual rights to life, liberty and security through due process of law.
- *Freedom of expression.* Individual freedom to seek, receive and impart information and ideas—orally, in writing or through any media— without any state-imposed restrictions, except to protect national security, public order and public health or to ensure respect for the rights or reputations of others.
- *Non-discrimination.* Equality of opportunity for individuals irrespective of gender, religion, ethnic group, national or social origin, language or wealth.

These four clusters can be related to the main institutions of a civil society that protect—or abuse—human rights. Thus, the legislature is responsible for political participation, the judiciary for ensuring the rule of law, the "fourth estate", the media, for protecting the freedom of expression and the executive branch for guaranteeing equal treatment to all citizens. Each cluster can then be measured by several indicators. For example:

Political participation. Single-party or multiparty elections; universal franchise; regularity and fairness of elections; freedom to form political parties; right of peaceful assembly; decentralization of decision-making powers; continuity and sustainability of democratic institutions.

Rule of law. No arbitrary arrests, torture or cruel treatment or killings by the state; no disappearance of political opponents; no police brutality; fair and open trials; competent, independent and impartial tribunals; presumption of innocence until proved guilty; judiciary independent from executive control; equality before the law.

Freedom of expression. No restrictions on public or private speech; no censorship or other limits on media; independent ownership and control of media; recourse to legal institutions to protect freedom of speech.

Non-discrimination. No discrimination based on gender, religion, ethnic group, national or social origin, language or income and wealth, whether by law, by government action or inaction or through actual practice.

Information can be collected on each of these indicators from several national, regional and international sources. The more frequently used sources are Amnesty International, Freedom House, Human Rights Watch, Inter-Parliamentary Union, US State Department reports, Lawyers Committee for Human Rights, Nordic human rights institutes and records of the United Nations Commission on Human Rights. These need to be supplemented by monitoring in each country by NGOs, media and other members of the civil society. Often, information must be checked and cross-checked to eliminate biases. A computerized data system can be built up over time through a systematic examination of all available sources of information for each country.

One of the main difficulties is to translate qualitative information into quantitative data. This can be done by panels of eminent experts, who can compare and discuss all available information.[1]

Equal weights can be used for the four clusters. There is no reason to rate any one aspect of political freedom more highly than another. But whether weighting is relevant could vary depending on the aim of a research enquiry.

Political freedom index for 1994

On the basis of this method, an illustrative political freedom index is presented, ranking 100 nations in four broad categories of political freedom:

highest, fairly high, fairly low, and lowest (annex 5.1). Extensive data from sources mentioned above were used to arrive at an assessment of each variable in the index. While there will be excited quibbling over the precise ranking of countries, there is likely to be consensus on the broad category in which each country belongs (table 5.1).

Should the HDI and the political freedom index (PFI) be integrated or kept separate? Several arguments have been advanced for keeping them separate. The HDI is more stable over time, while the PFI can change with every palace coup or democratic transition. Witness the recent political fluctuations in Bangladesh, Cambodia, Haiti, Rwanda, Somalia, Viet Nam, and the formerly socialist countries of the former Soviet Union and Eastern Europe. Moreover, the HDI is more advanced in its evolution while the PFI is still in its infancy and needs considerably more work. For these reasons, separate presentation of the two indices carries distinct advantages.

Even so, much can be learned by multiplying the HDI and PFI values to construct a modified HDI. What is revealing is the difference between the modified HDI (HDI x PFI) rank and the HDI rank. The Democratic Republic of Korea, Iran, Iraq, Libya, Myanmar, Saudi Arabia and Syria fall dramatically in their overall rankings because of their very low ranking on the political freedom index. But Benin and India show a dramatic improvement in their overall ranking, reflecting the freedom in their societies.

Eventually, the coverage of the HDI will have to expand to cover many aspects now excluded—not only political freedom, but also sustainable development discussed in the next chapter. For the time being,

Table 5.1 Most and least politically free nations, 1994

Freest industrial nations [a]	Freest developing nations [a]	Least free nations [b]
Sweden	Costa Rica	Iraq
Finland	Uruguay	Afghanistan
Norway	Trinidad and Tobago	Rwanda
Switzerland	Jamaica	Sudan
Belgium	Benin	Korea, Dem. Rep. of
Denmark	Argentina	Iran, Islamic Rep. of
New Zealand	Botswana	Syrian Arab Rep.
Netherlands		Myanmar
Germany		Saudi Arabia
USA		Libyan Arab Jamahiriya

a. Ranked in descending order from highest political freedom index value.
b. Ranked in ascending order from lowest political freedom index value.
Source: Annex 5.1.

however, work must proceed in many academic institutions to further refine a political freedom index before it can be used with confidence and before it can be merged with the more established HDI.

Note

1. The Human Development Report Office in 1991 consulted four experts, who, working independently, gave nearly the same rankings, with only a few minor exceptions, to 104 countries on the basis of detailed qualitative information made available to them.

Annex 5.1 Political freedom index for 100 nations, 1994

Country	Political participation	Rule of law	Freedom of expression	Non-discrimination	Political freedom index (PFI)
Highest political freedom index (80% and above)					
1. Sweden	100	98	98	100	99.0
2. Finland	100	100	100	95	98.8
3. Norway	100	100	100	90	97.5
4. Switzerland	100	100	100	90	97.5
5. Belgium	100	97	100	92	97.3
6. Denmark	100	95	100	90	96.3
7. New Zealand	100	100	100	85	96.3
8. Netherlands	100	97	90	95	95.5
9. Germany	100	94	100	85	94.8
10. USA	100	93	100	85	94.5
11. Costa Rica·	100	94	90	93	94.3
12. Ireland	100	100	90	85	93.8
13. Austria	90	94	100	90	93.5
14. Spain	100	94	90	90	93.5
15. France	100	97	95	80	93.0
16. Canada	100	100	95	75	92.5
17. Portugal	100	88	90	90	92.0
18. Uruguay	100	88	100	80	92.0
19. Trinidad and Tobago	100	94	100	70	91.0
20. United Kingdom ·	100	87	90	85	90.5
21. Italy	100	88	80	85	88.3
22. Australia	100	88	90	73	87.8
23. Hungary	80	96	96	75	86.8
24. Jamaica	90	70	100	85	86.3
25. Benin	65	93	100	83	85.3
26. Greece	100	94	80	65	84.8
27. Argentina	100	64	90	83	84.3
28. Botswana	100	94	90	45	82.3
29. Japan	100	88	80	60	82.0
30. Poland	70	82	95	80	81.8
31. Ecuador	80	80	80	80	80.0
Fairly high political freedom index (between 60% and 80%)					
32. Venezuela	100	58	90	70	79.5
33. Nicaragua	80	64	82	90	79.0
34. Papua New Guinea	90	70	80	75	78.8
35. Panama	80	74	80	75	77.3
36. Bolivia	85	65	95	60	76.3
37. Chile	80	76	70	70	74.0
38. Colombia	100	55	70	68	73.3
39. India	90	71	70	55	71.5
40. Mexico	80	50	70	85	71.3
41. Singapore	55	82	70	75	70.5
42. Malaysia	76	64	60	80	70.0
43. Korea, Rep. of	80	64	50	85	69.8
44. Senegal	86	46	70	76	69.5
45. Dominican Rep.	65	82	70	60	69.3
46. Bangladesh	80	66	70	60	69.0

Country	Political participation	Rule of law	Freedom of expression	Non-discrimination	Political freedom index (PFI)
47. Honduras	90	46	70	70	69.0
48. Bulgaria	55	90	60	70	68.9
49. Romania	60	82	70	60	68.0
50. Côte d'Ivoire	50	88	50	80	67.0
51. Zimbabwe	40	82	60	85	66.8
52. Thailand	50	76	70	70	66.5
53. Peru	100	28	70	65	65.8
54. Brazil	70	50	90	52	65.5
55. Zambia	50	64	70	75	64.8
56. Pakistan	80	52	80	45	64.3
57. Philippines	80	40	70	65	63.8
58. Paraguay	60	64	70	55	62.3
59. El Salvador	40	76	70	60	61.5
60. Jordan	40	76	70	60	61.5
61. Togo	20	82	60	80	60.5
62. Tunisia	50	75	40	75	60.0
Fairly low political freedom index (between 30% and 60%)					
63. Sri Lanka	90	13	60	70	58.3
64. Tanzania	40	82	40	70	58.0
65. Turkey	70	51	50	60	57.8
66. Nepal	45	64	60	60	57.3
67. Guatemala	65	28	70	65	57.0
68. Sierra Leone	20	76	70	60	56.5
69. Haiti	40	50	60	75	56.3
70. Nigeria	30	46	70	65	52.8
71. Kenya	20	52	70	65	51.8
72. Yemen	20	73	60	50	50.8
73. Cambodia	50	50	30	70	50.0
74. Kuwait	30	60	50	55	48.8
75. Uganda	20	27	70	75	48.0
76. Ghana	20	82	30	58	47.5
77. Egypt	40	34	50	65	47.3
78. Mozambique	20	46	60	60	46.5
79. Algeria	35	40	50	55	45.0
80. Indonesia	30	50	40	50	42.5
81. Viet Nam	40	40	40	50	42.5
82. Zaire	15	28	60	65	42.0
83. Cameroon	15	70	20	60	41.3
84. Morocco	30	50	40	45	41.3
85. Oman	10	73	20	55	39.5
86. Ethiopia	20	30	40	65	38.8
87. China	10	50	20	72	38.0
88. Malawi	10	64	10	65	37.3
89. Cuba	10	50	10	78	37.0
90. Angola	20	19	10	80	32.3

Country	Political participation	Rule of law	Freedom of expression	Non-discrimination	Political freedom index (PFI)
Lowest political freedom index (below 30%)					
91. Libyan Arab Jamahiriya	10	53	10	40	28.3
92. Saudi Arabia	10	60	20	10	25.0
93. Myanmar	10	13	10	65	24.5
94. Iran, Islamic Rep. of	30	25	10	30	23.8
95. Syrian Arab Rep.	10	20	10	55	23.8
96. Korea, Dem. Rep. of	10	10	10	55	21.3
97. Sudan	10	23	20	30	20.8
98. Rwanda	10	15	30	15	17.5
99. Afghanistan	10	15	10	25	15.0
100. Iraq	0	10	5	20	8.8

Source: Amnesty International, *Amnesty International Report 1994,* London, 1994; Freedom House, *Freedom in the World: 1993–1994,* New York, 1994; Charles Humana, *World Human Rights Guide,* New York: Oxford University Press, 1993; Human Rights Watch, *Human Rights Watch World Report 1994,* New York, 1994; Lawyers Committee for Human Rights, *Critique: Review of the Department of State's Country Reports on Human Rights Practices for 1993,* New York, 1994; Organization of American States, *Annual Report of the Inter-American Commission on Human Rights 1993–1994,* Washington, D.C., 1994; United Nations Commission on Human Rights, reports by special rapporteurs and the Secretary-General, Geneva, 1993–94; data from the United Nations Committee on the Elimination of Discrimination against Women and the United Nations Committee on the Elimination of Racial Discrimination; US Department of State, *Country Reports on Human Rights Practices for 1993,* Washington, D.C., 1994.

Chapter 6

A Framework for Sustainable Development

"O Oysters," said the Carpenter.
"You've had a pleasant run!
Shall we be trotting home again?"
But answer came there none—
And this was scarcely odd, because
They'd eaten every one.

— Through the Looking Glass

The call for sustainable development is not simply a call for environmental protection. Instead, it implies a new concept of economic growth—one that provides fairness and opportunity for all the world's people, not just a privileged few, without further destroying the world's finite natural resources and carrying capacity.

Sustainable development is a process in which economic, fiscal, trade, energy, agricultural, industrial and all other policies are designed to bring about development that is economically, socially and ecologically sustainable. This means that current consumption cannot be financed for long by incurring economic debts that others must repay. It also means that enough must be invested in the education and health of today's generations to avoid creating a social debt for future generations. And it means that natural resources must be used in ways that do not create ecological debts by overexploiting the earth's carrying and productive capacity. All postponed debts—whether economic, social or ecological—mortgage sustainability.

Sustainable development is concerned with replicable models of material consumption, models that recognize the limitations of the environment. They do not treat the ecosphere as a free good, to be plundered at will by any nation or individual. They put a price on this space, reflecting its relative scarcity today and tomorrow. And concerned with sensible asset management, they treat ecological space as any other scarce asset.

76   REFLECTIONS ON HUMAN DEVELOPMENT

Implementing such models of sustainable development requires far-reaching changes in both national and global policies. At the national level, a new balance must be struck between the efficiency of competitive markets, legal and regulatory frameworks that only governments can provide—and social safety nets for those with unequal access to the markets. Sustainability demands a balance between the compulsions of today and the needs of tomorrow, between private initiative and public action, between individual greed and social compassion. Sustainability also requires a major restructuring of budgetary priorities—from military spending and inefficient public enterprises towards more human investment and environmentally safe technologies—as well as the mobilization of additional resources.

At the global level, sustainable models of development require no less than a new global ethic—a clear understanding that the world cannot be made safe for anyone without the willing cooperation of everyone. Concern for common survival must lead to policies for a more equitable world order, based on fundamental global reforms.

Such a world order cannot be based on the passive perpetuation of today's international economic system. That system denies more than $500 billion of economic opportunities each year to poor nations because of their restricted or unequal access to global markets of trade, labour and capital. And it leads to a net resource transfer of more than $50 billion a year from poor to rich nations. In that system, richer nations reluctantly spare only 0.35% of their GNP in official development assistance for the 1.2 billion absolute poor in the developing world while earmarking budgetary resources equal to 15–20% of GNP for social safety nets for their own 100 million poor. And income disparities between the top 20% and the bottom 20% of the world's people have doubled over the past three decades, with the ratio of the two groups' incomes now at a staggering 150 to 1.

In such an unequal world of poor and rich, the concept of one world and one planet cannot be realized without some basic reforms. Nor can responsibility for the health of the global commons be shared without some measure of shared global prosperity. Without global justice, global sustainability will always remain an elusive goal.

The concept of sustainable human development

It is necessary, first, to define an operational concept of sustainable development. The Brundtland Commission's definition, useful as it is, is more a slogan than a framework for action. The commission defined sustainable development as "development that meets the needs of the present without compromising the ability of future generations to meet their own needs."

That definition begs more questions than it answers. What are the needs of the present and future generations? Developing countries are not satisfied with their present levels of consumption and have no intention of sustaining poverty. And industrial countries are not entitled forever to an 85% share of the world's income and to the perpetuation of their present patterns of consumption. In fact, the preservation of the global environment raises serious issues about the distribution of global income and assets in the present. There is no easy or clear link between present and future needs. The Brundtland report acknowledges these issues, but its definition of sustainable development is fairly static.

What we need to sustain is human life. Sustaining the physical environment is a means, not an end, just as GNP growth is only a means towards human development. The environmental debate must be given a human perspective to save it from the excesses of environmental fanatics, who often seem more interested in saving trees than in saving people. A more meaningful concept, therefore, is sustainable human development, putting people at the centre of the environmental debate.

If the basic concept is sustainable human development, each generation must meet its needs without incurring debts it cannot repay. That means avoiding the accumulation of environmental debts (by polluting or exhausting natural resources) as well as financial debts (through unsustainable borrowing), social debts (by neglecting to invest in human development) and demographic debts (by permitting unchecked population growth or urbanization). All these debts rob our children. Human development must allow each generation to balance its budget in each of these four areas.

The concept of sustainable human development would immediately focus on the nature and quality of economic growth, and avoid the sterile debate over zero growth. Growth is essential, but sustainable development requires that it be different. It must become more respectful of the physical environment. And it must translate into human lives. The concept of sustainability raises profound questions about the distribution and character of future global growth, but it sets no physical or technological limits on such growth.

One of our first challenges, therefore, is to give an operational framework to the concept of sustainable human development.

Some analysts interpret sustainability as a framework to preserve all natural heritage—all species, wildlife and forms of natural resources. There is much confusion here between ends and means, for what must be sustained is human life. Preservation or regeneration of natural resources is only a means towards this end. Throughout history, technological progress has altered the balance of the natural resources we need to sustain human life, and whether we believe in technological fixes or not, it is quite obvious that the natural resources needed to sustain present living standards will be quite different 50 years from now. Development opportunities and human choices must be preserved for future generations—not each and every form of natural capital or every ecological resource or every species. If more efficient substitutes are available, they must be used, as they have been throughout history. What must be sustained for the next generation is the capacity to enjoy at least the level of well-being that our own generation enjoys.

The concept of sustainable development should thus focus attention not only on the future but also on the present. There is something distinctly odd about worrying about unborn generations if the present generations are poor and miserable. And there is something clearly immoral about sustaining the present levels of poverty. Development patterns that perpetuate today's inequities are neither sustainable nor worth sustaining. A major restructuring of the world's income and consumption patterns—especially a fundamental change in the current life styles of the rich nations—is a necessary precondition for any viable strategy of sustainable development.

Within this broad perspective, six basic policy messages and a ten-point action agenda can move us from the concept of sustainable development to a programme of concrete action.

Basic policy messages

1. **Environmental concerns are not science fiction—they are real. The facts of environmental degradation are far more than the exaggerations of excited minds. And they are shocking.**

- Over the past 40 years, the world's population has more than doubled, to reach six billion people, and it is likely to double again over the next 40 years, increasing the pressure on natural resources.

- About 10% of the planet's potentially fertile land has already been turned into desert or wasteland through human interference or indifference, and another 25% is endangered. Every year, 8.5 million hectares are lost through erosion and silting, and more than 20 million hectares of tropical forests are cut down each year.

- Most poor people live in the most ecologically vulnerable areas: 80% in Latin America, 60% in Asia and 50% in Africa.

- About 1.3 billion people lack access to safe drinking water, 2.3 billion lack access to sanitation facilities, and 1.5 billion lack sufficient fuelwood for cooking and heating.
- The 1980s were the warmest decade of the century. If the present trend in emissions of carbon dioxide and other "greenhouse" gases continues, and the temperature continues to rise, the sea level could reach dangerous levels, with many unpredictable consequences for plants, animals and worldwide ecosystems.
- In Europe (excluding the former Soviet Union), the number of trees affected by air pollution is about 14 times greater than the number annually harvested in the region. Europe needs to spend $60 billion a year for the next 25 years to protect its forests from acidic and other air pollution.
- The OECD nations produced 9 billion tons of solid waste in 1990, including 300 million tons of hazardous waste. About 70% of that hazardous waste was disposed of in landfills, with possible consequences for human health and safety.
- American and European researchers have recently discovered that the depletion of the protective ozone layer is no longer a problem only in far-off Antarctica: it is about to occur over densely populated zones in the Northern Hemisphere.
- The social and economic costs of environmental degradation, though often heavy, are not counted in national income accounts. In Germany, the social cost of damage caused by transport noise is estimated at nearly 2% of GNP. In Costa Rica, the accumulated depreciation of its forests, soils and fisheries amounted to more than $4.6 billion (in 1989 dollars) between 1970 and 1990, about 6% of its GDP in that period. In Indonesia, the accumulated depreciation of forests, soils and petroleum resources between 1971 and 1984 amounted to $96 billion (in 1989 dollars), about 9% of its GDP in that period.

Environmental losses are a reality. They affect the lives of billions of people, in industrial and developing countries alike. And beyond the screaming headlines about global warming and depleted ozone are solid facts about environmental damage that affect the daily livelihood and quality of life of many people—reminders that current growth patterns do not respect nature.

2. A thoughtful response to these environmental concerns is not to stop economic growth or to continue previous patterns of growth, it is to design new models of sustainable development. The issue is not how much economic growth but what kind of growth, for zero growth can be as detrimental to the environment as rapid growth. It is the composition of GDP—the product mix and the types of production processes—that alone can tell whether the overall impact on the environment is positive or negative.

Continuing today's poverty would be one of the greatest threats to the sustainability of the planet, not just to the sustainability of human life. Poor people and poor countries depend on the soil for food, the rivers for water and the forests for fuel. Because they need these resources desperately, they have little choice—without assets or income—but to overuse and to destroy their natural environment simply to survive. In so doing, they threaten their health and the lives of their children. Economic growth is vital for giving more options to poor societies, but their models of development must become less energy intensive and more environmentally sound.

For industrial countries, too, stopping growth or even seriously slowing it is not much of an option for protecting the global environment. Their slower growth would imperil growth in the poor nations, which are dependent on the markets of the rich nations. Moreover, their continuing growth is needed to generate new environmentally safe technologies and the extra margin of resources needed for transfer to poor nations. But the growth models of industrial nations must change drastically. The current emphasis on the quantity of growth should be replaced by more concern with its quality. This should not, however, be confused with zero growth, which is largely a sterile, disruptive concept.

A consensus is growing that the character of future models of development must differ from that of today's models. But there is also a school of thought that believes that little change is necessary and that the present environmental debate is greatly exaggerated. It contends that, even on the most pessimistic assumptions, global warming would cause damage equivalent to only half a year's growth of world GNP over the next half century. It also argues that the only requirement for sustainability is that the financial savings rate should exceed the depreciation of natural, man-made and human capital every year, so that enough savings are always available to replace such capital.

These views are both facile and dangerous. There will be little comfort in such calculations if global warming raises the seas to dangerous levels. And financial savings will not be sufficient for sustainability if some natural resource required to sustain life (water or oxygen) becomes seriously depleted or if some essential human skills are missing. In short, financial savings alone may not be able to recreate natural resources.

3. The new models of sustainable development must focus on people as their primary concern, incorporate new environmentally safe technologies into all investment planning and seek ways to reflect the scarcity value of environmental resources in decision-making. The new models of sustainable development must be based on at least four guiding principles.

First, the models must place people at the centre. Environmental protection may be vital, but it is not an end in itself. Like economic growth, it is a means. The primary objective must be to protect human life and human options. Every environmental measure must be tested against how much it adds to the human welfare of the majority of the world's population. In other words, we must opt for sustainable human development. And we must begin to recognize that, in many places on our planet, people are the most endangered species.

Second, the new models of development must be based on environmentally sound technologies, particularly in energy. Emphasis on natural gas, clean coal technologies, unleaded fuel and catalytic converters could reduce emissions of particulates by 99%. There is also tremendous scope for reducing energy inputs per unit of output. For example, energy consumed in kilograms of oil equivalent per $100 of GNP is 13 in Japan, 18 in Germany, 35 in the United States, and 50 in Canada. If all industrial countries increased their energy efficiency to Japan's level, world consumption of energy would drop by around 2,300 billion kilograms of oil equivalent, or 36% of global energy consumption. The possibility for improvement is even greater in developing countries, where energy consumed in kilograms of oil equivalent for every $100 of GNP is 187 in China, 154 in Algeria, 132 in India and 105 in Egypt. New technologies and new patterns of production can thus drastically reduce energy inputs per unit of output and curtail the environmentally damaging emissions from each unit of energy used.

Third, powerful incentives are needed for economic agents to reflect the correct value of the environment in all decision-making. Markets and private investors often regard the environment as a free resource: its scarcity value is seldom reflected in investment decisions. The only effective way to underscore the value of the environment is to put a price on it. This must be done nationally, by correctly pricing environmental resources, particularly energy, and by making the polluters pay for the damage they cause. And it can be done globally, by issuing transferable national quotas for carbon dioxide emissions. Whatever the mechanism, the point is that the sustainability of development cannot be ensured unless environmental resources are properly priced.

REFLECTIONS ON HUMAN DEVELOPMENT

Fourth, sustainable development models must be participatory and community-based. They must mobilize all sectors of civil society because everyone has something valuable to contribute. They must ensure control by local communities over their natural resources. They must draw on local wisdom, experience and traditions for the sustainable management of water, land, soils, forests, rangelands, pasturelands, fisheries and wildlife. Unless local communities believe in and contribute to sustainability, national models of sustainable development will languish as theoretical exercises.

4. The concept of sustainability raises profound questions about the character and distribution of future global growth. A question often raised is whether the present material wealth of the rich nations can be replicated all over the world and whether the natural carrying capacity of the planet can bear such a burden. The answer: a resounding no. The North has roughly one-fifth of the world's people but consumes 70% of the world's energy, 75% of its metals, 85% of its wood and 60% of its food. To replicate the same material standards in the South would require 10 times the present consumption of fossil fuel and roughly 200 times the mineral wealth. And within 40 years, these requirements would double again as the world population doubles. Thus, the character of growth models must thus change. Can it change only for the developing world while the North continues to pursue the same levels of material consumption? Not in a world drawn close together in a global village.

The distribution of global consumption and global wealth must undergo a fundamental change. The North is not entitled forever to 85% of global income. Nor can its material consumption patterns be replicated across the entire world. The limited carrying capacity of the planet raises questions about the material life styles of the rich, about simpler and less energy intensive life styles all over the world and about a major redistribution of future development opportunities.

5. There are critical differences between the environmental priorities of the developing and the industrial nations. If we are to build a bridge of understanding between the North and the South, we must concede that environmental priorities can differ greatly at different stages of development. Industrial countries are now preoccupied with global warming, depletion of the ozone layer and disposal of hazardous wastes. Developing countries are concerned with much more basic elements of human survival: water and land.

Polluted water is a threat to life: 1.3 billion people in the developing countries still do not have access to safe drinking water. Eroded land is a threat to livelihood: in 1984 an estimated 135 million people lived in areas affected by desertification (up from 57 million in 1977).

It is unfortunate that "loud" environmental emergencies (global warming) receive more media attention than "silent" emergencies that affect the lives of many more people. For instance, 750 million children suffer from acute diarrhoeal diseases each year (and 4 million die) and 500 million people suffer from trachoma, 200 million from schistosomiasis and 800 million from hookworm. Just the provision of safe drinking water and sanitation and some education in hygiene can alleviate these environmental problems and relieve much human suffering. Surely, these issues should have as great a claim on the attention of the international community as the louder environmental emergencies.

Environmental standards for projects and programmes also differ vastly in developing and industrial countries. Poor nations, confronted with the struggle for daily survival with limited resources, naturally discount the future at a higher rate than do the rich nations. They cannot, and need not, adopt the environmental standards of Pittsburgh or Lancashire at their stage of development. That is why they may have to make their choices from a whole range of environmentally safe technologies.

6. Sustainable development models must avoid the false distinction between national and global environmental problems. Such a distinction is enshrined in the operations of the Global Environment Facility (GEF), meant to deal only with global warming, destruction of biological diversity, pollution of international waters and depletion of the ozone layer.

But every global environmental problem results from a national action and cannot be tackled without examining its national origins and root causes. The link between national and global environmental problems is important for another reason. Although much global pollution can stem from overconsumption by the rich, global poverty is one of the greatest threats to the global environment. If development policies are not adopted to overcome this poverty, poor people will continue to cut down trees and overuse their natural habitat merely to survive. The consequent environmental pollution and depletion of the world's oxygen reserves will affect all nations, not just the poor lands. In other words, the consequences of poverty cannot be contained within national borders. They travel all over the world, without a passport, in the form of global pollution. So, tackling global pollution requires tackling global poverty.

An agenda for action

Within the broader perspective of environment and development, the international community must make some critical decisions to protect the health and sustainability of the global commons. With today's crowded environmental agenda, the need is for selectivity to ensure that all the crucial tasks are undertaken. A ten-point agenda is given below for consideration by the international community.

1. Ecological resources must be correctly priced to reflect their scarcity value.

• At the national level, energy pricing must be re-examined to induce greater efficiency in energy use. Significant economies are possible. For instance, if Russia and other countries of the former Soviet Union, which account for two-thirds of the $232 billion in global energy subsidies, let fossil fuel prices rise to the world market level, carbon emissions would decline by roughly 6% globally. If all developing countries—including China, which accounts for about 20% of worldwide carbon emission from coal use—eliminated their energy subsidies, global carbon emissions would fall by 10%. And, as already noted, the adoption of Japan's energy use model by all industrial countries would reduce global energy use by 36%.

• Polluters must be made to pay for the environmental damage they cause. This principle should be built into the tax structure of every country.

• A significant carbon tax on fossil fuels should be considered. A tax of, say, $5 per barrel of oil, collected at the source by producers or exporters, would help encourage energy efficiency. But it could also yield more than $100 billion a year even if consumption shrinks (with about three-quarters of the revenue coming from industrial nations). An equivalent carbon tax on coal could yield more than $60 billion. Even a tax of $1 per barrel of oil and its equivalent on coal would yield a revenue of around $40 billion a year, but it might not have much effect on energy demand.

• Ration certificates for carbon dioxide emissions, to reflect for each country the extra cost of its using up ecological space, could automatically transfer resources from rich nations to poor. Tradable environmental permits issued to all nations—50% on the basis of their population and 50% on GNP—would transfer as much as 5% of the GNP of the rich nations to the poor.

2. In some environmental areas, mandatory quotas and compulsory audits may need to be introduced. Correct pricing is normally better than rationing. But mandatory quotas are needed in some areas.

• Mandatory ceilings on emissions of chlorofluorocarbons (CFCs) and other ozone-depleting substances have already been established by the Montreal Protocol.

• Many countries prescribe minimum energy efficiency standards for industrial undertakings, motor vehicles and human settlements—standards that are mandatory and that are monitored through regular audits. Information on successful national experiences in these areas should be made accessible to all countries.

• Some countries have already legislated clean air acts; all countries should adopt such legislation, adapted to their own conditions.

• International monitoring and regulatory mechanisms should be set up to ensure that the global mandatory quotas and national compulsory audits are efficiently implemented. Penalties may have to be assessed for non-compliance (along the lines of GATT and ILO practice).

3. A comprehensive framework should be established to encourage the use of environmentally safe technologies in future development. That framework will contain many components:

• A fiscal incentive system, based on a judicious system of tax credits, for the development of environmentally safe technologies.

• A global information system so that information about such technologies is made available to all nations, and at no cost to poor nations.

• A bar on long-term national patents and copyrights for environmentally safe technologies, so that a global market develops in these technologies, rather than protected and closely guarded monopolistic preserves.

• A mechanism to bring the private sector to the important task of such technology transfers.

• A global fund to make available at least 80% of the incremental costs of environmentally safe technologies to poor nations as grants, so that they can use cleaner technologies.

• A mechanism for paying to the developing countries the full incremental costs of any mandatory global quotas, as envisioned in the Montreal Protocol.

4. The national capacity of the developing countries to implement sustainable development policies and programmes must be strengthened. Few developing countries have the capacity to formulate, plan, implement and manage environmental programmes and to incorporate these programmes into their overall human development efforts. Strengthening national capacity for these purposes naturally means training people and setting up appropriate institutions. It also means creating self-supporting capacities in formulating and managing environmental policy, in generating and assimilating appropriate technologies and in developing community awareness and support for the environmental issues and opportunities. A comprehensive programme for national capacity building should comprise at least the following three elements:

• Environmental management planning, to help developing countries prepare their own national plans for implementation of the actionable agenda accepted at the Earth Summit.

• A capacity building window, perhaps as a separate window of the Global Environment Facility, making available 10–15% of the global environmental funds needed for building and strengthening indigenous capacity.

• Sustainable development networks, to enhance cooperation among developing countries through the exchange of information and policy experience about sustainable development.

5. Significant financial resources must be raised for both the environment and development through some practical international agreements. Words must give way to actions, and rhetoric to financial planning. Three promising ideas deserve the full attention of the international community:

• *A peace dividend.* All countries, industrial and developing, should commit themselves to reducing military expenditures in the 1990s by at least 3% a year. That has, in fact, been the actual trend over the past five years, though the peace dividend that materialized has not yet been committed to sustainable development. If this trend in reducing military spending is continued and a big part of the ensuing peace dividends mobilized for sustainable development, it is likely to yield during the course of the next decade a total peace dividend of around

$1.5 trillion, $1.2 trillion in the industrial countries and $300 billion in the developing countries.

• *Debt swaps.* A transformation of Third World debt into investment in sustainable development should be seriously considered. This debt has reached a staggering $1.3 trillion, increasing with each rescheduling and casting a dark shadow on the economic recovery prospects of developing countries. A sizable proportion of this debt needs to be written down—say, one-third—in exchange for a commitment by the beneficiary countries to invest the released resources in programmes and policies of sustainable development.

• *International taxation.* The compulsions for common survival may yet lead to an agreement for a system of international taxation to protect the global commons. Of many proposals for international environmental taxation, the more promising ones are:

- International taxes on fossil fuels.
- Greenhouse gas permits to emit a certain quantity of greenhouse gases.
- International taxes on arms sales, since the use of arms often destroys environment.
- Global commons taxes to reflect each country's usage of the global commons, such as the oceans (for fishing, transportation or seabed mining), the Antarctic (for mining) or space (for communication satellites).

6. Global institutional frameworks must be set up to assist in and finance the formulation of national sustainable development programmes. Several proposals for new funding mechanisms for sustainable development need to be considered. Of these, the proposal for establishing a sizable, general purpose "Green Fund", based on assessed contributions from rich nations and a system of international taxation, deserves serious consideration. But donors have been reluctant so far to go beyond some expansion of the resources of the Global Environment Facility. The GEF, while a useful start, needs to be modified:

• The mandate of the GEF should be enlarged to recognize more fully the links between national, regional and global problems and to include such concerns as desertification, acid rain, urban degradation, water pollution, land erosion and national capacity building.

• The enlarged mandate would require some $5 billion to $10 billion a year (compared with less than $1 billion at present), which could come from both voluntary contributions and new forms of international taxation.

REFLECTIONS ON HUMAN DEVELOPMENT

7. The need is urgent to formulate global environmental policies, particularly for energy, agriculture, population, tropical rain forests, climate, international trade and technology transfer. It would be ambitious, and totally unrealistic, to think in terms of global planning. Yet in some areas of environmental policy, clear policy signals are needed to avoid an uncertain and chaotic situation.

An international policy for energy is required, to economize on the use of fossil fuels and to increase the use of new and renewable energy sources. Energy must be included in any East-West or North-South agenda, and all policy-makers must be prepared to raise the national and international prices of fossil energy considerably.

An international policy for sustainable agriculture is needed, directed to securing sufficient food for everyone. This policy must give priority to increasing food production in the developing countries themselves, with as much emphasis as possible on agricultural methods and techniques that are sustainable and that demand little energy, capital or other inputs.

A global compact on slowing population growth rates should include national and global actions by 2000—to spread family planning knowledge and techniques to at least 80% of couples, to provide basic education and health care to all the people in the developing world (since human development is one of the most potent contraceptives) and to treat pressures from additional population on par with those from additional consumption in any pricing schemes for ecological space. The decisions at the UN-sponsored International Conference on Population and Development in September 1994 have made significant advances in this direction.

An international policy is also needed for conservation, aimed at the preservation and protection of tropical rain forests, at reforestation, at the maintenance of river basins and at the preservation of the soil's natural fertility. Such a policy would combat soil erosion and desertification, pollution by waste materials and poisoning by the dumping of dangerous substances. It would require international agreements, regulations and aid programmes. It could even mean that the international community would have to assume joint responsibility for areas whose ecological value far exceeds the financial resources of the countries or areas in which they are located. Examples include the Amazon region, the Antarctic, certain seas, and certain areas constituting the "common heritage of mankind"

An international policy on climate should be based on concrete, enforceable objectives for limiting emissions of carbon dioxide and other greenhouse gases to levels that can guarantee sustainable development.

An international trade and investment policy should not merely aim at liberalization and growth. It should also meet environmental criteria. Countries should not be allowed to export their pollution through trade. Nor should they be allowed to use strict environmental criteria as trade barriers. The best course is to agree on some minimum international environmental standards for exports and imports. This should be regarded as a priority area for the new World Trade Organization.

An international policy for technology transfers should ensure that environmentally sound technologies are not closely guarded, as all other technologies are, but made more freely available in the interest of common survival.

8. All countries should be encouraged to prepare environmentally sensitive national income accounts ("green GNP") to reflect the impact of environmental damage on national and global output each year. With each year, the world's resources steadily depreciate. Natural resources are used up, physical capital wears out, and the skills of human beings need to be replaced from one generation to the next. If the present generation in any country does not cover this depreciation with sufficient savings and investment, the base for future production will erode. And even if savings are sufficient, bottlenecks may develop if critical natural resources or human skills are missing.

Traditional economic indicators, such as GNP and GDP, are inadequate measures of sustainability. They may measure production, but they provide little information about people or about the state of their living environment. If a deteriorating environment causes disease, pushing up health expenditures and thus GNP, the higher GNP would be interpreted as a higher level of development even though people and their environment are worse off. Similarly, current income measures do not factor in the inevitable future costs of today's resource depletion.

As noted earlier, there may have to be significant adjustments to national income accounts if the depreciation of natural capital is taken into account. Costa Rica's GNP between 1970 and 1990 would be reduced by 6%, and Indonesia's between 1971 and 1984 by 9%. And this is only a partial adjustment, one that does not reflect all the depreciation in natural capital or the depreciation in human capital. Preparation of environmentally adjusted national income accounts would constantly remind us of what we are doing to nature and what it is costing us in turn.

9. A three-year timetable should be proposed for the formulation of sustainable human development strategies by both developing and industrial countries, coordinated and monitored at the global level. Because concrete action can be implemented only at the national level, all countries should be encouraged to prepare comprehensive sustainable human development strategies. These strategies should embrace all long-term national exercises now under way, such as the followups to the Jomtien Conference on Education for All and to the World Summit on Children, and the long-term strategies for Africa. Such sustainable human development plans should be prepared by both developing and industrial nations and submitted to the United Nations Sustainable Development Commission, which has the responsibility to coordinate and monitor national plans and to suggest global initiatives on that basis.

10. An Economic Security Council should be set up within the United Nations to formulate and implement a policy framework for new concepts of "people-centred security" and human justice, including ecological and economic security. The United Nations offers the world community a potentially effective system of global governance. But it still lacks a manageable and credible forum for coordinating global development policy. As development issues become increasingly global and universal, there is an urgent need to set up an Economic Security Council (chapter 16). Such a council should review security in its widest sense—security for people, not just for land—embracing all the issues from food security to ecological security.

One of the first tasks of this council should be to discuss and agree on the framework of an earth charter, for ratification by all nations. The earth charter should spell out the environmental obligations of all countries and have some real teeth. For instance, it should include:

- Mandatory quotas for carbon emissions and other forms of global pollution.
- Concrete elements of a global energy policy.
- Pricing policy for ecological space.
- Some form of international taxation or assessed contributions to raise resources for sustainable development.

The Economic Security Council must also recognize that environmental stress and human deprivation arise almost invariably from injustice between groups, between regions and between nations. An unjust system can never be sustainable. The council must, therefore, also address the much larger issue of global poverty—for without the alleviation of this poverty, there can never be environmental peace.

The Earth Summit in June 1992 offered a unique opportunity to strike a new global compact between rich and poor nations. It resulted in a consensus on the far-reaching Agenda 21 as a blueprint for sustainable development in the 21st century.

But the Earth Summit was the beginning, not the culmination, of a long-term process. If people finally discover that their survival is linked to the survival of all, if concern for the global commons finally creates a common resolve and bridges the North-South divide, if there is a greater awareness of the need for social justice on this shrinking planet, then the Earth Summit would have marked the beginning of a new understanding, a new era of cooperation, a new journey of hope.

REFLECTIONS ON HUMAN DEVELOPMENT

Chapter 7

Human Development Strategies in South Asia

> *"Well, in our country," said Alice, still panting a little, "you'd generally get to somewhere else—if you ran very fast for a long time, as we've been doing."*
>
> *"A slow sort of country!" said the Queen. "Now, here, you see, it takes all the running you can do, to keep in the same place. If you want to get somewhere else, you must run at least twice as fast as that!"*
>
> — Through the Looking Glass

*T*he battle for human development is going to be won or lost mainly in Asia because that is where 70% of the developing world's people live. Asia has made significant human progress in the past three decades. Average life expectancy has increased by 18 years—from 46 years in 1960 to 64 years in 1990. Average primary enrolment has increased from 57% to 71%. Infant and child mortality rates have been about halved. And the immunization coverage for one-year-olds is now around 85% in East Asia—higher than the average for industrial countries.

But there is a distressing and lengthening agenda of human deprivation. More than 700 million people live in absolute poverty. More than 600 million people cannot read or write, two-thirds of them women. And about half the people have no access to safe drinking water.

More disturbing are the wide disparities within Asia. South Asia, with more than one billion people, has a life expectancy 12 years lower than that in East Asia and a literacy rate 34 percentage points lower, 47% compared with 81%, and the lowest of all regions. Three-quarters of the world's illiterate people live in the five most populous Asian states—China, India, Pakistan, Bangladesh and Indonesia.

The contrast in the investment in people is sharp between the East Asian industrializing tigers and South Asia's economies. Annual per capita expenditure on human priority areas of basic education, primary health care, family planning, safe drinking water and nutritional programmes is $2 in Bangladesh, $3 in Pakistan and Indonesia and $9 in India. Contrast that with $133 in the Republic of Korea and $123 in Malaysia. East Asia has also invested a lot in technical and vocational education and in scientific and technological research. That is why the Republic of Korea today has 46 scientists and technicians per thousand people, compared with only 3 in India and Pakistan.

Investing in human development has been a key strategy of economic growth in East Asia. In the Republic of Korea, labour productivity grew by 11% a year between 1963 and 1979—with only half that growth due to increased capital investment. During 1985–90, Thailand increased its labour productivity by 63%, and it is now beginning to outstrip the pace earlier set by the Republic of Korea. At the heart of the East Asian economies' development strategies is a massive investment in people and technology—a strategy still missing in many countries of South Asia. So, even today, all countries of South Asia, except Sri Lanka, fall in the category of low human development.

The task ahead is clear. Sustainable human development must move to the top of Asia's priority agenda for 2000. The most important goals are universal access to basic education, primary health care for all, provision of family planning facilities, elimination of serious malnutrition and provision of safe drinking water to all. These goals are more relevant for the poorer economies of South Asia, still at a very low level of human development. Achieving them by 2000 will cost an additional $14 billion a year during the 1990s.

It is essential today that Asian economies prepare their own national human development strategies, cost them fully and reflect them in their investment and budget frameworks. One persistent question is whether adequate resources are available for accelerated human investment. It is abundantly clear that these resources can be mobilized if the necessary political will is there.

Agenda for action

Asian countries should consider freezing their military spending, to release additional resources for human development. The arithmetic of military spending in Asia is depressing. Asia currently spends $85 billion a year on its military. It imports $11 billion of arms every year. Some countries spend several times more on their military than on the education and health of their people. Soldiers outnumber teachers in many countries: Afghanistan and the Lao People's Democratic Republic have twice as many soldiers as teachers. South Asia's share in global income is only 2%, but its share in global arms imports is around 20%. India ranks

100th in the developing world in per capita income but number one in imports. In Pakistan, soldiers outnumber physicians by 10 to 1, in Viet Nam by 47 to 1.

There is a new window of opportunity in the 1990s to divert potential increases in military spending to social development. In the post–cold war era, it should become obligatory for the big powers to phase out their military bases in the Third World, convert their military assistance into economic assistance and restrict shipments of sophisticated arms. It is also necessary to build new structures of peace and security in the Asian region under a strengthened UN umbrella. And it is imperative for the Asian countries to find new avenues of peaceful accommodation with one other. If the Asian countries manage just to freeze their military spending in the 1990s—not cut it by 3–4% every year as industrial nations are beginning to do—it could potentially create a peace dividend of around $150 billion over the next decade, enough to finance all their essential human goals.

The need for such a freeze on military spending is particularly imperative in the countries of the South Asian Association for Regional Cooperation (SAARC)—containing a billion of the poorest people in the world, half of them without access to clean drinking water. The current military expenditures of around $20 billion a year in South Asia mock the extremes of human deprivation in the region. It is a challenge for the entire international community to create a new framework of peaceful accommodation in this region, so that the limited resources of these nations can be earmarked for their essential human needs.

Asian governments should get out of the productive sectors and into the social sectors. In many countries—particularly in South Asia—governments are overextended in production and trade. They overregulate their economic systems, leading to inefficiency and corruption. The losses of public enterprises could be avoided by privatizing some of these activities, so that much-needed resources could be diverted to social sectors. For example, South Asia spends only 6.6% of its combined GNP on education and health. The losses of public enterprises often amount to around 3% of GNP. A more thoughtfully defined role for the public sector could easily increase resource availability for social services by as much as 50% in many Asian countries.

Within the social sectors, governments must ensure that money is spent efficiently. There are far too many examples of inefficiencies and inequities: urban hospitals for a privileged few rather than primary health care for all; enormous subsidies for the universities while basic education goals await their turn in the budgetary queue; piped water for the higher-income groups rather than standpipes for the masses. Pakistan spends only 14% of its limited social sector budget on basic education and primary health care, but earmarks 86% for higher education and urban hospitals. This is a very wasteful use of precious resources. Of the roughly $10 billion spent each year on water supply in developing countries, an estimated 80% goes to services for the better-off. To provide safe water through standpipes would cost only $5 a person per year. It is ironic that in many countries the wealthy receive good services very cheaply while the poor get inadequate services at a higher price.

If the Asian countries make a determined effort to achieve these human development goals by 2000, the international community must lend a helping hand—in three ways. The first is to restructure aid allocations. Despite its grinding poverty, South Asia receives only $5 per person in official development assistance (ODA) each year—compared with $55 for aid-receiving countries of the Middle East, which have more than three times South Asia's per capita income. India has 27% of the world's absolute poor, yet it receives only 5.2% of total ODA. The second is to change aid priorities in favour of the human priority areas of basic education, primary health care and safe water. The third is to progressively dismantle trade barriers so that Asian countries can share more of the global economic opportunities. This is more significant now that many of the large South Asian countries, including India and Pakistan, are beginning to open up their economies.

A proposal for SAARC 2000
Nowhere is the need for a coordinated human development strategy as great as in the SAARC region, with 1.2 billion people in seven countries: Bangladesh, Bhutan, India, Maldives, Nepal, Pakistan and Sri Lanka. The region has an average real per capita income of around $1,260, compared with $14,860 in the industrial countries. Many people in this region still live in "absolute poverty", without the possibility to meet minimum nutritional requirements and other basic needs, including 78% of the people in Bangladesh, 40% in India and 28% in Pakistan. Set up as a cooperative regional arrangement in 1985, with many hopes and great promises, SAARC has achieved little in its first ten years of existence.

Even more distressing are the dismal human development indicators in the region, except in Sri Lanka. Literacy rates are low (generally below 40%). Infant mortality (an average of 94 per thousand live births) and population growth rates (between 2.2% and 3.1%) are quite high. Healthcare coverage is inadequate, and the per capita daily calorie supply is below internationally accepted standards. Even when these societies increase their production, they pay scant attention to the rapid development of their only real and abundant resource—their human capital. This relative neglect is reflected not only in their investment priorities but also in their budgetary expenditures on social services relative to their military expenditures.

In this context, the SAARC leaders should seriously consider a coordinated human development plan for 2000. Other avenues of cooperation—particularly trade—can raise controversies at this stage. But there can be no such controversy in the competition for accelerated human development.

At least three concrete steps are essential in developing an action programme:

First, each country in the SAARC region should prepare targets for 2000 for literacy, primary health care, nutrition, shelter and population planning. While national planning is the sovereign right of each country, it will be desirable to aim at universal primary education, complete immunization coverage, safe drinking water, minimum levels of nutrition and shelter for the entire population and a significant reduction in the population growth rate. The Bangalore Summit Declaration in 1987 "subscribed to the goals of universal immunisation by 1990, universal primary education, maternal and child nutrition, provision of safe drinking water and adequate shelter before 2000 AD." The next step is to broaden these goals into a comprehensive human development plan, to translate each target into a series of interlocking national five-year plans, to earmark necessary financial resources for these targets and to strengthen the administrative machinery and institutions required for their implementation.

Second, the SAARC Secretariat must provide technical assistance for the preparation of these national plans and should formulate a consolidated SAARC 2000 perspective based on individual country plans. The Secretariat, with fairly limited manpower resources at present, will have to draw on specialized expertise from the region. Bangladesh has done rather well in family planning, Pakistan in children's immunization, India in non-formal education and Sri Lanka in improving the overall quality of life. Their socio-economic environments have many similarities, so it is easier to transfer such experience from one country to another, a role that the SAARC Secretariat can perform.

To institutionalize intellectual analysis and policy studies in these areas, it would be useful to set up a SAARC Institute for Human Development, where the region's best scholars could assemble to carry out professional work on concrete strategies and programmes for human progress in the SAARC region. Such an institute could also monitor the yearly progress in implementing the objectives of SAARC 2000 and present an independent and objective annual report to each SAARC Summit on the State of the Human Condition within the SAARC region. Such reports, a refreshing change from the routine monitoring of GNP and investment growth, would go to the heart of the human equation in the development process. A special focus in these reports should be the status of women, because all objective indicators show that they have suffered most in the process of socio-economic change.

Third, preparation of a human development plan for SAARC 2000 would offer an opportunity for external donors to provide generous assistance on soft terms to a region where more people live in absolute poverty than anywhere else in the world. It could also elicit coordinated efforts from UN specialized agencies—such as UNICEF, WHO, UNESCO, UNFPA, and UNDP—to assist in the formulation of the SAARC 2000 perspective and in its implementation. The SAARC 2000 plan would become even more attractive if it persuaded the political leadership in these countries to accept a mutually agreed freeze—or even a significant cut—in military spending to release the necessary resources for their human development.

For human development strategies to succeed in the SAARC region, they must be embraced by both India and Pakistan, whose cooperation will be vital for any successful regional cooperation. Normalization of political relations between the two countries is essential for this purpose. With the recent unexpected developments for peace in East-West relations, and between Israel and Palestine, the end of apartheid in South Africa and the cease-fire by the Irish Republican Army—it is only logical that India and Pakistan should seek some mutually acceptable resolution of their bitter confrontation of the past five decades.

During the past few years, India and Pakistan together have spent twice as much on the import of arms as Saudi Arabia, which is about 25 times richer. At a time when their human development indicators are among the lowest in the world and economic and social despair among their poor is coming to a boil, their confrontation is costing them $20 billion a year on defence spending. Each jet fighter acquired by these countries costs them over one million children in primary schools. If both were only to freeze military spending for the next decade, they could finance the costs of universal basic education, universal primary healthcare, safe drinking water for all and many other basic social services.

If the proposal for SAARC 2000 is to succeed, both India and Pakistan must embrace it enthusiastically, since more than 80% of the SAARC population lives in these two countries.

Human development strategy for India

Despite considerable social progress in the past, India's life expectancy of 60 years and adult literacy rate of 50% are significantly lower than the average for all developing countries. By contrast, China has a life expectancy of 70 years and adult literacy rate of 80%. In 1990, more than 350 million people were estimated to live below the poverty line in India, more than one-fourth of the world's absolute poor. About 75 million children (of which 54 million are girls) are not in school. Nearly 70 million children under five are malnourished. About 216 million people are without access to safe drinking water.

A concrete agenda for action is needed that would not only accelerate economic growth but also eradicate all these forms of human deprivation—so as to provide an environment where this great mass of humanity can fully develop and both contribute to and benefit from development.

Indian planners need to draw up a long-term human development strategy covering the next 10–15 years. Such a strategy should clearly identify the human development objectives that India hopes to reach—particularly in education, health and technology—through judicious investment in its human capital. These human development goals should be fully costed and reflected in a broadly based growth and investment strategy—with a timetable. Many developing countries have already embarked on the formulation of such comprehensive human development strategies, with technical support from UNDP at the request of their governments. In Asia, such strategies are currently being prepared in Bangladesh, Indonesia, Pakistan and Viet Nam. The basic decision to prepare and implement long-term human development strategies must be taken by the government itself since it requires tremendous political commitment and must be primarily an indigenous exercise.

No worthwhile human development objectives can be achieved or sustained without a generous injection of economic growth. It is encouraging that India has broken away from its low growth trap of only 1.5% annual growth in per capita income from 1965 to 1980 to a much more respectable growth rate of 3.3% during the 1980s. But even this growth rate will need to be accelerated considerably in the next decade if worthwhile objectives are to be achieved for human development. The recent courageous experiments in abolishing stifling economic controls and privatizing some public enterprises will help. But a note of caution: when markets are freed, there is even greater need for social action.

Markets are not particularly friendly to the poor and the vulnerable, who may require considerable investment in their human potential before they can begin to compete on equal footing in the market-place. Even in laissez-faire economies such as the United States, about 15% of GNP is recycled towards the lower-income groups through medicare, food stamps, unemployment benefits, education subsidies, nutritional supplements and various forms of welfare payments. In Sweden, the ratio is over 35%. The need for social safety nets in poor developing countries is obvious—existing income distribution is very uneven, and democratic accountability generally limited. The new ideology of the market-place must thus be tempered with a judicious amount of social compassion so that efficiency and equity march in step.

India must increase its social expenditure. Its present expenditure on human priority concerns—basic education, primary health care, safe drinking water, child nutrition, family planning—is only 2.5% of its GNP, compared with 12.7% in Zimbabwe, 7.7% in Botswana, 6.3% in Malaysia and 5.5% in Jordan. India also makes fairly limited investments in science and technology, despite having some of the most outstanding institutes in this field. There are only 3 scientists and technicians in India for every thousand people, compared with averages of 9 for all developing countries and 85 for industrial nations. India clearly is investing far too little in its human capital, and it will have to explore several avenues to find additional resources for human investment. The most feasible and promising is restructuring existing budgetary priorities. Reducing the losses of public enterprises through phased privatization will definitely help. So will restructuring development priorities towards programmes that have a beneficial impact on poorer groups. But the biggest potential lies in military spending.

There is no doubt that a more favourable global economic environment will help India considerably in accelerating its economic growth and sustainable human development in the coming decade. It is not clear why official development assistance provides India only $2 per capita while Botswana gets $124, Jamaica $105, Jordan $70 and Egypt $30. India's size has often discriminated against it: as noted earlier, with 27% of the world's absolute poor, it gets only 5% of total ODA. A lack of concessional assistance has obliged India to incur hard debts—which exploded over the past decade, mortgaging India's future options. Nor has the trade environment been favourable, with barriers heaviest on labour-intensive exports, particularly textiles and footwear.

But India's real battle for human development lies at home, not abroad. If human investment is adopted as a major priority in national planning, India can soon convert its large population into a competitive advantage and bring the fruits of economic growth closer to its people.

Human development strategy for Pakistan

Few countries in the world show a wider gap between their investment in physical production and their investment in human capital than Pakistan, which has neglected investing in its most precious wealth—its people. The results are obvious. Pakistan has yet to translate the benefits of its fairly reasonable economic growth rates into the day-to-day lives of its people. Pakistan's adult literacy rate of 36% is 33 percentage points below the average for all developing countries (69%). Its net enrolment ratio in basic education is around 50%, compared with 100% in China and Sri Lanka, 97% in Indonesia, 90% in Malaysia and 68% in India. And its infant mortality rate (100 per thousand live births) is significantly higher than the average for the developing world (70).

Most of Pakistan's education, health, nutrition and other social indicators lag considerably behind those of other developing countries at a comparable per capita income, and within Asia, the comparisons are distressing. Pakistan's per capita income compares favourably with those of China and Sri Lanka. But on the Human Development Index, as shown in *Human Development Report 1994*, Pakistan ranks 132, compared with 90 for Sri Lanka and 94 for China. In adult literacy, Sri Lanka has already reached 89% and China 80%—compared with Pakistan's 36%, despite similar per capita incomes.

Despite Pakistan's income being much higher than India's, its people suffer much greater human deprivation because personal income is unevenly distributed and because Pakistan's governments have consistently neglected the provision of basic social services. Pakistan is 70% ahead of India in its real income, according to World Bank estimates, but far behind in human development: its adult literacy rate is 36%, compared with India's 50%; its combined enrolment at all levels is 24%, compared with 50%; and its access to safe drinking water is 50%, compared with 75%.

The magnitude of human deprivation in Pakistan boggles the mind: 55 million people have no access to safe drinking water or primary health care services; 95 million are deprived of sanitation services; 35

million people are below the absolute poverty line, with limited access to even the very basic needs for human survival; 42 million adults are illiterate, two-thirds of them women; 4 million children under five are severely malnourished.

Pakistan is simply not preparing for the technological challenges of the 21st century. It spends only $3 per capita on real human priority concerns, compared with $133 in the Republic of Korea, $123 in Malaysia and $9 in India. Besides, too few students go for scientific and technical skills—only 1.6% at the secondary school level, compared with ten times that many in the Republic of Korea. Pakistan has yet to recognize that the quality of human capital changes the destiny of any country.

The neglect of Pakistan's human resources arises from a feudal society that places a low value on the lives of the ordinary people—except at election times. Accumulating over the past four decades, this human neglect cannot be reversed overnight. It will require considerable investment in human development over a fairly long period of time—and tough decisions on resource allocations. There will be no quick results or facile solutions.

Pakistan needs to spend a minimum of 10% of its GNP on the provision of basic social services to its people—particularly education and health. Until 1990, Pakistan was spending around 3% of its GNP. The size of recent allocations, after the launching of its Social Action Programme, remains unclear—though it is possible that the budget provision has increased to over 5% of GNP. Still, at least a doubling of current allocations is called for. This will be impossible if debt servicing continues to consume 6% of GNP, if defence spending consumes another 7% and if tax revenue does not rise above the present 14% of GNP. If social expenditure is to have its rightful place in the national budget, rather than remain a mere residual, a complete restructuring of fiscal management is required. Domestic debt must be reduced through the sale of major public assets. And defence spending must be brought into a better balance with social spending, without compromising the legitimate requirements of national security.

If Pakistan is to make any strides on the road to human development, it must strike a much better balance between investment in arms and investment in its people. Pakistan is spending 125% as much on its military as on the education and health of its people. It has 50% more soldiers than teachers. The human cost of current arms purchases is prohibitive. As *Human Development Report 1994* points out, Pakistan ordered 40 Mirage 2000 E fighters and three Tripartite aircraft from France in 1992 at a cost that could have provided clean water for two years for all 55 million who lack safe drinking water, plus family planning services for the estimated 20 million couples in need of them, plus essential medicines for the nearly 13 million people without access to health care, plus basic education for the 12 million children out of primary school. Just one year's purchase of arms by Pakistan could have financed most of its essential social agenda. In 1994, Pakistan also purchased three submarines at a reported cost of $1.2 billion, a sum that could have provided safe drinking water for about half the country's population or extended basic education to all children currently out of school. Of course, Pakistan cannot unilaterally undertake a reduction in military spending. A SAARC agreement on joint reductions in military spending is needed so that no nation within the region is put at a comparative disadvantage.

Since Pakistan's budgetary resources will remain tight, it needs to squeeze the maximum mileage out of its funds. This means giving a greater priority (and subsidy) to basic education rather than to university buildings, to primary health care rather than to expensive hospitals, to cost-effective community water taps in rural areas rather than to piped water in high-income urban neighborhoods. It is the poor who need government patronage, not the rich, who can afford to pay for the services they get. But only 14% of social expenditure goes for priority needs in Pakistan, compared with 68% in Malaysia and 50% in Zimbabwe. Despite limited resources for social development, Pakistan's priorities still are not tilted in favour of the poor majority. To mobilize grass-roots community efforts, government spending must be supplemented by providing liberal incentives to NGOs and the private sector. Self-help by the community must play an increasingly larger role, and that requires a thoughtful policy framework.

Pakistan must also place much greater emphasis on science and technology. Technical schools—imparting training in the technological skills of the 21st century—should be opened in every district, some financed through foreign assistance, particularly from Japan and UNDP. But what is needed is not just new technical schools—it is a change in the entire national culture. Pakistan should start giving modern science and technical skills their proper place in the society. Technical schools should issue degrees, not just diplomas. Technicians should be properly rewarded: the special allowance for Ph.D.s and computer technicians in the 1985 and 1988 budgets was only a small recognition of this need. Private industry should be exposed to greater competition through lower tariffs—so that it realizes that profitability depends on new technology, not sheltered markets. In other words,

Pakistan must start thinking like a modern, scientific nation: Republics of Korea are not built on feudal attitudes.

Given unpredictable budgetary pressures, it is wise to segregate some financial resources in a special fund for social needs. The *Iqra* surcharge levied under the 1985 budget on all imports (yielding 8 billion rupees) was meant for this purpose, and there was an accompanying suggestion for a separate *Iqra* fund and an eminent *Iqra* board. But the fund was not separated from the general budgetary pool—a major mistake and a betrayal of national trust. What is needed now is the establishment of a national human development fund that can receive a share of the proceeds of various taxes and be protected from the vicissitudes of political change.

Pakistan should also begin to attract the return of its considerable human capital from abroad—far more valuable than the return of foreign bank deposits. To begin with, a complete inventory of this human capital should be prepared by the government and supplied to the private sector—to open the prospect of matching demand and supply. The educated youth abroad will return only if Pakistan's society is built on merit, on democratic values and on the rule of law. The exodus of Pakistan's best human capital has been a revolt against the feudal values that have dominated the society.

Pakistan's investments in education are investments in change, and female education is the most potent weapon in advancing socially and economically and in reducing population growth. Such investments are likely to give Pakistan a political and economic payoff that no other investment can promise.

Pakistan has a long way to go in its search for a viable human development strategy. It shares a gross neglect of human investment with other Islamic countries. This neglect does not arise from its Islamic cultural heritage—which has always taken pride in advances in education and science and technology—but from its prevailing feudal system. But there is a curious similarity with other Islamic countries that are also trying to shake off feudal traditions and enter the modern world of human enterprise. The next chapter explores this issue in the broader context of the entire Islamic world.

Chapter 8

Human Development Potential in the Islamic World

> *"Take some more tea," the March Hare said to Alice, very earnestly.*
> *"I've had nothing yet," Alice replied in an offended tone, "so I can't take more."*
> *"You mean you can't take* less," *said the Hatter: "it's very easy to take* more *than nothing."*
>
> — Alice in Wonderland

he human development ranks of Islamic countries are generally lower than their per capita income ranks, showing that their income has not been fully translated into the lives of their people. The overall Human Development Index (HDI) for 49 Islamic countries is only 0.393, placing the Islamic world in the low human development category. Many Islamic countries have HDI ranks far below their per capita GNP ranks: for example, the difference is 54 for Oman, 52 for the United Arab Emirates and 41 for Iraq (table 8.1). This difference reveals the considerable potential in these societies for enhancing their human development.

Some non-Islamic countries enjoy much better education and health than Islamic countries at similar per capita incomes (table 8.2). In access to health services, safe water and sanitation—and in combined primary and secondary enrolment ratios—the Islamic world lags behind the developing country average. Within their respective regions, the Islamic countries are generally behind the regional average in most social indicators of development.

While this picture is true for most Islamic countries, there is a brighter side. Some Islamic countries, particularly Jordan, Malaysia and Tunisia, show that much can be done in human development if the political determination is there. Jordan and Tunisia, at per capita incomes of $1,060 and $1,500, enjoy literacy levels higher than Saudi Arabia's, which has a per capita income five times higher. Similarly, Malaysia, starting from a fairly low level of human development in 1960 (HDI of 0.331), achieved the largest absolute increase in HDI during 1960–92 (with an HDI of 0.794 in 1992).

There are some critical gaps in the human development record of most Islamic countries:

• There is significant income and wealth inequality. For example, the latest data for Pakistan indicate that the poorest 20% of the households receive only 8% of national income while the wealthiest 20% receive 46%. In Morocco, the comparable figures are 10% and 40%.

• The disparities are also reflected in the ownership of land and the feudal structure of power. The Gini coefficient of land distribution, a measure of inequality in landownership (with perfect equality at 0 and perfect inequality at 1), was as high as 0.83 in Saudi Arabia, 0.64 in Yemen and 0.54 in Pakistan in the 1980s.

• Widespread poverty prevails in many Islamic countries. In Ghana, Mali and Tanzania, more than half the rural people are in absolute poverty, and in Bangladesh 86% are.

• Another critical human gap is in the status of women. In such indicators as maternal mortality, average age at first marriage, literacy and primary enrolment, women in the Islamic countries are generally far behind their counterparts in the rest of the developing world.

• The Islamic countries also lag behind other nations in their accomplishments in scientific and technical education. Many high school students prefer to go for general education rather than for technical education. For instance, secondary technical enrolment as a per-

Table 8.1 GNP and HDI rankings of selected Islamic countries

Country	GNP per capita rank	HDI rank	GNP per capita rank minus HDI rank
Oman	38	92	−54
United Arab Emirates	10	62	−52
Guinea	129	173	−44
Iraq	59	100	−41
Libyan Arab Jamahiriya	41	79	−38
Algeria	72	109	−37
Qatar	20	56	−36
Saudi Arabia	31	67	−36
Senegal	114	143	−29
Bahrain	33	58	−25
Kuwait	28	51	−23
Iran, Islamic Rep. of	64	86	−22
Lebanon	83	103	−20

Source: UNDP, Human Development Report 1994, New York: Oxford University Press, 1994.

centage of total secondary enrolment is only 1.6% in Pakistan and 2.5% in Uganda, compared with a ratio ten times higher in the Republic of Korea.

The picture is not so bleak that nothing much can be done—the reverse is true. Many Gulf states have made rapid progress in human development in the past two decades, particularly after the rise in oil prices increased their resources and policy options (table 8.3). In most human development indicators, the change in the Arab region during 1970–90 was much faster than in the rest of the developing world. Between 1960 and 1990, the HDI of Saudi Arabia nearly doubled and that of Morocco increased by 60%. Between 1970 and 1985, the HDI of the Yemen Arab Republic more than tripled, and there was an increase of more than 60% in Algeria, Jordan and Syria. This shows that there is no cause for despondency—and that rapid human progress is possible once the right development priorities are set and sufficient financial resources are made available.

But if the Islamic countries wish to finance higher levels of human development, they must reconsider their military expenditures, often among the highest in the world (table 8.4). In the Arab States, an average of 7.1% of GNP goes into military spending—as much as 18% in Saudi Arabia and 16% in Oman. There are 27 times as many soldiers as doctors in the Arab world, compared with a ratio of only 4 to 1 in the industrial nations. Many Islamic countries spend much more on their military than on education and health. For instance, the ratio of military spending to spending on education and health in 1990 was 511% in Iraq, 500% in Somalia, 239% in Pakistan and 177% in Saudi Arabia.

Table 8.2 Similar incomes but different human development

Country	GNP per capita (US$) 1991	HDI rank	Life expectancy (years) 1992	Adult literacy rate (%) 1992	Infant mortality rate (per 1,000 live births) 1992
Low-income					
China	370	94	70	80	27
Pakistan	400	132	58	36	99
Middle-income					
Colombia	1,250	50	69	87	30
Jordan	1,060	98	67	82	37
High-income					
Barbados	6,650	20	75	99	10
Saudi Arabia	7,900	67	68	64	31

Source: UNDP, *Human Development Report 1994,* New York: Oxford University Press, 1994.

No one should take lightly the national security requirements of these nations, particularly in their difficult geopolitical context. But a balance must be struck between territorial security and human security. Without an educated and trained population, sophisticated weapons systems often become useless and irrelevant. And many nations have discovered that their real defence lies in the training and scientific education of their people.

A few proposals

It is time for an annual report on human development in the Islamic world. Such a report would regularly update all information on human development progress in the Islamic countries, focus on selected policy issues requiring the attention of the region's top policy-makers and highlight relevant country experience in the Islamic world. The Islamic Development Bank might take the lead in financing the production of such a report by an independent group of experts from the Islamic region. The network of research institutions in Islamic countries could do the background analysis.

Beyond this report, all Islamic countries should formulate their own human development strategies. They need to fix a time horizon of 10–15 years for this purpose, choosing practical targets and costing them realistically. Then they should formulate a practical financial strategy, by

Table 8.3 Human development progress in the Arab States
(index)

Indicator	Arab States	Developing world
Life expectancy		
1960	100	100
1991	133	136
Infant mortality per 1,000 live births		
1960	100	100
1991	41	48
Daily per capita calorie supply as % of need		
1965	100	100
1990	139	118
Adult literacy		
1970	100	100
1990	170	141
Combined primary and secondary enrolment		
1970	100	100
1990	154	132
Real GDP per capita (PPP$)		
1960	100	100
1990	258	228

Source: UNDP, Human Development Report 1993, New York: Oxford University Press, 1993.

restructuring their existing priorities, mobilizing additional domestic resources and seeking additional outside assistance. Bangladesh and Pakistan have already produced human development strategies and discussed them with international consortia led by the World Bank. They are now implementing ambitious social action programmes to overcome critical human development gaps. Morocco and Tunisia are embarking on the preparation of national strategies. The demand for national human development strategies now exists in most of the Islamic countries. What they need is a helping hand.

The Islamic world has many countries rich in financial resources. It is their development priorities that are out of tune with their human investment needs. It is time to consider the establishment of an Islamic fund for human development, with generous contributions from the richer members of the Islamic community. This fund should be devoted to overcoming the Islamic world's existing gap in science and technology in the shortest possible time—by establishing relevant institutes of science and technology, by sending students for advanced training abroad, by instituting "Nobel Prizes" to recognize the talents of the Islamic countries' best scientists. There should be only one goal for such a fund: to prepare the young generations in the Islamic countries for the challenges of the 21st century, to recapture the scientific tradition of the Islamic world's past. In this context, a concrete proposal for an Islamic Science Foundation—by the only Nobel Laureate in physical science in the Islamic world, Professor Abdus Salam—is reproduced below.[1]

Table 8.4 Weight of the military scenario in Islamic countries

| Country | Military expenditure as % of GDP | | Military expenditure as % of education and health spending | | Soldiers per doctor |
	1977	1990	1977	1990	1987
Morocco	2.0	4.5	88	52	46
Libyan Arab Jamahiriya	1.2	8.6	29	56	14
Egypt	5.5	4.6	341	57	7
Tunisia	2.2	3.2	35	58	11
Kuwait	..	6.5	88	83	5
Jordan	16.7	10.9	183	128	26
Indonesia	5.8	1.6	94	143	13
Saudi Arabia	5.7	17.7	137	177	4
Pakistan	5.5	6.6	214	239	10
Somalia	..	3.0	91	500	130
Iraq	8.7	20.0	212	511	105

.. Not available.
Source: UNDP, *Human Development Report 1993*, New York: Oxford University Press, 1993.

Proposal for an Islamic Science Foundation

No Muslim country possesses a high level of scientific and technological competence. While the world economy is getting more and more global, the gap between the industrial countries and the Muslim communities continues to widen, and scientific and technological advances remain confined to the rich countries of the North.

The Islamic countries could make a decisive breakthrough by creating an Islamic Science Foundation. The Foundation would be sponsored by Muslim countries and operate within them. It would be non-political, purely scientific and run by eminent people of science and technology from the Muslim world.

The Foundation would have two principal objectives. First, to build up high-level scientific institutions and personnel—strengthening existing communities of scientists and creating new ones where none currently exist. Second, to build up and strengthen international institutions for advanced scientific research, both pure and applied, relevant to the needs of Muslim countries, and with an emphasis on international standards of quality and attainment.

The Foundation would initially concentrate on five main areas:

• *High-level training*—Scholars would be sponsored abroad to acquire knowledge in areas where gaps exist in the Muslim countries. Some 3,000 would be supported annually with continued support for 1,000 after they return home—about 15% of the Foundation's budget.

• *Enhancing research quality*—Contracts will be awarded to university departments and research centres to strengthen their work in selected scientific fields—about 25% of the budget.

• *Contact with the world scientific community*—To promote the interchange of ideas and criticism on which science thrives, the Foundation will support 3,000 two-way visits of scholars and fellows, as well as the holding of international symposia and conferences—about 10% of the budget.

• *Sponsoring applied research*—To strengthen existing institutions and create new ones devoted to the problems of the Middle East and the Arab world—including health, technology, agriculture, environment and water resources—about 40% of the budget.

• *Popularizing science*—To help make the population of the Islamic countries more scientifically and technologically minded, by making use of the mass media, scientific museums, libraries and exhibitions. It would also help modernize science and technology syllabi, and award prizes for discoveries and inventions.

The Foundation would have its headquarters at the seat of the Islamic Conference and would be open to sponsorship by all its members. Its Board of Trustees would consist of representatives of governments, professors and scientists. It would also have an Executive Council of eminent scientists which would be free from political interference.

The Foundation would be a non-profit tax-free body, which as a non-governmental organization would build up links with the United Nations, UNESCO and the UN University system. It would have an endowment fund of at least $5 billion and a projected annual income of $300 million to $350 million. It is envisaged that the sponsoring countries would pledge the endowment fund as a fixed proportion of export earnings and provide it in four annual installments.

Creating such a Foundation should be an urgent priority for the Muslim world. It would enable Muslim countries to recapture their glorious heritage of scientific pre-eminence and to compete as equals in the world of tomorrow.

Note

1. Permission to reproduce the proposal is gratefully acknowledged. The original proposal appears in UNDP, *Human Development Report 1994*, New York: Oxford University Press, 1994, p. 81.

Part 2

Towards a New International Dialogue

"I know what you're thinking about," said Tweedledum: "but it isn't so, nohow."

"Contrariwise," continued Tweedledee, "if it was so, it might be; and if it were so, it would be; but as it isn't, it ain't. That's logic."

— Through the Looking Glass

Chapter 9

New Imperatives of Human Security

"Take off your hat," the King said to the Hatter.
"It isn't mine," said the Hatter.
"Stolen!" the King exclaimed, turning to the jury, who instantly
made a memorandum of the fact.
"I keep them to sell," the Hatter added as an explanation: "I've
none of my own. I'm a hatter."
"Give your evidence," said the King; "and don't be nervous, or
I'll have you executed on the spot."

— Alice in Wonderland

The world is entering a new era in which the very concept of security will change—and change dramatically. Security will be interpreted as:

• Security of people, not just territory.
• Security of individuals, not just of nations.
• Security through development, not through arms.
• Security of all the people everywhere—in their homes, in their jobs, in their streets, in their communities, in their environment.

Another perception will change as well. Human security will be regarded as universal, global and indivisible. The same speed that has brought many modern products and services to our doorsteps has brought much human misery to our backyards.

Every drug that quietly kills, every disease that silently travels, every form of pollution that roams the globe, every act of terrorism that destroys life senselessly—imagine for a moment that they all carried a national label of origin, much as traded goods do, and there will be a sudden shocked recognition that human security concerns are more global today than global trade.

A third perception will change—it will be recognized that poverty cannot be stopped at national borders. Poor people can be stopped. But not the tragic consequences of their poverty. Those consequences travel without a passport—and in unpleasant forms. Drugs, AIDS, pollution and terrorism stop at no national frontier today. They can strike with devastating speed in any corner of the world. When people travel, they bring much dynamism and creativity with them. When only their poverty travels, it brings nothing but human misery.

One more perception will change—it will be recognized that it is easier, more humane and less costly to deal with the new issues of human security upstream rather than downstream. Did it make sense to incur the staggering cost of $240 billion in the past decade due to HIV/AIDS when even a fraction of that amount invested well in primary health care and family planning education could have prevented such a fast spread of this deadly disease? Is it a great tribute to international diplomacy to spend $2 billion in a single year on soldiers to deliver humanitarian assistance in Somalia when such an amount invested much earlier in increased domestic food production might have averted the human tragedy—not for one year but for a long time to come? Is it a reflection of human ingenuity that we are willing to spend hundreds of billions of dollars on drug prevention and rehabilitation, but not even a small part on alternative livelihoods in the poor nations that supply drugs?

We need today a new concept of human security—reflected in the lives of the people, not in the weapons of their countries.

Human security is not a concern with weapons. It is a concern with human dignity. In the last analysis, it is a child who did not die, a disease that did not spread, an ethnic tension that did not explode, a dissident who was not silenced, a human spirit that was not crushed.

A powerful, revolutionary idea, the emerging concept of human security forces a new morality on all of us through a perception of common threats to our very survival. But many of the most profound changes in human society have come from crises—from war, economic depression, natural disaster. While great religions often move the human spirit through the sublimeness of their messages, they also carry in their messages the fear of eventual punishment. Much human change comes from a fear for human survival.

Human security is a concept emerging not from the learned writings of scholars but from the daily concerns of people—from the dread of a woman that she may be raped in a lonely street at night, from the anguish of parents over the spread of drugs among their children, from the choked existence of prosperous communities in increasingly polluted cities, from the fear of terrorism suddenly striking any life anywhere without reason. A people's concept and a people's concern, human security is reflected in the shrivelled faces of innocent children, in the anguished existence of the homeless, in the constant fear of the jobless, in the silent despair of those without hope.

From the emerging concept of human security flow many hopeful insights and policy prescriptions. Human security can also serve as the basis for a new human world order. This would require at least five determined steps.

A new concept of development

Step 1. Seek a new concept of development. There must be a search for models of development that enhance human life, not marginalize it; treat GNP growth as a means, not as an end; distribute income equitably, not concentrate it; replenish natural resources for future generations, not destroy them; and encourage the grass-roots participation of people in the events and processes that shape their lives.

The issue is not growth per se but its character and distribution. Those who postulate a fundamental conflict between economic growth and sustainable human development do no service to the poor nations. To address poverty, economic growth is not an option—it is an imperative. But what type of growth? Who participates in it? And who derives the benefits? These are the real issues. To benefit the masses, growth's opportunities must be equitably distributed. And they must be sustainable from one generation to the next.

The heart of this concept is equity—within and between generations. But it is equity in opportunities, not necessarily in results. What people do with their opportunities is their concern—but they should not be denied an equal opportunity to develop their human capabilities. Such equity, however, requires many structural reforms: better distribution of productive assets (including land and credit), open access to market opportunities, a conducive policy environment for job creation and social safety nets for those bypassed by markets.

The emerging concern with sustainability takes this dialogue a step further. Development opportunities must be provided not only to present generations but to future generations. This does not mean protecting every form of natural capital or every resource or every species. If more efficient substitutes are available, they must be used. What must be protected is human life—for human beings are the most threatened species on earth. Economic growth or environmental protection are mere means. The real end is human welfare.

The ethical and philosophical foundation of the new development paradigm lies in acknowledging the universalism of life claims. No new-born child should be denied development opportunities merely because that child happens to be born in the "wrong class" or in the "wrong country" or is of the "wrong sex". For people, the purpose of development must be to increase their options, to equalize their opportunities and to enable them to enter the market on an equal footing. That is the real essence of sustainable human development strategies (chapter 2).

There is an increasing consensus on this new paradigm of development. And the next real challenge is operational: to translate this message of equality of opportunity into action through the formulation of national development policies, through the dialogue on development cooperation and through the workings of the international institutions.

A new phase of disarmament

Step 2. Move from arms security to human security and use the emerging peace dividend to finance the lengthening social agenda of humankind. The cold war is not over yet. The job is only half done. We have phased out the cold war in East-West relations. But we have forgotten to phase it out in the Third World. No leader from the Third World participated in the disarmament talks at Geneva: it was entirely an East-West affair.

Isn't it time to ask the leaders of the Third World these questions:

• Why do they insist on spending two or three times as much on arms as on the education and health of their people?

• Why do they have 20 times more soldiers than doctors?

• How can they find the resources for air-conditioned jeeps for their military generals when they lack even windowless schoolrooms for their children?

And isn't it time to ask the leaders of the rich nations to stop the continuing arithmetic of death and destruction in the Third World— where 22 million have died in more than 120 conflicts during the "peaceful transition" since the Second World War? Should they not fix a concrete timetable—say, the next three years—to:

• Close all foreign military bases in developing countries?

• Convert all existing military aid into economic aid?

• Stop the arms shipments of more than $35 billion a year that make huge profits from poor nations that cannot even feed their people?

• Eliminate subsidies to arms exporters and retrain their workers for jobs in civilian industries?

The next challenge is to curtail the huge arms spending of $130 billion a year in the poor nations and to invest this money instead in the welfare of their people. The big powers that launched the cold war have a moral obligation to defuse global tensions, to build new alliances for peace and to help developing countries make a smooth transition from arms security to human security.

Nor should we give up on the peace dividend. Global military expenditures have begun to decline for the first time in our lifetime. Between 1987 and 1994, they fell by enough to yield a cumulative peace dividend of $935 billion. Where has this peace dividend gone? Why is it not available for the neglected social agenda held over from the days when societies were accumulating arms and their people were praying that the arms race would stop? This issue is discussed in the next chapter.

In the rich nations, the preoccupation is with balancing budgets. But does it take a genius to discover how to balance financial budgets without unbalancing human lives? Why should rich societies find it impossible to provide resources for their unvaccinated children, for their homeless or for their decaying cities in an era of such rapidly falling military expenditures?

In the poor nations, unfortunately, the decline in military spending is still slow and hesitant. In fact, military expenditures are still going up in two of the poorest regions of the world—Sub-Saharan Africa and South Asia. Obviously, the poverty of their people is no barrier to the affluence of their armies. Even a freeze on current military spending in the Third World would release sufficient resources to take care of its essential human agenda.

Look at Sub-Saharan Africa. Its ratio of military spending to GNP increased from 0.7% in 1960 to 3.5% in 1990—a fivefold increase at a time that some African countries were cutting social spending in the name of structural adjustment.

And look at South Asia: an expenditure of $20 billion a year on defence by India and Pakistan when they contain the largest number of the world's poorest people. During 1988–92, India and Pakistan imported twice as many arms as Saudi Arabia, which is 25 times richer.

It is time for one final push, to ensure that arms security is replaced by human security—particularly in the poor lands, where every new jet fighter costs one million additional children in school.

A new framework of development cooperation

Step 3. Form a new partnership between the North and the South. This partnership would be based on justice, not charity; on an equitable sharing of global market opportunities, not aid; on two-way compacts, not one-way transfers; on mutual cooperation, not unilateral conditionality or confrontation.

Foreign aid has often dominated North-South relations since the Second World War, even though this aid was often marginal and misdirected. Consider one sobering comparison: rich nations channel an average of 15% of their GNP to their own 100 million poor—those below a poverty line of around $5,000 a year. But they earmark only 0.3% of their GNP for poor nations, which contain 1.3 billion poor people with incomes of less than $300 a year. What a telling contrast between national and international social safety nets! And yet a public perception persists in the rich nations that their aid money could be better employed at home. The rich nations may not recognize that even if all their aid stopped today, their domestic social safety nets would only increase from 15% of GNP to 15.3%—perhaps not the most handsome bargain in history.

It is not just the marginal role of aid that matters. Its distribution also leaves much to be desired. Aid today carries all the scars of the cold war era. It was often given to strategic allies rather than to poor nations. Consider aid's link to the oft-repeated objective of eliminating global poverty. Only one-third of ODA is earmarked for the ten countries containing two-thirds of the world's absolute poor. Twice as much ODA per capita goes to the wealthiest 40% in the developing world as to the poorest 40%. Egypt receives $280 a year per poor person, India receives only $7. And less than 7% of bilateral ODA is directed towards human priority concerns—primary health care, basic education, safe drinking water, nutrition programmes and family planning services.

Consider yet another dimension of aid: most was directed towards strategic allies in the cold war, to authoritarian regimes, to high military spenders. Even today, two and a half times as much per capita ODA goes to high military spenders as to low military spenders, with strategic allies getting preference over poor nations. For example, El Salvador receives 16 times as much ODA per poor person from the United States as does Bangladesh, even though Bangladesh is five times poorer.

A final irony: while aid transfers so few resources to the developing world, the denial of global market opportunities through trade protection, immigration barriers and an increasing debt burden takes away several times more. According to *Human Development Report 1992*, such global losses are about ten times the aid that poor nations receive.

What is crucial for poor nations is equitable access to global market opportunities, not charity. What we must battle for today is the removal of trade barriers, particularly for textiles and agriculture, which would yield at least $100 billion a year in additional exports for the developing world. What we must insist on today is a compensation package from rich nations for imposing immigration controls, since free labour flows were supposed to be an essential component of a liberal international economic system that would equalize global opportunities. What we must negotiate today is a market in global environmental resources that would oblige the rich nations to pay their due share for their overuse of the common heritage. They could end up paying as much as 5% of their GNP, according to some recent studies on tradable environmental permits. This is not aid. This is not charity. This is merely taking the logic of the market-place back to the rich nations.

For too long, we have missed the real essence of a new system of development cooperation between rich and poor nations. When we should have sought participation in markets, we sought exemption from these market rules. When we should have constructed a comprehensive design for relations between the North and the South—including all flows of trade, labour, investment and technology—we got hopelessly stuck on the 0.7% aid target. When we should have sought fair rules for international competition, we kept counting our diminishing aid dollars.

It is time to advance from a charitable aid relationship to a more respectable development relationship. It is time to build a new design for development cooperation between the North and the South, one that enables the poor nations to gain more equitable access to global market opportunities (chapter 11). It is also time to create a new mechanism to facilitate payments by one country to another for services rendered that are mutually beneficial and by their nature cannot be mediated by markets. Examples include environmental services, control of narcotic drugs and control of contagious diseases.

There is also a need to create a new mechanism to facilitate compensation for damages when one country inflicts economic injury on another. Compensation can be thought of as fines payable by countries that depart from internationally agreed rules of good conduct. Some examples of conduct leading to economic injury: encouraging the brain drain from poor nations, restricting the migration of low-skilled labour and restricting exports from poor countries. These compensations would be voluntary in a sense because they could be avoided by refraining from engaging in objectionable behaviour.

Aid will have only a marginal role in this new design of development cooperation—as a global social safety net for the very poorest nations and, hopefully, as a more predictable and obligatory commitment by the rich nations. Aid is needed to address some of the darkest aspects of poverty but it must be far better targeted than in the past.

We need, therefore, a design of development cooperation much broader than just aid—a design that draws new strength from domestic reforms in the South, that recognizes that real human security in the North will ultimately depend on an investment in reducing global poverty, that secures equitable access to global market opportunities for all people all over the globe.

A new framework of global governance

Step 4. Fashion a new framework of global governance. In the search for a human world order, global markets or automatic mechanisms cannot achieve justice for all nations or all people. Global institutions are needed to set rules, to monitor "global goods" and "global bads", to redress widening disparities. Paradoxically, these global institutions are weakening just as global interdependence is increasing. All global institutions desperately need both strengthening and reform.

Take, for example, the Bretton Woods institutions (chapter 14). What should worry us today is not their seeming arrogance but their growing irrelevance. They are no longer institutions of global governance. They are institutions to direct economic management only in the developing world.

• The writ of the IMF runs only in developing countries, responsible for a mere 10% of global liquidity. The G-7, not the IMF, influences the global monetary system today. The rich nations hold their collective breath for the pronouncements of Alan Greenspan, not those of Michel Camdessus.

• The World Bank has a limited role in recycling global surpluses. It collects more in debt repayments each year than it lends to the developing world. Private capital markets recycle resources—but three-fourths of those resources go to about ten better-off developing countries, in East Asia and Latin America. The other countries wait for World Bank interventions that never materialize on the scale originally envisaged.

• The GATT's jurisdiction was excluded until recently from most of the important items of international trade: textiles, tropical products, agricultural commodities, services, labour and investment flows. And the GATT stands, on the sidelines, strangely silent as the United States and Japan get ready to launch a disastrous trade war.

• The United Nations has never become the strongest pillar of human development that it was intended to be. Most donors preferred the one-dollar, one-vote governance of the Bretton Woods institutions to the one-country, one-vote governance of the United Nations. So, UN development programmes never got the support they deserved. Limited finance led to diminished efficiency, and diminished efficiency became the justification for even more limited finance.

What are our real options today? Bashing international institutions is tempting. But it is self-defeating when global governance is already so weak.

Instead, we must form alliances for change within these institutions and with their governance. The goal should be reform, not demolition. We must convince these institutions to focus more on human development strategies, to formulate adjustment programmes that place much greater burdens on the rich than on the poor and that balance budgets without unbalancing the lives of the people, and to evolve governance patterns that give a much greater voice to the poor nations.

All sorts of scenarios can be drawn up for the global economic and financial institutions of the 21st century—but one thing is certain. As distances shrink and we become a global village, we are likely to witness an evolution at the global level similar to the evolution that we have already seen at the national level in the past century. That is why we should start giving serious thought to possible structures for a world central bank, a global taxation system, a world trading organization, an international investment trust and even a world treasury. Some of us may not live to see all these global developments, but our grandchildren surely will. So, let us at least begin with the rough architecture.

Whatever the shape of this new architecture, it is becoming essential to set up an Economic Security Council in the United Nations as the highest decision-making forum for dealing with threats to global human security and for agreeing on the actions to take to address these threats (chapter 16). Such a council must deal with all issues confronting humanity—from food security to environmental security, from global poverty to jobless growth, from international migration to drug trafficking. Its membership should be kept small and manageable, but it should represent all world constituencies and carry no country veto. It should oversee the policy directions of all international and regional institutions. And it should be served by the ablest professional staff, formulating enlightened policy options on the economic and social dilemmas facing humankind. Indeed, it is impossible to think of democratic global governance for the 21st century without such an Economic Security Council, in one form or another.

A global civil society

Step 5. Move towards a global civil society. Future changes will not depend exclusively on governments. Instead, they will come primarily from the actions of people at the grass roots—people who will hold their leaders increasingly accountable for all their actions.

The forces of democratic change have swept the world in the past decade. In one country after another, people are standing up to their authoritarian regimes and bending them to the popular will. The nation-state is under much pressure today. The age of the people may finally have arrived.

This new momentum for change carries both dangers and opportunities. There are dangers of anarchy and social disintegration if people are denied their legitimate economic and political rights. But there is also a unique opportunity to build a new global civilization at this hinge of history.

In poor nations, a realistic process of change has already begun. These nations are opening their economies, carrying out painful structural adjustments and passing through a rapid phase of democratic change. Seeking justice, not charity, they no longer blame the North for all their troubles. They are beginning to recognize that the real battle of poverty will be fought and won in the South.

Unfortunately, at a time of such profound change in human affairs, the North is becoming somewhat passive, cautious, conservative and almost reactionary—fearing that it may lose some of its privileges.

- While the poor nations are beginning to open up their economies, the rich nations are beginning to close theirs.

- While the poor nations are undergoing structural adjustment at very low levels of income, the rich nations are resisting any adjustment in their life styles.

- While the rich nations preach democracy to the poor nations, they resist democracy in international institutions and in global governance.

- While the rich nations rightly condemn corruption in poor lands, they fail to discipline their own multinationals that offer bribes or their banks that gladly accept corrupt money and for a handsome profit.

- While the rich nations have started advocating reduced military spending to developing nations, they have quietly turned around and increased subsidies to their own arms exporters.

A new partnership between North and South will demand a new ethics of mutual responsibility and mutual respect. The North does not realize yet that, through its constant advocacy, it may have unleashed

REFLECTIONS ON HUMAN DEVELOPMENT

forces of change that will transform not only other nations but also its own life styles. Democracy is rarely so obliging as to stop at national borders. Its vast sweep will change global governance in the 21st century. The real choice is to accept the evolution of such a global civil society and speed its arrival—or to resist it in the name of old-fashioned power balances and plunge the world into utter confusion.

These five steps can lead towards a new human world order. A unique opportunity to build such an order emerged at the World Summit for Social Development in Copenhagen in March 1995. The Social Summit was expected to review the progress made by humanity in the past 50 years and construct the new architecture of peace and development for the next 50 years. This was a time to fashion a new concept of sustainable human development, to take concrete steps to capture the peace dividend, to design a new structure of international development cooperation, to initiate some work on the architecture of a new global governance and to speed the evolution of a global civil society and human world order. Unfortunately, however, the Social Summit proved to be only a modest first step on a very long road. A vision for the 21st century is still wandering in search of leadership.

Chapter 10

What Happened to the Peace Dividend?

> *"We must have a bit of a fight, but I don't care about going on long," said Tweedledum. "What's the time now?"*
> *Tweedledee looked at his watch, and said "Half-past four."*
> *"Let's fight till six, and then have dinner," said Tweedledum.*
> *"Very well," the other said, rather sadly: ... "I generally hit everything I can see—when I get really excited."*
> *"And I hit everything within reach," cried Tweedledum, "whether I can see it or not."*
>
> — Through the Looking Glass

There is a popular view these days that the much-talked-about peace dividend has failed to materialize. Like many popular views, it is false. There was a significant peace dividend between 1987 and 1994. But the global community did not spend it very wisely. We let it slip right through our fingers.

Actual peace dividend

There has been a sizable reduction in global military spending since 1987, for the first time in the lifetime of the generation that grew up after the Second World War. The relaxation in East-West tensions and the end of the cold war led to a cut of almost one-quarter in military spending, from nearly $1 trillion in 1987 to $767 billion in 1994 (in 1991 prices). This cut of around 4% a year was led by the United States and the former Soviet Union. The reduction in the developing world was somewhat smaller—about 2% a year.

On a global scale, the cumulative peace dividend—calculated as the accumulated savings from reduced military spending—was $935 billion during 1987–94. Never in history has there been such a large peace dividend. Yet the perception persists that the end of the cold war produced no peace dividend whatsoever.

There are at least two reasons for such a perception. First, reduced military spending in the industrial nations has not resulted in greater attention to their social services or human development programmes. In the United States, most savings in the military budget have been committed to reducing the budget deficit and the national debt. In Eastern Europe and the former Soviet Union, the near collapse of economies wiped out all the savings from military spending. And Western Europe and Japan have barely cut their military budgets. Hence the pervasive feeling that no peace dividend materialized. The reality, however, is that the peace dividend was very significant, but it was not linked to any direct improvement in human lives.

Second, the task of disarmament has scarcely begun in the Third World. Most reductions in military spending have come in the more affluent parts of the Third World—for example, in the Middle East and Latin America. In the Middle East, arms embargoes enforced lower arms purchases, whether desired or not. The most disturbing trends have been in South Asia and Sub-Saharan Africa, two of the poorest regions in the developing world. High military spending levels seem to be the privilege of the poorest nations.

Is it not odd that Western nations have declared victory in the cold war, yet forgotten the possible use of the peace dividend for their neglected social agendas and the real threat of continuing armament in the Third World?

Potential peace dividend

Although global military spending has declined to less than $800 billion a year, it still is a major burden on the world's economic and environmental resources. To put it in perspective, global military spending now equals the yearly income of about half the world's people. Military arms also pose the greatest threat to the global environment. And defence establishments all over the world are the chief consumers of the best scientific talent, which could otherwise be used for productive technology.

The human costs of military spending remains high. Consider these estimates in *Human Development Report 1994:*[1]

• A 12% cut in global military spending could eliminate severe malnutrition and reduce moderate malnutrition by half, provide safe drinking water for all, and provide primary health care for all, including the immunization of all children.

• An 8% cut could finance a basic family planning package for all willing couples and help stabilize world population by 2015.

- Even a 4% cut could cover the cost of reducing adult illiteracy by half, providing universal primary education and educating women to the same level as men.

A considerable peace dividend could be realized if global military spending were cut further. For example, a 3% annual reduction in military spending would yield a potential peace dividend of $460 billion during 1995–2000—$385 billion in the industrial world and $75 billion in the developing nations. That would be enough to finance a large part of the lengthening social agenda of the global community.

What are the chances that such potential will be realized? Not all that good, in the Western world or in the transition economies. The United States may be reluctant to cut its military arsenal further, especially after the recent triumph of the Republican Party in the US Congress. In any case, reductions in the budget deficit are likely to take precedence over social objectives or programmes in the United States for some time. In Eastern Europe and the former Soviet Union, economic problems are already forcing reductions in military spending. But there is little chance for a peace dividend because of the large fall in their national output. Japan now spends less than 1 percent of its GNP on defence. If anything, it is likely to increase its defence spending moderately to compensate for the gradual withdrawal of the US defence umbrella from East Asia and to meet its growing international obligations for UN peacekeeping operations. That leaves Western Europe, where the scope for a cut in military spending is large but where there has been the least adjustment to a post–cold war world. Western Europe is likely to feel more vulnerable without a US defence umbrella and is far more exposed to a latent threat from the East.

So, the real scope for a peace dividend lies in the developing world—where it is most needed and where the task of disarmament has barely begun.

Military spending in the Third World

It is surprising how little attention has gone to the rapid rise of military spending in the Third World. At its peak, this spending rose three times as fast as that of the industrial nations between 1960 and 1987—7.5% a year, compared with 2.8%. During this period, the developing world more than doubled its share of global military spending, from 7% in 1960 to 15% in 1987—a dubious distinction, since its share of global income stayed well below 6% and declined in many of the poorest regions.

Let's review some shocking facts:

- Today, 24 developing countries spend more than 5% of their GNP on defence. Of these, 12 countries spend more than 10%. The average for the more affluent industrial world is 3%.

- In 1992, 18 developing countries still spent much more on their military than on the education and health of their people. Of these, at least 8 (Angola, Ethiopia, Mozambique, Myanmar, Pakistan, Sri Lanka, Somalia, Yemen) belong to the group of the poorest nations. The human costs of their military spending were thus extremely high.

- In the Third World, there are 20 soldiers for every doctor, even though the chances of dying due to preventable diseases and malnourishment are about 33 times greater than the chances of dying in a conflict.

- India and Pakistan together spend around $20 billion a year on defence—despite having 450 million people in absolute poverty, 500 million without access to safe drinking water and 340 million illiterate adults. These two countries also outbid Saudi Arabia in purchases in the global arms bazaar during 1988–92—spending twice as much as Saudi Arabia did (at international prices) even though Saudi Arabia is 25 times richer.

- Even though nearly two-thirds of the people in Sub-Saharan Africa are slipping into absolute poverty and many African societies are undergoing a socio-economic disintegration, the region has increased its military spending fivefold in real terms in the past three decades—from 0.7% of their combined GNP in 1960 to 3.5% in 1990.

- Some of the poorest African nations spend excessive amounts of their scarce resources on the military: $23 per capita in Sudan, $15 in Ethiopia, $11 in Chad and $10 in Burkina Faso.

Why such public indulgence for armies in the midst of so much squalor? There does not appear to be much of an external threat to the territorial security of many of these poor nations. But in many cases, armies have been used by authoritarian regimes to repress their own people. The rich nations have lent a hand as well, often subsidizing their arms exporters to win markets in the developing world. About 75% of the global arms trade is now directed to poor lands, and 86% of the arms are supplied by five permanent members of the Security Council. This was not the role envisaged for the guardians of international security!

To reverse this trend requires a new political assessment on all sides. The industrial powers should recognize that it is not smart to ship arms to unstable regimes during one decade and then try to take them out in the next decade—as in Afghanistan, Iraq, Rwanda and Somalia.

Nor can the restructuring of defence industries be postponed for long by exporting arms and tensions to other parts of the world.

Developing countries need to recognize that the real threat now comes from the socio-economic deprivation of their masses. Diverting scarce resources to military equipment only increases this threat—as Iraq, Nicaragua and Somalia found to their sorrow. These countries had the highest ratios of military to social spending in 1980 but were unable to protect either their territorial security or the security of their people in the ensuing decade.

And international donors need to recognize that supporting high military spenders with foreign aid largesse (as has been the practice, discussed in the next chapter) is a short-sighted strategy at both ends. If a new political perspective is created along these lines, a comprehensive plan can be designed for peace and development in the Third World.

A peace agenda

In the light of the foregoing analysis, a five-point agenda for peace in the Third World is offered here:

1. *Start at the source.* The real or perceived threats to national security should be contained through international action or regional understanding. The major powers carry a moral responsibility to diffuse some of the tensions created during the cold war era. It is only fair that, since the cold war was fought by proxy on the soil of the Third World, the major powers should now forge new alliances for peace. Some of the more intractable conflicts are nearing resolution—for example, the Israeli-Palestinian conflict, apartheid in South Africa, terrorist activities by the Irish Republican Army. The major powers, particularly the United States, should take a proactive role in persuading countries to find a peaceful solution to their continuing tensions. For example, they can gently lean on India and Pakistan to find a mutually acceptable way out of their military confrontation, which is foreclosing socio-economic options in both countries.

2. *Create forums to discuss Third World disarmament openly and frankly.* The present disarmament dialogue has proceeded mainly in forums concerned with East-West relations: Geneva disarmament talks, START treaties, NATO, the Warsaw Pact. No leader from the developing world has ever been invited to these talks.

The Third World lacks its own forums for a discussion on disarmament. As a matter of long-established practice, the Non-Aligned Movement or regional forums (ASEAN, SAARC, OAU, OAS) seldom take up these issues. This must change. The most relevant forums for disarmament talks must be found at the regional level. Several issues that may be difficult to tackle bilaterally could be taken up in these forums. For example, the SAARC forum could be used to agree on a timetable for mutual cuts in military spending in all seven SAARC nations, including India and Pakistan. It would be far more difficult for the governments of those two countries to commit to such cuts unilaterally or bilaterally as their domestic critics might accuse them of gambling with national security.

The United Nations should show more interest in Third World disarmament. It should do far more work on Third World military expenditures than it has done. And it should be willing to provide strong secretariat support for any concrete moves by Third World countries towards disarmament.

3. *Have industrial countries play a major role in stopping the mindless arms race.* The industrial countries could phase out their existing military bases and military assistance. They could agree on a timetable for eliminating subsidies to arms exporters. They could ban the shipment of sophisticated arms to all developing countries and even conventional arms to potential trouble spots. And in the present unstable situation, they should at least stop all arms shipments to Sub-Saharan Africa and South Asia.

The trouble is that the industrial countries have not devised a coherent strategy for disarmament in the Third World, perhaps assuming that it is none of their concern. They have often—without even realizing the potential for global disruption—pushed more and more arms into politically fragile nations. But short-term profits in arms can be earned only at a very high long-term cost in global human security. It is essential for the industrial world to realize that greater armament of the Third World will threaten its own stability and the stability of the rest of the world.

4. *Add military spending to the aid dialogue.* External donors—bilateral or multilateral—should increasingly consider it legitimate to discuss military spending with recipient countries as a part of a new and benign aid conditionality.[2] Normally, aid donors have been reluctant to discuss tough domestic issues—such as military spending or land reforms—brushing them aside as political issues. This is a cop-out. Unless external donors are willing to put a squeeze on powerful vested interests within the system, the squeeze will inevitably fall on the weakest and most vulnerable groups in society.

External assistance should be regarded as an alliance not with governments—which often change—but with people, an issue discussed in the next chapter. Only then will the objectives of such assistance be better appreciated in the recipient countries. For example, as a part of the new benign conditionality, donors might stipulate that countries that insist on spending more on their armies than on their people will not be eligible for foreign assistance. Similarly, during discussions of adjustment programmes, donors could insist that military spending be cut ahead of social spending. And the IMF could place credit ceilings on military debts, in addition to those on civilian or development debts. (Military debts are already one-third of the total debts of many large developing countries.)

The emerging détente of the 1990s offers donors an opportunity that they must seize with real courage and imagination. It is encouraging to note that the World Bank and the IMF are already beginning to raise this issue, at least at the global level. So are some bilateral donors, notably Japan and Germany. It is essential to establish some international consensus on this issue and to agree on a global strategy for linking aid policy dialogue with military spending levels in the recipient countries.

5. *Increase the transparency of information on military spending.* It is amazing how much secrecy still surrounds military data. In industrial countries, it is almost impossible to get honest information on subsidies to arms exporters, even though these subsidies come from taxpayers' money. Secrecy also leads to significant corruption in arms purchases and to a culture of no accountability. Such data must be supplied in budgets as a matter of course.

In the developing world, the information about military spending or arms purchases or military debts is totally inadequate. It should be mandatory for international organizations (the World Bank, the IMF and the UN system) to collect and publish such data. No honest dialogue can proceed without such information—nor can pressure for change be mobilized from the members of civil society, particularly from the mass media. More readily available information on military spending must be regarded as one of the most essential steps towards Third World disarmament. Ultimately, the pressure for change will arise within these countries—once their people begin to realize the enormous social and human costs of military budgets.

The future of the peace dividend depends, therefore, on a comprehensive strategy for disarmament in the Third World. It is time to consider this as the next step in making the world safe for peace and for human development. Without peace, development cannot proceed. And without development, peace will always be at risk.

Notes

1. UNDP, *Human Development Report 1994,* New York: Oxford University Press, 1994, p. 50.

2. I have consistently opposed aid conditionality and argued for persuasion, rather than coercion, in aid policy dialogue. But I have always made one exception: linking aid with the level of military spending. Since military establishments are extremely powerful in developing countries, there must be powerful pressures from outside to provide a countervailing force, in support of those within the system who are trying to contain military spending. On this, there should be no compromise.

Chapter 11

A New Framework of Development Cooperation

I passed by his garden, and marked, with one eye,
How the owl and the panther were sharing a pie;
The panther took pie-crust, and gravy, and meat,
And the owl had the dish for his share of the treat.
When the plate was divided, the owl, as a boon,
Was kindly permitted to pocket the spoon:
But the panther obtained both the fork and the knife,
So, when he lost his temper, the owl lost his life.

— Through the Looking Glass

*T*he end of the cold war opens up new opportunities for reallocating aid to improve its quality and effectiveness. In fact, a major improvement in the quality of aid could argue most powerfully for an increase in its quantity.

Today, there is no clear link between aid and several global objectives that donors normally avow as goals—because aid still carries the scars of the cold war:

• High military spenders among developing countries receive more than twice as much official development assistance per capita as more moderate military spenders.

• El Salvador gets more aid than Bangladesh, even though Bangladesh has 24 times more population and a fifth the income.

• Of the $21 billion that the United States provides each year in foreign assistance, about half is still military assistance.

The link between aid and the global objective of poverty alleviation is weak:

• Only one-third of ODA is earmarked for two-thirds of the world's poor.

• India, with 27% of the world's absolute poor, receives only 5% of total ODA.

• Egypt receives $280 a year per poor person, India only $7.

• The richest 40% of the developing world's people receive twice as much per capita ODA as the poorest 40%.

- The much poorer South Asia receives $5 in ODA per capita each year, the much richer Middle East $55 per capita.

- According to an Overseas Development Council study, the United States provides $250 per capita a year to high-income developing countries and only $1 per capita to low-income countries.

Nor is there a strong link today between the ODA allocations and the global objective of supporting priority human development goals:

- While the education sector received around one-tenth of bilateral aid in the 1980s, only 7% of these funds were earmarked for primary education.

- Of the ODA channelled to the health sector, only 27% was for primary health care.

- The rural share of aid earmarked for water supply and sanitation was only 19%.

- Only 6.5% of bilateral assistance is earmarked for human priority concerns—basic education, primary health care, rural water supply, nutrition programmes and family planning services.

- Of the aid to low-income countries, only 2% is for primary health care and 1% for family planning.

- In Sub-Saharan Africa during the 1980s, only $1 of assistance was provided per primary pupil, $11 per secondary pupil and $575 per university pupil.

These priorities reflect, of course, the priorities of the developing countries themselves. The point is that many donors do not try to influence or correct these distorted priorities but often willingly go along with them because of their commercial interest in brick-and-mortar projects.

And despite considerable shrill rhetoric on this subject, there is no clearly established link between aid and human rights:

- Recent studies by US scholars have established a perverse correlation between US aid and human rights violations during the 1980s: strategic alliances in the cold war era took precedence over human rights considerations.

- Bangladesh, Pakistan and the Philippines found that their per capita ODA allocation went down, not up, after they lifted martial law. Donors often like political stability and economic management policies under martial law regimes, despite their protests to the contrary.

Nor has there been a link between aid and decentralized governance, despite donors' avowed support for decentralization. According to *Human Development Report 1993,* aid, almost all of which is negotiated with central governments, has had a very centralizing impact.

Although it is not necessary for central authorities to spend the aid directly through the central government, that is what has happened. Few developing countries are keen to pass aid funds on to local bodies after having guaranteed repayment at the central level. And only a few donors have insisted on a more decentralized implementation, through local authorities or NGOs, of the projects they support.

There is also little discernible link between technical assistance and the sacred mantra of national capacity building. After 40 years of technical assistance, 95% of these funds (more than $12 billion a year now) still go to foreign consultants, despite the outstanding national expertise within the developing countries. Africa receives around $6 billion a year in technical assistance, yet its human development indicators are the lowest in the world. It has received more bad advice per capita than any other continent. No other form of assistance deserves radical surgery as much as technical assistance does today.

The purpose of the analysis here is not so much to indict aid as to indicate the opportunity for considerable improvement in aid allocation priorities. Development cooperation has had significant successes, but much more mileage can be squeezed from existing funds. In this spirit, a determined attempt must be made to improve the quality of assistance and to design a new framework of development cooperation to fit the post–cold war realities. The following proposals are offered as a contribution towards this objective.

First, find a new motivation for development cooperation, based on fighting the growing threat of global poverty rather than the receding threat of the cold war. Security may no longer be threatened by the prospect of a nuclear holocaust, but it is certainly threatened by the travel of global poverty across international frontiers in the form of drugs, AIDS, pollution, illegal migration and terrorism. While the chances of a global nuclear suicide were always small, the chances of every family being affected by these new threats are very great. Can the rich nations convince their people of this looming threat to their own human security?

To create a new motivation for aid, countries should put aside around 2% of existing ODA budgets (about $1 billion a year) for cultivating the new constituencies of change—half of it to be spent bilaterally and half through international channels. In this age of communications, powerful vested interests exploit the resources of the media for their own narrow ends. Why should we hesitate to use the same channels to promote a new framework of development cooperation to safeguard global human security?

Second, persuade the nations of the world that the cold war must be phased out in the Third World as well. The cold war is not over yet. The job is only half done. We have phased out the cold war in East-West relations. But we have forgotten to phase it out in the Third World. This issue was discussed in the preceding chapter.

Third, demonstrate to skeptical publics that the essential human development agenda can be financed even by reallocating priorities in existing budgets. Consider a new 20:20 vision. The developing countries would commit an average of 20% of their budgets to human priority concerns rather than the present 10%—by reducing military expenditures, by privatizing inefficient public enterprises and by eliminating low-priority development expenditure. The rich nations would raise their human priority allocations from the present 7% of ODA to around 20%.

This new global human compact can be financed entirely by recasting existing allocation priorities. It requires no new resources, but it does require considerable courage and skill. And it would yield $30 billion to $40 billion in additional allocations for the urgent human development agenda in the poor nations, three-quarters through their own decisions and one-quarter from the international community. The human pay-off of such a compact could be enormous. Within ten years, all children could be in school, primary health care and clean drinking water could be available to all the people, family planning services could be provided to all willing couples, and severe child malnutrition could be eliminated.

Many grand designs have been constructed on elusive additions of aid. Isn't it time to become realistic and show the world what can be accomplished even with existing resources? Isn't the best strategy to convince reluctant legislatures and sceptical publics that they must support additional aid by showing them the potential mileage from existing resources—by showing the doable, the possible, the achievable? This proposal is elaborated in chapter 15.

Fourth, redress the growing imbalance between short-term emergency assistance and long-term development support. While the United Nations spent less than $4 billion on peacekeeping missions during the first 48 years of its existence, it spent more than $4 billion on such missions in 1994 alone. And for every dollar of humanitarian assistance, about ten times as much goes for soldiers—as in Somalia. It is time to review this strange and disturbing imbalance. And it is time to recognize that if there are diminished funds for socio-economic development, there are likely to be many more emergencies in the future.

This imbalance has at least two policy implications. One is that the donors must be convinced that allocations for UN peacekeeping operations should come out of their defence budgets, not out of their limited ODA budgets. After all, peacekeeping operations are an extension of their security requirements, not a gift to the poor nations. The other is that the developmental role of the United Nations must be strengthened. The Agenda for Peace must be complemented by an Agenda for Development. This means that the United Nations must be given a mandate for sustainable human development, be provided more assured sources of development financing and have a forum for global economic decisions at the highest level in an Economic Security Council (chapter 16).

Fifth, search for a more innovative model of development cooperation based on human security, not on outmoded ideas of charity. That model would embrace three new mechanisms:

• A new mechanism to facilitate payments by one country to another for services rendered—services that are mutually beneficial and by their very nature cannot be mediated by markets. Examples include environmental services, the control of narcotic drugs and the control of contagious diseases (such as AIDS).

• A new mechanism to facilitate compensation for damages when one country inflicts an economic injury on another. Compensation can be thought of as fines payable by countries that depart from internationally agreed rules of good conduct. Some examples of conduct leading to economic injury: encouraging brain drain from poor nations, restricting the migration of low-skilled labour in search of international economic opportunities and restricting exports from poor countries. Compensations for such injuries would in a sense be voluntary, because they could be avoided by refraining from engaging in objectionable behaviour.

• A new mechanism of automatic resource mobilization for global objectives that embrace common human survival. To be seen essentially as a shared price for shared human existence, financing should be mobilized particularly for environmental protection, where huge sums may need to be raised through tradable permits for carbon emissions, through an international carbon tax or through other such measures that make attending to matters of human survival automatic, not subject to national legislative approval.

Sixth, broaden development cooperation to include trade, investment, technology and labour flows. Comprehensive accounts should be prepared to ensure that what is given with one hand is not taken away with the other and that the focus of efforts continues to be on opening up global market opportunities. Recall the startling conclusion of *Human Development Report 1992:* developing countries are denied $500 billion of global market opportunities every year while receiving a mere $50 billion in aid. A broadened framework of development cooperation is perhaps the most urgently needed policy initiative today—to move the North-South dialogue from aid and charity to a more mature partnership.

Seventh, link the aid policy dialogue to the new issues of reduced military spending, better national governance and greater emphasis on sustainable human development. Persuasion is better than coercion. Constructive alliances for change with domestic policy-makers are better than outside intervention. An enlightened policy dialogue is better than an inflexible conditionality. And a two-way compact is better than one-way pressure.

More important, however, is to change the substance of the policy dialogue. Aid has been unpopular at both ends because the policy dialogue is entirely between governments—not people—with no discernible objectives defined or served. It certainly is difficult to sell the message of aid to suspicious publics if its link with global objectives is not clearly spelled out and regularly monitored. Much greater transparency must be introduced in the data on aid. It is impossible today to monitor aid on the basis of its link with laudable global objectives: even the limited illustrations at the start of this chapter took considerable research. And it is impossible today to get any data on military assistance, military debts, military bases or subsidies to arms exporters. The OECD's Development Assistance Committee should be given a mandate to collect and publish such data, something that would make its annual reports significant international events.

These issues are controversial, but an honest dialogue must begin around them. The post–cold war era requires an entirely new framework of development cooperation. It is simply amazing how little thought has been given to this subject by national and international policy-makers.

Chapter 12

The Myth of the
Friendly Markets

He said "I look for butterflies
That sleep among the wheat:
I make them into mutton-pies,
And sell them in the street.
I sell them unto men," he said,
"Who sail on stormy seas;
And that's the way I get my bread—
A trifle, if you please."

— Through the Looking Glass

he development pendulum is swinging once again, from over-commitment to the public sector to an overenthusiasm for the private sector. A "garage sale" of public enterprises is going on all over the world—from New Delhi to Rio, from Moscow to Warsaw—enough to warm the heart of any ideologue of capitalism. And professional shock therapists roam the globe in search of willing victims, delivering the message of overnight change. This long overdue return to the market is welcome, but the pendulum may once again swing too far.

Why the overcommitment to the public sector in many developing countries in the first place? Pursuing a wide range of social objectives, in addition to higher economic growth, many developing countries lost their way in trying to liberate their societies from poverty. An innocent flirtation with socialism mixed up the ends and means. The means chosen were a large role for the public sector—but that often meant bureaucratic capitalism, not the pursuit of social objectives. The economy was handed on a silver platter to the civil servants, often ill trained and ill paid. Many times they used controls and regulations not to enrich the economy but to enrich themselves.

A very strange world emerged in the past 30 years. Public enterprises in agriculture, industry, trade—all the productive sectors—were mainly inefficient money-losers. In Cameroon, the annual losses of the public enterprises exceeded the government's total oil revenue. In the

140 REFLECTIONS ON HUMAN DEVELOPMENT

Philippines, these losses were 2–3% of GNP—and but for these losses, the country could have increased its education and health spending by about 30%. In Sri Lanka, two-thirds of the budget deficit was due to public enterprise losses. In Argentina, public enterprise losses exceeded 11% of GNP before the major privatization programme of the past few years. These countries wasted their scarce financial resources, and even more their scarce management skills, on inefficient public enterprises that could have been privatized with greater benefit to all sides.

Many developing countries committed scarce resources and energies to things that the private sector could have done more efficiently, leaving too few budgetary resources to do the things that only the government could do, particularly investing in education and health and providing many social services. Then they complained about the poverty of their resources. But it was not the lack of resources that was decisive—it was the lack of political will. Military spending in these nations often exceeded their spending on education and health. Restructuring priorities in their budgets would have given them the resources they needed for urgent human development.

Despite all this, the new and rather aggressive market ideology emerging globally is a cause for worry. In many countries, markets are not free, efficient or equitable. Unless the state is a good regulator, and unless free markets are combined with social compassion, there may be many social and political upheavals.

Markets and the poor

One important point: markets are not very friendly to the poor, to the weak or to the vulnerable, either nationally or internationally. Nor are markets free. They are often the handmaidens of powerful interest groups, and they are greatly affected by the prevailing distribution of income. If the richest 20% of the population has 26 times the income of the poorest 20%, as in Brazil, the market allocates resources to the rich. Brazil does spend 12% of its GNP on social services, but the main beneficiaries are higher-income groups. About 88% of its public sector health budget is spent on expensive urban hospitals for the few rather than on primary health care for all. Brazil gives 18 times more in subsidies to university students than to primary education, and only 1% of enrolments in its universities come from the poorest 20%. That is why Brazil has four times the infant mortality rate of Jamaica, despite having twice the per capita income and despite spending more on social services.

And one important concern: is everybody in a position to compete in the market, or will some people fall outside the market-place because they do not have enough education, health and nutrition to compete on any footing, let alone an equal footing? That is why much better distribution of income and assets, of credit, of power structures and certainly of knowledge and skills are vital to making markets work more efficiently. Markets cannot become neutral or competitive unless the playing field is even and playable.

Efforts to distribute income and assets more equitably encounter many practical problems, including political constraints. But distributing knowledge and skills quite equally is possible in many countries, and is a tremendous leveling force in the market. And unless there is a tremendous investment in human capital in many countries, the markets will continue to work inefficiently and inequitably—and be hijacked by the rich.

The same is true of global markets. *Human Development Report 1992* analysed whether global economic growth trickles down to poor nations and poor people. Consider some dramatic conclusions about global markets:

- Developing countries are denied at least $500 billion of economic opportunities in the global markets every year because of trade restrictions, immigration controls and uneven capital flows. That is about ten times the amount of annual foreign assistance they receive.

- The poorest 20% of the world's population receives only 0.2% of global commercial credit, 1% of world trade and 2.7% of global foreign private investment.

- The indebted nations of Latin America paid four times higher real interest rates in the 1980s than did the industrial countries (17%, compared with 4%) because of the big fall in commodity prices.

- Capital markets in the 1980s worked in such a way that the poor nations were transferring a net $50 billion a year to the rich nations by the end of the decade.

- Commodity markets worked in such a way that prices of primary commodities (excluding oil) declined to their lowest levels since the Great Depression. Sub-Saharan Africa alone lost more than $50 billion in export earnings between 1986 and 1990 because of depressed commodity prices.

- Sub-Saharan Africa's share in global trade markets declined from 3.8% in 1970 to 1.0% in 1989, despite many trade concessions.

- The ratio of the real income of the wealthiest 20% to that of the poorest 20% of the world's population exploded to 150 to 1 by 1990—more than twice the ratio of 1960—as a natural outcome of the workings of the global markets.

The point again is that markets do not automatically favour the poor, the weak, the vulnerable. Unless policy steps are taken to enable the poor to compete on an equal footing, they stand to lose much from the workings of the unregulated market system. While policy-makers must accept the logic of the market-place, they must also turn around and make markets work more efficiently in the interests of all people. It is people-friendly markets that are needed. After all, markets are only a means—people, the end.

Establishing people-friendly markets—accessible to all the people, encouraging full participation in the mainstream of economic life, extending benefits to everyone rather than to a privileged few—has several preconditions. There must be a more equitable distribution of income, productive assets (particularly land) and credit. There must be enough human investment to enable people to compete on an equal footing. There must be open market entry—with no religious, ethnic, gender or other barriers. There must be competitive market conditions and regulation of monopolistic practices—to prevent a powerful few from bending the market rules to serve their narrow interests. There must be regulation to ensure that the pursuit of private greed does not create external "bads" (such as environmental pollution) and that the greedy are made to pay for the bads they create. People-friendly markets thus require a very activist government—not to overregulate economic enterprises but to create conditions of more equitable access to competitive markets.

Even when markets are fully competitive, some people will fall outside the market-place and require a social safety net. Where the preconditions for people-friendly markets are missing, as they are in many developing countries, the need for such a social safety net increases. Every society develops a certain social consensus on how to balance market efficiency and social compassion. In the United States, the New Deal articulated a new social consensus on the balance between markets and government action—a social contract still valid today, despite some recent weakening. The United States now transfers around 15% of its national income to the more vulnerable groups in society through medicare, food stamps, unemployment benefits and other social security programmes. The Nordic countries transfer more than 30%.

Many developing countries spend less than 5% of their national income on such social safety nets—despite generally worse income and asset distributions, less competitive markets, more formidable barriers to market entry and less institutionalized systems of democratic accountability. And yet many international consultants and financial

institutions advise these developing countries to dismantle their mea-
gre social safety nets in the pursuit of market growth.

Shock therapy

A new cadre of professional shock therapists, often emerging from the
inner sanctums of Harvard and Yale with their academic innocence
intact, carry the message of instant change to far-off lands whose cultures and political systems they do not understand. Mr. Conrad, former
Deputy Prime Minister of Czechoslovakia, says that the doctrine of
shock therapy is out of touch with reality and ignores the impact of such
an approach on the worst-educated skill classes of Eastern Europe. In
Czechoslovakia, after radical reforms had been in place for a year, the
outcome in 1991 was a 22% fall in industrial output, a rise in unemployment from 2.5% to 8.5%, a 33% decline in domestic demand and a 40%
drop in GDP. Conrad admits that these trends are the consequence of
40 years of communist mismanagement but contends that their sudden
intensity results from shock therapy. He notes that Margaret Thatcher
took 12 years to privatize Britain while East Europe got only two years.
He concludes with the sad observation that shock therapy is untested
beyond the economic laboratories of Cambridge, Massachusetts.[1]

The record of shock therapy is dismal. It has failed in many societies. And the unacceptable human and social costs of change have often
led to political upheavals.

Take China and its unprecedented GNP growth of 8–10% a year in
the 1980s. But what happened to social progress? Many social indicators began to weaken. Life expectancy went down, particularly for
women. Health indicators deteriorated because, with the disappearance
of the communes, the nationwide system of primary health care, nur-
tured by barefoot doctors, also disappeared. And unemployment and
inflation emerged in a society with no recent experience of such phe-
nomena. People had not yet begun to share the fruits of market productivity when they started witnessing the human distress in freer
markets, and the weakening of the social safety net that used to be taken
for granted.

Why the weakening of social indicators in a society experiencing
higher income growth? That question is at the heart of the confronta-
tions in Tiananmen Square. The despair that led to upheaval was economic, not political, though some dissenters tried to exploit it for
political purposes. And Chinese policy-makers are perhaps right in
keeping the pace of change gradual and watching more carefully the balance of economic and social progress.

Now consider Sri Lanka, regarded for a long time as a model of human development but recently beset with ethnic conflict. What changed? Sri Lanka has long experienced high literacy and long life expectancy, with Tamils and Sinhalese living together for many decades. In 1979, an adjustment package formulated by the IMF directed that the free rice rations given to every family be targeted more narrowly (and more efficiently, it was suggested) on the very poor through a scheme of food stamps. The scheme made it easier for civil servants to hijack the free nutrition that poor families had been getting. By trying to focus the food stamps only on the very poor, Sri Lanka ended up excluding many poor families from the scheme. The nutritional levels of the poor declined significantly in the 1980s, while average per capita income growth accelerated. The consequent upheavals—social and economic grievances that simply boiled over—should have come as no surprise.

Sri Lanka ended up spending more on its police and its security apparatus than it had spent on food subsidies. What a cruel choice for a finance minister—to put bullets in the stomachs of his people rather than food, even when bullets cost more. And how unnecessary, since higher income growth should have permitted higher, not lower, social spending—all because the IMF was monitoring spending on food subsidies but not spending on police and security.

Many professional shock therapists forget that the opening of markets need not inflict unacceptable social and human costs. The challenge is to design strategies that can combine rapid change with minimal human costs. It is no use shrugging away the social pain with the banal observation that pain is inevitable in a major transition to the market. The most critical question is the distribution of pain: is it borne only by the masses or also by the privileged economic groups? Much of the pain for poor people can be avoided if the burden of adjustment is placed on the favoured strata of society—the military establishment, industrial tax evaders, feudal rentiers, corrupt civil servants, higher income earners. The international institutions should calculate the distribution of the pain of adjustment in a society and try to protect the poor, rather than nonchalantly ignore the issue. How lightly outside consultants and institutions treat the distribution of pain can be illustrated by just one example: their criminal silence on military spending in the Third World in the past three decades. That spending increased by 7.5% a year, three times faster than in the industrial countries. It rose from 7% of global military expenditures in 1960 to 18% in 1985. And yet there was more tolerance for military subsidies than for food subsidies. International institutions carried out no serious economic analysis of military spending in the developing countries. No attempt was made to collect data on military debts—a frightening omission. No information was made available on military assistance. No international outcry went up against powerful military establishments in the Third World. Those who pride themselves on designing "rational" aid conditionality for poor nations should pause to consider whether they should also stand up to powerful vested interests.

If some irrational spending priorities are changed, the painful transition to the market can be combined with social safety nets for the poor. We have come to a crossroads where individual initiative must be combined with social objectives. Not one, not the other, but both. The course of the world's societies may well depend on how skilfully they combine market efficiency with social compassion.

Some analysts have contended that recent years have seen the triumph of capitalism and the demise of socialism. If this is the triumph of capitalism, let us hope that it is not the triumph only of private greed. And if this is the demise of socialism, let us hope that it is not the demise of all social objectives.

Note

1. *New York Times*, 5 January 1992.

Chapter 13

Policy Direction of the World Bank

> *"Where do you come from?"* said the Red Queen. *"And where are you going? Look up, speak nicely, and don't twiddle your fingers all the time."*
>
> Alice attended to all these directions, and explained, as well as she could, that she had lost her way.
>
> *"I don't know what you mean by your way,"* said the Queen: *"all the ways about here belong to me—but why did you come out here at all?"* she added in a kinder tone. *"Curtsey while you're thinking what to say, it saves time."*
>
> — Through the Looking Glass

*A*lthough the senior management and the Executive Board of the World Bank never ignored politics in their economic decision-making, that was not true of Bank staff—young, self-confident professionals from the world's leading universities who treated the latest economic theories and development models as gospel.[1] They were repeatedly told to focus only on the technical and economic aspects of projects and programmes—thus the narrow technical judgements of the Bank staff were linked with the much broader economic and political perspective of senior management and the Executive Board.

The original charter of the World Bank was often quoted to young officers to ensure that their sights were fixed on narrow economic analysis: "The Bank shall make arrangements to ensure that the proceeds of any loan are used only for the purposes for which the loan was granted, with due attention to considerations of economy and efficiency and *without regard to political or other non-economic influences or considerations*" (emphasis added).

Only recently has the Bank recognized the folly of such a narrow, technocratic interpretation of its charter. The revisionist interpretation, articulated in 1992 in *Governance and Development,* states with a certain air of discovery: "Good governance is synonymous with sound development management."[2] It then goes on to suggest what the Bank should not have taken so long to discover: "The Bank's experience has shown that the programmes and projects it helps finance may be technically sound but fail to deliver anticipated results for reasons connected to the quality of government action." On "the quality of government action", the document mentions such issues as improved public sector management, a democratic system of accountability, a sound legal framework for development, access to information and transparency, systematic checks against corruption and reduced military expenditures.

This refreshing departure from the past practice of ignoring the broader issues of national governance in project appraisal or country policy dialogue is most welcome. A review of the Bank's lending patterns during 1960–90 shows that Bank staff missed many opportunities to link their lending policies to the broader objectives that the Bank itself advocated, and that narrow project conditionality often triumphed over broader policy dialogue regarding national governance. A credibility gap arose because the Bank staff was often oblivious to the larger policy issues that the Bank's management was espousing in its single-minded focus on country creditworthiness and rates of return on projects. In addition, the Bank staff shied away from many legitimate issues—such as land reform, income distribution, military spending and corruption—in the belief that politics would be dragged into pure economic analysis. Having found stirring articulation in the speeches of the senior management, these issues were often forgotten by the time project reports or country economic memoranda were written.

Link with military spending

During the cold war decades after the Second World War, several strategic considerations influenced the distribution of bilateral ODA. The most dominant was to shore up various defence alliances around the globe with generous injections of economic assistance. The pattern of bilateral aid allocations during this period strongly indicates a close link with the level of military spending in recipient countries, particularly for US assistance. Even in 1990, the distribution of bilateral ODA still showed the scars of the cold war (table 13.1). If recipient countries are classified by their military spending, the highest military spenders (with military spending of more than 4% of GDP) were receiving 80% more ODA per capita than more moderate military spenders (2–4% of GDP) and 30% more than low military spenders (less than 2% of GDP). The United States earmarked more than half its bilateral economic assistance in 1989–90 for only five countries, on the basis of strategic geopolitical considerations: Israel, Egypt, Pakistan, the Philippines and El Salvador.

The World Bank's lending pattern reveals no such preference for high military spenders. The per capita share for the highest military spenders is slightly higher than that for moderate spenders but much lower than that for low military spenders. What this lending pattern shows is a neutral stand on the military spending of developing countries rather than an activist policy. This neutrality of the World Bank towards the military spending appetites of its member countries is even more obvious over time (table 13.2). Unlike many bilateral donors, the World Bank revealed no distinct preference for the highest military spenders in its lending during 1960–90. The Bank was obviously guided by country creditworthiness, quality of economic management and soundness of projects and programmes rather than by any geopolitical or strategic considerations in the allocation of its funds.

It could be argued that the strictures on "political neutrality" in the World Bank charter have worked in the larger interest of global economic development in this case. That may well be true. But the World Bank's neutrality bordered on indifference to the military spending habits of its borrowers. Military spending levels were not analysed as a part of regular budget analysis. Nor was the trade-off between military and social spending made a major issue in World Bank policy dialogue or loan conditionality. That is all the more important to remember

Table 13.1 Military spending and bilateral and World Bank assistance, 1990

Category	Share of population (%)	Share of bilateral ODA (%)	Share of bilateral ODA as % of population share	Share of World Bank loans (%)	Share of World Bank loans as % of population share
Low military spenders (less than 2% of GDP)	27.7	30.6	111	43.0	155
Moderate military spenders (2–4% of GDP)	54.7	43.9	80	39.9	73
High military spenders (more than 4% of GDP)	17.6	25.5	145	17.1	97

Note: The table is based on a group of 84 countries, with 66% of the developing countries' population. Categories are based on military spending figures of 1989. Bilateral ODA is based on net disbursements. World Bank lending is based on average annual commitments in fiscal 1989–91 and includes both IDA and IBRD loans.
Source: World Bank data; and UNDP, *Human Development Report 1992,* New York: Oxford University Press, 1992.

because of the recent—and most welcome—emphasis by the World Bank management on reducing military expenditures in the developing countries and the observation in the World Bank's recent publication that "the Bank is interested in military expenditures because of their crowding-out effect on development spending".[3] The same publication points out that the Bank's "main concern is that the country systematically ensures that all its expenditures, including military expenditures, are properly assessed and prioritized, that they are transparent, and that they are subject to expenditure controls and auditing".[4]

Obviously, no such considerations had bothered the Bank in the preceding four decades of its operation. There is no evidence that the level of military spending and its "crowding-out effect on development spending" ever played a major role in the allocation of World Bank funds to member countries.

This was a major opportunity lost, and one that the World Bank is now trying to capture. It is particularly pertinent to analyse the adjustment experience of some of the poorest countries in the 1980s, when social expenditures were cut while military expenditures actually increased, to realize how the "human face" of the adjustment process was distorted because of World Bank reluctance to raise the issue of military spending with its borrowers.

Table 13.2 World Bank lending to low, moderate and high military spenders
(percent)

	1960s			1970s			1980s		
	Share of loans	Population share 1965	Share of loans as % of population share	Share of loans	Population share 1975	Share of loans as % of population share	Share of loans	Population share 1985	Share of loans as % of population share
Low military spenders (less than 2% of GDP)	61.7	65.8	94	31.9	20.7	154	27.8	20.6	135
Moderate military spenders (2–4% of GDP)	19.6	9.1	215	50.2	63.4	79	36.4	48.3	75
High military spenders (more than 4% of GDP)	18.7	25.1	75	17.9	15.9	113	35.8	31.1	115
Groups' share of total population of developing countries (%)		60			67			66	

Note: IDA and IBRD commitments by fiscal year. Country groups for the 1960s, 1970s and 1980s are based on military spending in 1960, 1974 and 1985.
Source: World Bank data; UNDP, Human Development Report 1992, New York: Oxford University Press, 1992; Ruth L. Sivard, World Military and Social Expenditures 1993, Leesburg, Va.: World Priorities Inc.; and Stockholm International Peace Research Institute, SIPRI Yearbook 1992: World Armaments and Disarmament, New York: Oxford University Press, 1992.

During 1960–85, military spending in the Third World increased at a frightening 7.5% a year—three times faster than in the industrial countries. The share of the Third World in global military expenditures rose dramatically—from 7% in 1960 to 18% in 1985. Even the poorest developing countries were not immune to this madness in arms spending. Many of them started spending two to three times as much on their military as on the education and health of their people: Iraq, Somalia, Nicaragua, Ethiopia, Pakistan, Uganda, Zaire. In Sub-Saharan Africa, military spending rose from 0.7% of GNP in 1960 to 3.5% of GNP in 1990—a fivefold increase in a resource-strapped continent. In South Asia (principally India and Pakistan), military expenditure has now reached more than $20 billion a year.

And where was the World Bank when all these alarming developments were taking place? It could not pretend that these developments were not the most important events affecting prospects for economic change. Yet no World Bank country economic reports carry an analysis of military expenditures during this period. No effort was made to collect data on military expenditures or military debts.[5] No policy position was adopted by the Bank management on the "crowding-out" effect of military expenditures. Obviously, the narrower technical focus prevailed over larger policy cross-currents.

The Bank, some would argue, could not have exercised much influence on military spending in its member countries even if it had chosen to make a major policy issue out of it. That simply is not true. Greater transparency of information and more analysis of trade-offs between military and social spending would have generated a healthy national and international debate. In any case, there are anti-military-spending lobbies in all countries, and they could have used some constructive support from the World Bank.[6]

A major test for the World Bank (and the IMF) arose during the phase of adjustment policies in the 1980s. Most developing country budgets needed drastic measures to balance them, particularly on the expenditure side. The real question was, could these countries balance their financial budgets without unbalancing the lives of their future generations? Would defence expenditures be cut ahead of social expenditures? As it was, in several countries where the World Bank supported adjustment programmes, social expenditures were drastically curtailed (sometimes by more than 50%) while military expenditures increased.[7] The bitter controversy over the need for structural adjustment programmes during this period often missed the real point. Of course, the budgets needed to be balanced. But the real issue was, what expenditures were being reduced? A very disturbing picture emerges: poor countries slash their education and health expenditures while increasing their expenditures on the military, with the World Bank and the IMF watching silently from the sidelines.

Some apologists argue that the Bank could not violate the sovereignty of the developing countries by making military spending a major issue. The Bank, they maintain, was in no position to judge countries' national security requirements. This argument rings hollow. The Bank never hesitated to violate the sovereignty of its borrower countries when it came to eliminating food subsidies, increasing taxes or imposing severe social costs on a vast majority of their people. Did it develop a conscience only when it had to confront powerful military establishments in the developing world, along with the vested interests of its donors in continuing arms exports? And why has this argument of protecting the sovereignty of developing countries vanished in the aftermath of the cold war, when the basic interests of the big powers have changed?

Military spending has been picked up here as only one significant illustration of the opportunities that the World Bank missed for a broader policy dialogue with its member countries. There are many other examples. Attention to such issues as land reform, income inequality, ethnic discrimination, gender bias and regional disparities is crucial in designing any viable, long-term economic framework—though it may bruise delicate national sensitivities. These broader issues failed to attract much of the Bank's attention in the past, issues the Bank is now trying to deal with under the umbrella of "national governance".

Link with poverty alleviation

To what extent were World Bank lending policies guided by analysis of each country's creditworthiness and the relative merits of individual projects? And to what extent were they influenced by some overall policy objective, such as alleviation of poverty in the developing world? The poverty alleviation objective was openly embraced by the Bank management, particularly in the McNamara era (1968–81). It was, of course, often seen more as a technical issue ("raising the productivity of the poor") than as a political issue ("changing the existing power structures"), which imposed its own constraints. But to what extent was the rhetoric on poverty alleviation translated into the Bank's distribution of funds among developing countries?

The record is not reassuring. It may be better than that of many bilateral donors, but it is by no means outstanding. Only 27% of total bilateral ODA was allocated to the ten countries containing 72% of the world's absolute poor in 1990, a poor link between total ODA and global poverty (table 13.3). The World Bank did better, allocating 39% of its funds (both IDA and IBRD) to the same nations. Overall, the developing countries with the largest concentrations of poor people received a much lower per capita allocation than more affluent nations did. The Bank did not manage to defy the tyranny of market creditworthiness as the crucial test, despite the emergence of the IDA. In recent years, only 43% of IDA funds have been earmarked for 72% of the world's absolute poor, compared with 38% of IBRD resources—a surprisingly small difference considering that the IDA was created to meet the needs of the poorest, least creditworthy nations.

The lack of a close link between Bank lending and global poverty is apparent throughout the period between 1960 and 1990 (table 13.4). Roughly 30% of the World Bank's total resources were earmarked for about 70% of the world's absolute poor in 1960 and 1970. The proportion

Table 13.3 The World Bank and the poorest people, 1990

Poor people in the ten developing countries with the greatest number of poor (millions)[a]	869
Poor in these countries as a percentage of total world poor	72.4
Bilateral ODA allocation to these countries as a percentage of total ODA	26.8
World Bank allocation to these countries as a percentage of total World Bank lending[b]	39.5
IDA	42.6
IBRD	38.4

a. India, China, Bangladesh, Indonesia, Pakistan, the Philippines, Brazil, Ethiopia, Myanmar and Thailand.
b. Average annual commitments, fiscal 1989–91.
Note: For details, see annex 13.1.
Source: World Bank data; and UNDP, *Human Development Report 1992,* New York: Oxford University Press, 1992.

Table 13.4 World Bank lending to the ten countries with the greatest number of poor people
(percent)

	1961	1970	1980	1990
IBRD lending	23.7	18.3	32.0	38.4
IDA lending	60.8	66.0	60.6	42.6
IDA plus IBRD lending	28.9	29.9	40.7	39.5
Population of the ten countries[a] as a share of population of all developing countries	70.8	70.4	69.4	67.9

Note: Lending shares are calculated using averages over three fiscal years.
a. India, China, Bangladesh, Indonesia, Pakistan, the Philippines, Brazil, Ethiopia, Myanmar and Thailand. The countries are chosen for the 1990 period; data for earlier periods are for the same group of countries.
Source: World Bank data.

rose to 40% towards the end of the McNamara era in 1980 and was still close to that level in 1990. The objective of poverty alleviation did not significantly influence allocations between poorer and richer developing countries. The developing countries with the largest concentrations of absolute poverty continued to receive a much lower per capita allocation than the richer ones did, largely owing to their poorer creditworthiness and their more limited capacity to generate good development projects. The role of the World Bank as an activist development agency—while apparent in some developing countries—was always somewhat exaggerated in global terms. In the end, the "banker" in the World Bank allocated its funds.

A much better picture emerges from World Bank lending to the least developed countries. On the recommendations of the UN Committee on Development Planning,[8] these countries have been classified as most deserving of international concessional assistance on the basis of their low per capita incomes, poor human and physical infrastructure, limited industrial base and low creditworthiness. At present, 45 countries, with around 10% of the developing world's total population, qualify as "least developed". Most of the larger poorest countries (China, India, Pakistan and Indonesia) have been deliberately excluded from this list. The World Bank has never officially endorsed or used the classification of "least developed countries", relying instead on a per capita income test to classify countries in low-, middle- and upper-income brackets.

The least developed countries have received about 40–50% of IDA funds during the past decade for a population that is only around 10% of the developing world's total population (table 13.5). In other words, these countries—many of them in Sub-Saharan Africa—have generally received four to five times the per capita allocation of poor countries not in the least developed category. Somewhat more surprising, the IDA share to least developed countries has been more generous in the post-McNamara era (46%) than it was in the McNamara era (33%). The main reasons for this are the increasing focus of the Bank on Africa and the gradual reduction of IDA lending to South Asia. In fact, the share of IDA lending going to the least developed countries has been roughly twice the share of ODA from OECD Development Assistance Committee (DAC) nations.

In overall terms, then, the World Bank has done fairly well in allocations to the smaller, least developed countries (particularly in the allocation of IDA resources), but its record for the more populous of the poorest nations is much less satisfactory. If poverty alleviation is seen in terms of the number of poor people affected rather than the number of poor countries reached, the Bank's performance leaves many questions about how seriously it actually pursued this objective in global allocations.

Three main conclusions emerge from this analysis of the reality (as distinct from the fiction) of the World Bank's focus on poverty reduction:

First, World Bank lending was biased against the countries with the largest number of poor people, a bias implicit in rationing IDA allocations to India and in not lending to China. India in particular suffered in the 1980s. According to World Bank data, India contained 34% of the world's absolute poor but received only 3.5% of global ODA (including World Bank assistance). It turned to private capital markets in the 1980s and incurred a debt of more than $50 billion, with a per capita income of $360. The Bank found itself helpless to do much about this situation, despite its constant noise about absolute poverty.

Second, within countries, it appears that World Bank lending was biased against the poor people. The proportion of "poverty loans" in country portfolios was much smaller than the proportion of people living in absolute poverty.

Third, Bank lending carried a distinct country bias. The Bank dealt with countries rather than with people. It doled out money to nations on the basis of its assessment of country creditworthiness and the avail-

Table 13.5 Lending to least developed countries
(percent)

World Bank fiscal years	Share of aid from DAC countries	Share of World Bank lending		
		IBRD	IDA	IBRD and IDA combined
1960s		6.1	15.8	8.2
1970s		2.9	32.6	11.0
1979/80	25			
1980s		0.5	44.1	10.6
1989	23			
1990	22	0.0	49.4	13.2
1991		0.1	37.9	10.6
McNamara era, 1968–81		2.8	32.9	11.2
Post-McNamara era, 1982–91		0.3	45.8	10.8

Note: The least developed countries are Afghanistan, Bangladesh, Benin, Bhutan, Botswana, Burkina Faso, Burundi, Cambodia, Cape Verde, Central African Republic, Chad, Comoros, Djibouti, Equatorial Guinea, Ethiopia, Gambia, Guinea, Guinea-Bissau, Haiti, Lao People's Democratic Republic, Lesotho, Liberia, Madagascar, Malawi, Maldives, Mali, Mauritania, Mozambique, Myanmar, Nepal, Niger, Rwanda, Samoa, São Tomé and Principe, Sierra Leone, Solomon Islands, Somalia, Sudan, Tanzania, Togo, Uganda, Vanuatu, Yemen, Zaire and Zambia.
Source: World Bank data.

ability of high-return projects. The objective of poverty reduction was generally an afterthought.

Link with human development

Another way to look at the World Bank record in meeting human concerns in the developing countries is to review the investment that the Bank was prepared to make in social services and in increasing people's access to social opportunities. McNamara always regarded the higher allocations that he achieved for social sectors, previously considered non-bankable, as one of his main contributions to converting the World Bank from a strictly banking orientation to a greater development orientation.[9]

The World Bank's allocations for social sectors have increased steadily over the past two decades (table 13.6). More than a quarter of its total funds are earmarked for social sectors, compared with 15% of total ODA. But less than half the social sector allocations are for the basic human concerns of the masses: basic education, primary health care, safe drinking water, adequate sanitation, family planning and nutrition programmes. More than half are earmarked for colleges and universities, urban hospitals, urban housing and other social programmes reflecting the preferences and vested interests of powerful groups in the developing countries.

The record of the Bank in allocations for basic human priority concerns is much better than that of the bilateral donors: 10.8% in 1990, compared with 6.5% for bilateral ODA. But the nagging feeling remains that—at a time of such resource scarcity—the Bank could have done a

Table 13.6 World Bank lending and human development
(percent)

Period or year	Social allocation ratio [a]	Social priority ratio [b]	Share of total funds for basic human priority concerns
1973–79	17.8	58.5	10.4
1980–89	18.4	62.6	11.5
1990	25.7	41.8	10.8
Memo item			
Bilateral ODA (1990)	14.8	43.7	6.5

Note: For details, see annex 13.2.
a. Percentage of total funds allocated to social sectors.
b. Percentage of social sector funds allocated to basic human priorities: basic education, primary health care, safe drinking water, adequate sanitation, family planning and nutrition programmes.
Source: OECD data; and UNDP, *Human Development Report 1992*, New York: Oxford University Press, 1992.

REFLECTIONS ON HUMAN DEVELOPMENT

much better job of standing up for allocation priorities that would have benefited the many rather than the few. The recent changes in the Bank's stance on human development are refreshing: it appears that the Bank will soon be earmarking as much as 20% of its total funds for human priority concerns, particularly in Africa, where the need for such allocations is the greatest.

Link with democratic transition

To what extent was the World Bank's allocation pattern influenced by the political complexion of a country? Did it make any difference whether a country was adopting a democratic framework or whether it was an authoritarian regime? Did the World Bank lending pattern change at all when a country got rid of its martial law regime and needed some room for manoeuvre in experimenting with democratic institutions? Was there ever a link between World Bank lending and a country's observance of human rights?

Difficult questions. Some studies have been done regarding the link between bilateral aid and human rights violations, particularly for US aid. The United States adopted a deliberate policy in the late 1970s of linking its assistance to greater respect for human rights in developing countries. But many recent studies have established that the actual link was more often perverse: more US assistance went to countries that violated the human rights of their citizens—this because the United States often sided with dictators in its search for allies in the cold war.[10]

No similar studies are available for the World Bank. A quick analysis shows, however, that World Bank lending was not much influenced by democratic transition in borrowing countries (table 13.7). For instance, the Philippines received roughly the same share of World Bank funds in the Corizon Aquino democratic era as it did under Ferdinand Marcos's authoritarian regime. In Bangladesh, the transition from martial law to democratic rule in 1991 seems to have made no difference for the commitment of World Bank resources. In Pakistan, there was a significant increase in World Bank lending after the termination of martial law in December 1985, but this increase was related more to the improved creditworthiness of the economy for which sound economic management during the earlier martial law period had prepared the basis—the increase was in IBRD lending, which rose fourfold. Only in China did the lending pattern register political change—and that because the United States prevailed upon the World Bank's Executive Board to freeze lending to China for some time after the Tiananmen Square upheaval, much against the wishes of the Bank management. On the whole, the Bank was influenced little by democratic transitions in considering its levels of lending to developing countries.

That does not mean that the Bank did not respond at all to gross violations of human rights. Its freeze of lending to Pakistan—during the pangs of Bangladesh's birth in December 1971—is a case in point. Similar tactical interruptions in lending were imposed by the Bank management in certain other cases of flagrant human rights abuses. But these interruptions were rare and always justified in economic terms ("inability to carry out projects efficiently" being a typical excuse) rather than in political terms—as a deferential nod to the provisions in the Bank charter. All in all, it would be fair to say that democracy has not been a precondition for Bank lending or a main policy preoccupation, nor has it been a strong selling point for countries trying to obtain higher Bank allocations.

The narrow, technocratic focus of the World Bank often confined it to considering a host of micropolicy economic issues while it missed out on the macropolicy horizon.

Table 13.7 World Bank lending and democracy
(loans in annual averages; US$ millions)

The Philippines	1980–85	1986–91
IBRD	389.6	550.8
IDA	—	11.0
IBRD plus IDA	389.6	561.8
Total IBRD and IDA loans	13,528.7	19,661.3
Share in total IBRD and IDA loans (%)	2.88	2.86
Pakistan	*1980–85*	*1986–91*
IBRD	129.7	490.2
IDA	197.8	203.3
IBRD plus IDA	327.5	693.4
Total IBRD and IDA loans	13,528.7	19,661.3
Share in total IBRD and IDA loans (%)	2.42	3.53
China	*1986–89*	*1990–91*
IBRD	860.4	300.8
IDA	540.3	783.9
IBRD plus IDA	1,400.7	1,084.7
Total IBRD and IDA loans	18,645.1	21,693.6
Share in total IBRD and IDA loans (%)	7.51	5.00
Bangladesh	*1988–90*	*1991*
IDA	397.0	459.7
Total IDA loans	4,971.4	6,293.3
Share in total IDA loans (%)	7.99	7.30

Source: World Bank, *The World Bank Annual Report,* Washington, D.C., various years.

In retrospect, the World Bank has interpreted its mandate far too narrowly. Its Articles of Agreement should have been interpreted as an injunction against lending for purely political reasons, not as a bar against considering the political dimensions of economic policy issues. The economic development process can never be divorced from the political process, and any attempt to do so is to bury one's head in sand. It may lead to a situation where—as the World Bank rightly points out now—"projects . . . may be technically sound but fail to deliver anticipated results for reasons connected to the quality of government action".

The World Bank has recognized the dilemmas inherent in its earlier, narrower interpretation of its Articles of Agreement and is now trying to broaden its role to encompass the larger issues of economic and political management in the name of national governance. It defines national governance as "the manner in which power is exercised in the management of a country's economic and social resources for development."[11] And it has obtained a fresh interpretation of its Articles of Agreement from its General Counsel. The new interpretation is still quite cautious, as befits the conservative image of the Bank, though it appears that it is merely to serve as a fig leaf.

The World Bank publication mentions that: "The General Counsel's memorandum identified five aspects of governance which are beyond the Bank's mandate: the Bank cannot be influenced by the political character of a member; it cannot interfere in the partisan politics of the member; it must not act on behalf of industrial member countries to influence a borrowing member's political orientation or behavior; it cannot be influenced in its decisions by political factors that do not have a preponderant economic effect; and its staff must not build their judgments on the possible reactions of a particular Bank member or members."[12]

Despite such a cautious interpretation, the Bank's actual interpretation of its new role is much less inhibited—both in theory and in practice. The same publication details some of the areas in which Bank intervention will now be legitimate. These include "weak institutions, lack of an adequate legal framework, weak financial accounting and auditing systems, damaging discretionary interventions, uncertain and variable policy frameworks, and closed decision-making which increases risks of corruption and waste . . . monopolies allocated to friends of those in power . . . discrimination against certain ethnic groups . . . lack of public accountability, corruption, and the 'capture' of public services by elites. . . ." In other words, the entire gamut of economic and political factors that guide the policy framework of any country.

In actual practice, too, the Bank is taking on issues that earlier were considered outside its limits. The Bank management recently expressed strong views on the increasing military spending in the developing world, and the Bank staff is beginning to analyse this issue in country reports. Although human rights violations are not openly mentioned as a cause for suspending aid commitments, the Bank is beginning to pay some attention to this issue. For example, in November 1991, the Bank agreed to postpone its aid consortium meeting for Kenya until Kenya organized new, multiparty elections and curbed its rampant corruption—though the Bank did this under obvious pressure from bilateral donors. The march towards a far more liberal interpretation of its Articles of Agreement has already begun.

It is refreshing that the Bank is beginning to interpret its Articles of Agreement more broadly. The Bank staff is discovering—rather belatedly—that the quality of governments, not just the quality of projects, often proves decisive. The Bank is dipping its feet, albeit cautiously, in the political waters that shape economic policies. This is a double-edged sword. The Bank's forays into such uncharted territory scare many developing countries. But it is far better to have an open dialogue among the senior management and the Executive Board on these issues than to maintain the fiction of political neutrality for Bank staff when, at the higher decision-making levels, no such neutrality has existed.

Notes

1. The author is grateful to Kees Kingma for his assistance with the statistical analysis discussed in this chapter, which required reprocessing a considerable amount of raw data obtained directly from the World Bank.

2. World Bank, *Governance and Development,* Washington, D.C., 1992.

3. Ibid., p. 46.

4. Ibid., p. 46.

5. I was informed that a recent attempt by the IMF to establish the size of Egypt's military debts has progressively revised the estimate from an earlier guesstimate of $5 billion to more than $40 billion. How can international institutions advise on balance of payments policies if they are not even aware of the substantial size of military debts?

6. I know from my experience as Planning and Finance Minister of Pakistan for seven years (1982–89) that my somewhat forlorn advocacy within the system—of the viewpoint that we simply could not afford military spending levels three times higher than education and health spending levels—would have gained tremendous strength and credibility if international institutions had been willing to raise this issue with both Pakistan and India.

7. See UNDP's 1990, 1991 and 1992 *Human Development Reports* (New York: Oxford University Press) for documentation of country cases.

8. A group of 20–25 distinguished economists and other leading thinkers who meet periodically in their personal capacities under the UN umbrella.

9. When both McNamara and I were leaving the Bank in 1981, I asked him how we were ever to meet the frequent charge that our emphasis on absolute poverty and marginal people was more rhetorical than operational. His quick response was: "At least 38% operational impact." When I looked mystified, he took out a statistical table showing that 38% of World Bank lending at that time was going to sectors not regarded as Bank-worthy before he came to the Bank in 1968 (non-formal education, rural electrification, rural water supply, family planning, nutrition, primary health care and so on).

10. See, for example, James M. McCornick and Neil J. Mitchell, "Human Rights and Foreign Assistance: An Update," *Social Science Quarterly* 70 (4, 1989): 969–79.

11. World Bank, *Governance and Development*, Washington, D.C., 1992, p. 3.

12. Ibid., p. 5.

Annex 13.1 ODA and World Bank lending to the poorest, 1990

Ten developing countries with greatest number of poor	Number of poor (millions)	Poor as % of total world poor	ODA per capita (US$)	IDA lending per capita (US$)	IBRD lending per capita (US$)	IDA + IBRD lending per capita (US$)
India	410	34.2	1.8	1.0	1.7	2.7
China[a]	120	9.9	1.8	0.6	0.4	1.0
Bangladesh	99	8.3	18.0	4.2	0.0	4.2
Indonesia	70	5.8	9.3	0.0	9.0	9.0
Pakistan	37	3.1	8.8	1.9	5.3	7.2
Philippines	36	3.0	20.3	0.4	12.3	12.7
Brazil	33	2.8	1.1	0.0	7.2	7.2
Ethiopia	30	2.5	17.7	1.5	0.0	1.5
Myanmar	17	1.4	4.7	0.0	0.0	0.0
Thailand	17	1.4	14.1	0.0	2.3	2.3
Total	**869**	**72.4**	**4.2**	**0.9**	**2.2**	**3.1**

Annex 13.1 ODA and World Bank lending to the poorest, 1990 (continued)

Ten developing countries with greatest number of poor	Share of total ODA (%)	Share of IDA lending (%)	Share of IBRD lending (%)	Share of IDA + IBRD lending (%)
India	3.5	15.9	9.1	10.9
China[a]	4.7	12.4	3.0	5.4
Bangladesh	4.7	8.5	0.0	2.2
Indonesia	3.9	0.0	10.2	7.6
Pakistan	2.5	3.9	3.7	3.8
Philippines	2.9	0.4	4.8	3.7
Brazil	0.4	0.0	6.7	5.0
Ethiopia	2.0	1.4	0.0	0.4
Myanmar	0.4	0.0	0.0	0.0
Thailand	1.8	0.0	0.8	0.6
Total	**26.8**	**42.6**	**38.4**	**39.5**

Note: ODA is expressed as net disbursements. World Bank lending is average annual commitments for fiscal 1989–91.

a. The number of rural poor in China is estimated by the World Bank at about 100 million. A rough estimate of 120 million is adopted here for the entire country, based on a rural poverty rate two and a half times the urban-poverty rate.

Source: World Bank data.

REFLECTIONS ON HUMAN DEVELOPMENT

Annex 13.2 Human priorities in bilateral and multilateral aid

Country or agency	Bilateral ODA (US$ millions) 1990	Bilateral ODA as % of GNP 1990	Social allocation ratio [a] 1988/89	Social priority ratio [b] 1988/89	Percentage of total ODA for human priorities 1988/89
Bilateral assistance					
Norway	1,207	1.17	27.2	72.3	19.7
Switzerland	750	0.31	35.8	50.6	18.1
Finland	846	0.64	38.0	41.4	15.7
Canada	2,470	0.44	23.8	45.9	10.9
Denmark	1,171	0.93	19.2	55.4	10.6
Netherlands	2,580	0.93	21.1	44.5	9.4
United Kingdom	2,639	0.27	13.4	65.8	8.8
Italy	3,395	0.32	18.0	47.3	8.5
USA	10,166	0.19	16.4	50.4	8.3
Austria	389	0.25	13.4	60.6	8.1
Sweden	2,007	0.90	17.0	41.5	7.1
France	6,277	0.52	11.0	35.9	4.0
Japan	9,054	0.31	10.7	25.5	2.7
Australia	955	0.34	6.4	31.4	2.0
Germany	6,320	0.42	8.9	21.4	1.9
Total	**50,226**	**0.35**	**14.8**	**43.7**	**6.5**
Multilateral assistance					
UNICEF			91.7	85.9	78.8
IFAD			16.8	100.0	16.8
IDB (including special)			27.8	54.4	15.1
AsDB (including special)			17.5	64.5	11.3
IBRD/IDA			17.5	47.7	8.3
AFDB/African Development Fund			16.6	32.4	5.4
Total			**19.1**	**49.1**	**9.9**

a. Percentage of allocations to all social sectors.
b. Percentage of social sector allocations earmarked for human priority concerns of basic education, primary health care, safe drinking water, adequate sanitation, family planning and nutrition programmes.
Source: UNDP, *Human Development Report 1992,* New York: Oxford University Press, 1992.

Chapter 14

Bretton Woods Institutions in Global Governance

"You are old, Father William," the young man said,
"And your hair has become very white;
·And yet you incessantly stand on your head—
Do you think, at your age, it is right?"

"In my youth," Father William replied to his son,
"I feared it might injure the brain;
But, now that I'm perfectly sure I have none,
Why, I do it again and again."

— Alice in Wonderland

The birth of the Bretton Woods institutions in the 1940s was a direct response to the dismal experience of the 1920s and 1930s. Many of those surveying the wreckage of the global economic system in the dreary days of the Second World War—among them, John Maynard Keynes, the dominant economic thinker of that time—came to a simple conclusion. The world's economic system needed honest referees. It could not be left to the mercy of unilateral action by governments or to the unregulated workings of international markets. It needed multilateral institutions of economic governance to lay down some mutually agreed rules for all nations on the conduct of their affairs. Thus emerged the International Monetary Fund (IMF), the International Bank for Reconstruction and Development (IBRD, or the World Bank) and, later, the General Agreement on Tariffs and Trade (GATT).

The starting point was the United Nations Conference on Money and Finance held in the United States in Bretton Woods, New Hampshire, in July 1944. Lord Keynes, representing the United Kingdom, and Harry White, of the US delegation, were the dominating intellectual figures setting the stage for a more orderly global economic transition after the Second World War. With memories of the Great Depression still fresh, the battle cry at the Bretton Woods conference was: "Never again!" Unemployment had been heavy—so the new objective was full employment. Trade and investment rules had broken down—so the new objective was to prevent beggar-thy-neighbour policies. The international monetary system had collapsed—so the new objective was to maintain stable currencies with agreed procedures for adjustment. Unilateral national policies had created world chaos—so the basic idea was to fashion new institutions of global monetary and economic governance, with clear objectives and with changes in global policies engineered through a broad international consensus.

The structure emerging from the Bretton Woods conference was supposed to rest on four pillars of multilateralism:

1. The International Monetary Fund, to maintain global monetary stability, primarily through the mechanism of fixed but adjustable exchange rates.

2. The International Bank for Reconstruction and Development, to reconstruct the war-torn economies of Europe and Japan and to stimulate the growth of the less developed regions in the Third World.

3. The International Trade Organization (ITO), to stabilize international commodity prices and to manage a liberal trading regime.

4. The United Nations (UN), to maintain peace among nations as well as to encourage social and human development within nations.

The first two pillars of this global economic system emerged in a fairly strong form. But the other two pillars were shaky from the start. The US Congress refused to consider the treaty setting up the ITO, negotiated at Havana in 1946. Established instead to police the world trading system was the GATT, in 1948, joined in 1964 by the United Nations Conference on Trade and Development (UNCTAD). UNCTAD generated some pressure—largely unsuccessful—for commodity price stabilization. The United Nations system was never given the role of a development agency as originally envisioned. Donors channeled most of their aid funds through the Bretton Woods institutions, whose governance was based on a one-dollar, one-vote formula that gave donors overwhelming control over the funds. The governance of the United Nations, by contrast, was based on a one-state, one-vote formula, much too democratic for the taste of the democratic regimes that constituted the donor community. So, the UN development system went into a tailspin—inadequate financing led to ineffectiveness and alleged inefficiency, and the inefficiency led to further erosion of its financial support.

The relationship between the UN system and the Bretton Woods institutions has always been somewhat ambiguous and tense. It started that way. Few realize that the offspring (the Bretton Woods institutions) were born a year earlier (in 1944) than the parent (United Nations, formed in San Francisco in 1945), an immaculate conception of institutions! From the start, the Bretton Woods institutions neither respected nor cared for the UN system, and they have worked largely independently—despite polite noises from time to time about mutual cooperation.

Impact of the Bretton Woods institutions

The Bretton Woods institutions had a major influence on the global economic environment in their first 25 years, but this influence has been on the wane in their second 25 years, as they have become increasingly marginalized in global economic governance. Their influence on economic management in the developing world nevertheless remains significant.

In the first 25 years after the Second World War (1945–70), industrial countries grew nearly twice as fast as in any comparable period before or since. In Western European countries, national output increased by 4.4% a year in the 1950s and by 4.8% in the 1960s. The corresponding annual growth rates in the United States were 3.2% and 4.3%, and in Japan, 9.5% and 10.5%. Even the developing countries grew at satisfactory rates, normally 5–6% a year. These healthy GNP growth rates bear a striking contrast to the rather pallid growth of recent decades.

Many factors contributed. The more liberal trading regime set up under the GATT rules helped considerably. The annual rate of export growth in the 1950s and 1960s was spectacular: 17% in Japan, 12% in West Germany and 5% in the United States. Such robust growth in trade kept feeding rapid economic expansion.

The strong economic performance during this period was also assisted by the global monetary stability established under the IMF rules. All nations established fixed exchange rates, which could be changed only in consultation with the IMF. In both rich nations and poor, the IMF rules had a major influence on domestic monetary policies.

The World Bank played a more marginal role in these first 25 years—with the spotlight often on the IMF and the GATT. The task of reconstruction and development of Europe and Japan was largely taken over by the Marshall Plan, with the World Bank playing only a limited role. The Bank's influence grew significantly in the developing countries, but mainly in the past three decades, particularly after the addition of its soft loan affiliate, the International Development Association

(IDA), in 1960 to provide concessional finance to low-income developing countries.

There were several reasons for the success of the Bretton Woods institutions in their first 25 years. The world economy was run by a small number of countries that enjoyed overwhelming influence in the weighted voting structures of these institutions. After the Second World War, US output was about 50% of world output, so the United States was in a position to lay down the global rules of the game and to keep the management of the Bretton Woods institutions firmly in line. At the same time, a good deal of growth was possible as economies that had been closed before and during the war were opened to global competition and as new technologies developed during the war were applied to civilian industries.

These favourable trends disappeared in the 1970s and 1980s. The collapse of the Bretton Woods institutions' influence started in a dramatic fashion in 1971, with the US decision to abandon pegged but adjustable exchange rates and to opt instead for a floating rate for the dollar. The gold parity established for the dollar ($35 for one ounce of gold) was given up, and the dollar began to float freely, as did all other major and minor currencies, one by one. The stable monetary regime introduced by the IMF was no more. The IMF was effectively dead, though it soldiered on in very difficult circumstances. The world had entered a new era of exchange rate instability.

Many other global developments began to undermine the influence of the Bretton Woods institutions during this period. The number of international players began to increase, along with their economic influence—for example, the OPEC nations, Japan, West Germany and newly industrializing countries. The institutions' management and voting structures were too slow and too rigid to respond to such shifts in global economic power. The US share in global output fell from 50% to 20%, yet its desire to control Bretton Woods institutions showed no comparable decline. And decisions on global economic policies started shifting to the Group of Seven industrial nations (G-7), often bypassing the framework of the Bretton Woods institutions.

Visions—and realities

Since their dramatic marginalization, the Bretton Woods institutions have had almost no role in the industrial nations or in the global economy. They only police the developing world. That is a sad decline, for they constituted a remarkable initiative on behalf of mankind. They need to be reformed rather than allowed to die.

The International Monetary Fund

The IMF in its present form is a pale shadow of Keynes's original vision. Keynes proposed a fund equal to one-half of world imports—so that it could exercise a major influence on the global monetary system. Even Harry White's more conservative proposal suggested IMF reserves of one-sixth of world imports. Today, the IMF controls liquidity equal to 2% of world imports, too insignificant to exercise much global monetary discipline. Speculative private capital flows of more than $1 trillion cross international borders every 24 hours at the push of a computer key in response to the slightest change in exchange and interest rates—capital movements that play havoc with the monetary stability of most economies.

Keynes envisioned the IMF as a world central bank, issuing its own reserve currency (the "bancors") and creating sufficient international reserves whenever and wherever needed. The IMF was authorized in the 1970s to create special drawing rights (SDRs), but the experiment was stillborn because of persistent US trade deficits and because the United States chose to finance its deficits by creating more dollars rather than accept the more painful adjustment. The SDRs also were made unattractive to hold by raising their interest rate nearer to the market rate during the 1970s. Today, SDRs constitute only 3% of global liquidity. The world economy is dollar-dominated. And for the world monetary system, the actions of the heads of the US Federal Reserve Board and the German Bundesbank are far more important than those of the IMF managing director—a long distance from the original Keynesian vision.

Keynes regarded balance of payments surpluses as a vice and deficits as a virtue—since deficits sustained global effective demand and generated more employment. This led him to advocate a punitive interest rate of 1% a month on outstanding trade surpluses. The situation today is exactly the reverse: deficit nations without a reserve currency of their own, particularly those in the developing world, come under tremendous pressure to undertake real adjustment. There is no similar pressure on the surplus nations to adjust. And deficit industrial nations can borrow endlessly to finance their deficits rather than adjust—especially the United States, which has the unique privilege of being able to borrow its own currency.

In the Keynesian vision, there would be no persistent debt problem because the IMF would use surpluses to finance deficits. No separate International Debt Refinancing Facility would be needed. Nor would the poor nations be obliged to provide a reverse transfer of resources to the rich nations (as they now do) to build their international reserves. These reserves would have been provided by the international currency issued by the IMF. The proposed automatic mechanism for meeting the liquidity requirements of developing countries has been replaced in practice by harsh policy actions to replenish foreign exchange reserves (as in Mexico recently).

The World Bank

Has the World Bank remained closer to its original vision than the IMF? Consider its role vis-a-vis the developing nations. The Bank was supposed to intermediate between the global capital markets and the developing countries. It was to recycle market funds to these countries using its own creditworthiness and help them gradually build up their creditworthiness so that they could gain direct access to private markets. Again, the reality is far from the original vision.

In some respects, the World Bank has done better than originally expected. It helped raise market funds at lower cost, for longer maturity periods, and for some social sectors (education, health, population, nutrition) that private markets would not have touched. It introduced the International Development Agency (IDA) in 1960 to lend to poorer nations. Started as a bank, the World Bank kept evolving into a development agency.

Where the World Bank is beginning to fail is in transferring significant resources to developing nations. In 1990, there was a global surplus of $180 billion—half of it from Japan. Most of it was recycled by the private capital markets, principally to the United States and other richer nations. And what role did the World Bank play? It recycled –$1.7 billion to the developing countries: its receipts of interest and principal from past loans exceeded its fresh disbursements. In fact, the Bank is now recycling repayments of its own debts rather than new resources.

The role of the World Bank in recycling market funds has thus become quite marginal. Private lending to developing countries has increased rapidly—and that is good. But three-fourths of this private market lending is still to about ten of the better-off economies in Latin America and South-East Asia. What about the other 117 developing countries? The Bank's role in these countries has been a modest one, and negative net resource transfers by the Bank to some poor nations have raised real questions about its development mandate. Its net resource transfers, including the funds of the IDA, the Bank's soft loan agency, have recently been –$1 billion to –$2 billion a year.

The Bank was supposed to build up the creditworthiness of individual developing countries so that they could turn with confidence to private capital markets. Except for the Republic of Korea, the Bank has few successes to boast of. Most of its clients had less creditworthiness in the 1980s than they had enjoyed in the 1970s—thanks to a severe global debt problem, which the Bank did not have the honesty to acknowledge as a general problem but kept treating case by case. The disastrous decision of the Bank's president in 1982 to link the IBRD lending rate to the private capital market rate compounded the debt problem. Rather than cushion the developing countries against the high market interest rates, this action gave an institutional blessing to fluctuating interest rates in private markets.

The resource profile of the Bank and the poverty profile of the developing world are out of sync. According to the Bank's own estimates, the number of absolute poor in the developing world has been increasing. Yet the availability of real IDA resources per poor person has been shrinking. This is the fault not of the Bank management but of its donors, which have refused to see the implications of such an imbalance. No wonder India contracted commercial debts of $50 billion in the 1980s—when its IDA allocations were rationed—acquiring a Latin-type debt problem at a per capita income of only $360.

Sources of fresh creativity are missing in the World Bank. After the innovation of the IDA in 1960, the Bank's inspiration has quietly gone to sleep. It is unable to respond innovatively to the changing global requirements. For example, the emergence of OPEC surpluses in the 1970s and of Japanese surpluses in the 1980s required a new intermediate window, something between the IDA and the IBRD—maybe with a 4% interest rate and a 25-year repayment period. That would have enabled the Bank to phase South Asia out of the IDA and into the new window while concentrating the softest IDA resources primarily on the poorest nations of Sub-Saharan Africa. But the Bank management made only one half-hearted attempt, in 1974, to set up a "third window" with OPEC financial surpluses. (It lasted only a year, because the Bank's traditional contributors refused to give an enhanced role to OPEC nations in the management of this new window, even while accepting their financial resources.)

The original Keynesian vision of the World Bank was as an institution for the expansion of global growth and employment—not as an instrument for deflationary policies. One of the most scathing criticisms of the Bank in the developing countries these days is that the Bank gets brow-beaten by the IMF into prescribing demand management and deflationary policies, particularly as conditions for its structural adjustment loans. Rather than engineering a healthy competition with the IMF, the World Bank has chosen a path of intellectual subservience.

The GATT

The third pillar of the Bretton Woods system—the GATT—has been even further removed from the original Keynesian vision than the IMF and the World Bank. Keynes envisioned an international trade organization that would maintain free trade and help stabilize world commodity prices. That is why he linked the value of his world currency (the "bancors") with the average price of 30 primary commodities, including gold and oil. In practice, the GATT excluded primary commodities, and only belatedly did the Uruguay Round of negotiations make an effort to include agriculture and tropical products in the global trade package. In the meantime, commodity prices have hit their lowest levels since the Great Depression, and Africa alone lost $50 billion in reduced earnings in the 1980s as a result of declining commodity prices.

The operations of the GATT system reflect the same disparity in global power as those of the two other Bretton Woods institutions do. The South and the former socialist bloc are opening their markets. The North, according to a recent OECD study, has been restricting its markets and adopting greater trade protection. But the GATT does not enjoy the political clout to bring some parity to nations' current trade liberalization efforts or to impose penalties for the growing trade protectionism in the OECD nations. It would be far-fetched to suggest that the GATT is in a position even to demand compensatory payments from the rich nations if they chose to impose greater trade or migration barriers.

Nor has the GATT prevented beggar-thy-neighbour policies or trade wars between powerful nations. Witness the current spectacle of the United States and Japan poised on the brink of a costly trade war, with no protesting voice emerging from the impotent citadel of the GATT, whose distinguishing feature is its overall irrelevance. The GATT's purview embraces only a small fraction of the world production entering trade markets—and excludes primary commodities, gold, oil, textiles, services, capital flows, labour flows and intellectual property resources. It is hoped that the World Trade Organization can reverse the growing marginalization of the international trade regime.

Fatal flaws

The real question is, was the original vision flawed? Or has the international community opted for inferior solutions?

Two aspects of the 50-year evolution of the Bretton Woods institutions are of particular concern. First, the IMF and the World Bank are no longer institutions of global governance. They are primarily institutions to police the developing world. In fact, no real institutions of global economic, monetary and financial management exist today (the World Trade Organization may be an exception). For the IMF, isn't it charitable to call a money manager with influence only on the monetary policy of developing countries, which account for about 10% of global liquidity, an international monetary fund? And isn't it optimistic to describe an institution recycling negative net financial transfers from the developing countries as a world bank?

Neither the IMF nor the World Bank has much impact on the economic or monetary policies of the industrial world. As global interdependence has increased, the institutions of global governance have weakened. We are back to ad hoc improvisations by rich nations, made either unilaterally or through loose coordination by the G-7.

A basic question today is, do we need the Bretton Woods institutions to influence only the policies of the developing countries, which account for a fifth of global output and a tenth of global liquidity? Or do we need them to be genuine institutions of global governance? Some criticism of these institutions by the enlightened lobbies of the Third World arises from a perception that the industrial countries are largely independent of the discipline of the Bretton Woods institutions. What's more, the industrial countries not only set their own rules, they also set the framework in which the Bretton Woods institutions and developing countries operate.

Second, the founders of the Bretton Woods institutions were seeking to promote expansionary economic policies, after a prolonged period of global deflation. Full employment was at the top of the international agenda in the 1940s. In recent decades, world leaders, particularly in the industrial nations, shifted their preoccupation to inflation. But the pendulum is beginning to swing once again, and jobs are returning to the top of the policy agenda.

Unfortunately, the developing countries must live with the consequences of the industrial world's changing policy agenda. Most of them, despite their real need for growth in jobs and output, have been subjected to deflationary policy conditions by the Bretton Woods institutions. Demand management often won out over supply expansion, in part because adjustment through supply expansion often takes more time and far more resources than the Bretton Woods institutions could afford.

This is not to suggest that demand management is unnecessary. It may sometimes even be a precondition for sound supply expansion. After all, budgets must be balanced, and borrowing curtailed. But the Bretton Woods institutions compounded their error of overemphasizing demand management by accepting the wrong priorities in the slashing of budgetary expenditures.

It doesn't take a genius to figure out how to balance budgets without unbalancing the lives of the people. There are many low-priority budgetary items. Military expenditures exceed expenditures on education and health in many developing countries. Budgetary subsidies to the rich often far exceed subsidies to the poor. Yet education and health expenditures have been cut ahead of military expenditures during periods of adjustment, and food subsidies to the poor have been slashed in preference to the tax and interest rate subsidies to powerful landlords and industrialists. The social and human costs of the adjustment programmes have been unnecessarily high, and the Bretton Woods institutions have been blamed for the consequences.

This image of insensitivity has been rather unfair to both the IMF and the World Bank. People in the Bretton Woods institutions do not chuckle about the harsh human conditions of their loans. It is a game of mirrors on both sides. The developing country governments find it politically convenient to squeeze the poorer and weaker sections of society and to pretend that it is because of external conditions.

But the Bretton Woods institutions must accept their part of the responsibility. They should pressure governments to cut their military spending rather than their social spending—something they have started doing only in the past few years. They should analyse the subsidies in a national budget and stand firm on slashing subsidies to the rich, elitist groups in a society before subsidies to the poor are touched. They should at least encourage transparent information and open policy dialogues by suggesting policy options for balancing budgets in their economic reports and analysing the impact of these options on various income groups. And they should spend as much time discussing such politically sensitive issues as land reform and credit for all as they now spend discussing distorted prices.

These are not easy issues. They require skilful engineering and political alliances for change within the system. But unless the Bretton Woods institutions are willing to take some political heat on these issues, the cause of the poor—always poorly defended in their own systems—will fall by the wayside. And as long as the Bretton Woods institutions are already taking so much abuse for human costs that they do not wish to cause, they might as well get more directly involved in the discussion of these politically sensitive areas.

Many policies of the Bretton Woods institutions require urgent re-examination and reform—from their weighted voting structures to their conditionality for structural adjustment loans. But whatever else is done, they must first be rescued from the swamp of global irrelevance into which they have been sinking for the past 50 years.

One central question today is whether to leave the fate of the global economic system to the ad hoc coordination of the G-7 or to the free workings of the international markets—or whether to have a minimum of global economic management through professional analysis and con-sultative processes in international financial institutions. That such a question needs to be asked again is rather frightening. Keynes and White thought that they had settled this issue in 1944 by persuading the international community to reject unilateralism in favour of multilater-alism. The experience of the 1920s and 1930s was never again to be repeated.

The 50th anniversary of the Bretton Woods institutions is the time to shape these pale relics of a forgotten past into institutions of genuine global governance for the 21st century. The IMF needs to become an international central bank, and the World Bank an international invest-ment trust. If they are not up to the challenge, we may need to invent new institutions of global financial and economic management.

A blueprint for reform

It is far better to build on the existing structure than to search for an entirely new one, because evolutionary change is our best hope. In this spirit, what reforms could reposition these institutions for the chal-lenges of the 21st century?

Let us start with the IMF. A global institution to ensure sound eco-nomic management and global monetary stability should be able to per-form five functions:

- Help stabilize global economic activity.
- Act as a lender of last resort to financial institutions.
- Calm the financial markets when they become jittery or dis-orderly.
- Regulate banks and financial institutions with an international reach.
- Create and regulate new international liquidity.

These five functions are the proper role of a world central bank. Even if the last function is de-emphasized as overly ambitious at this stage, the other four functions lie at the very heart of sound macro-economic management. And the IMF must carry them out if it is to reclaim its legitimate role in the global monetary system.

Whether there will be a move towards a world central bank in the 21st century is likely to excite much debate in the next decade. In a way, such a move is inevitable. Meanwhile, some cautious steps—eminently logical—can initiate a reform of the IMF in the right direction.

First, a new issue of SDRs must be seriously considered—in the range of 30 billion to 50 billion SDRs. Global inflationary pressures are low. Primary commodity prices have hit rock bottom. Most industrial countries are reducing their budget deficits. And an extra dose of global liquidity could help fuel world economic recovery. There could also be innovation in the distribution of SDRs—with some industrial countries passing on some of their allocations to developing countries through overdraft facilities.

Second, the Compensatory and Contingency Financial Facility of the IMF needs to be changed in several ways. There should be no quota restriction, so that countries can obtain full compensation for shortfalls in exports. The loan period needs to be extended, so that countries do not have to repay before the contingency is over. Even more important, policy conditions must go. If a country is reeling from external shocks outside its control, why add the shock of IMF conditions?

Third, in collaboration with the Bank of International Settlements, the IMF should acquire some regulatory control over international banking activities. The IMF should also administer the proposed Tobin tax of 0.5% on international currency transactions to curb excessive speculation, if this sensible proposal catches the imagination of the international community. This tax would give the IMF some control over international capital flows sweeping through global markets with hurricane force. It would also yield enormous revenue—about $1.5 trillion a year—to help finance World Bank and UN development operations.

Fourth, the IMF needs to acquire a greater role in global macro-economic management—reviewing the policies of all countries, whether or not they are active borrowers, and, in particular, having some influence over the macroeconomic policies of the major industrial powers. One possible mechanism for increasing the IMF's influence over the industrial countries' macroeconomic policies would be to have the Bank for International Settlements link the level of reserves that banks are required to hold against loans to these countries to the IMF's evaluation. That would affect the industrial countries' ability to raise funds from private banks and give the IMF important leverage over their policies.

These four steps would be only a beginning in IMF reform. They are not a blueprint for converting the IMF into a world central bank.

For the World Bank, several areas of reform are appropriate at this stage.

First, the Bank is the finest institution advising developing countries on economic growth policies. Where it needs to develop sensitivity and expertise is in linking economic growth to human lives, in analysing the distribution and sustainability of growth and in examining more participatory patterns of development. The issue is not growth for itself. The issue is the character and distribution of the growth. To benefit the masses, the opportunities that growth generates must be more equitably distributed. And they must be sustainable from one generation to the next. The World Bank talks about these issues. But its critics allege that its embrace of the need for sustainable, people-centred development is less than enthusiastic. It regards that need more as an irritation than as a central theme. All could gain if the Bank were to turn its professional rigour to the emerging concerns for sustainable human development.

Second, the Bank must find new ways of recycling much larger resources to the developing countries. Legislatures in the rich nations will not keep voting for larger IDA resources. In the 21st century, more innovative ways of raising global financing will have to be found to address the issues of global poverty. Such proposals as the Tobin tax, an international tax on non-renewable energy resources or on arms trade, or the sale of emissions permits—still regarded with healthy scepticism—may move to the centre of the international debate, especially when it is recognized that the new compulsions of global human security require some form of global financing. The Bank has been fairly conservative in its approach to new financing sources, and since the launching of the IDA in 1960, it has considered no significant innovation. Many of its well-wishers would like to see the Bank lead in exploring new avenues for raising international finance.

Third, the Bank must start considering prudent ways to restructure its debts. The Bank has advised all other creditors to restructure their debts to developing countries. But it claims an inability to reschedule its debts because of the limitations of its charter, and it sounds concerns about its triple-A credit rating in the capital markets. The obvious result: the Bank will end up owning more and more of the debt of its member countries, its net transfers will decline significantly, and in time, it will be recycling its own debts rather than new resources. Having already reached that position for several developing countries, the Bank must begin to convince its contributors and the capital markets that it has to act as a development agency, not as a global money lender, and that prudent rescheduling of debts must be a part of its operations.

Fourth, the Bank must become an international investment trust—selling bonds to nations with a surplus and lending the proceeds to developing countries. Developing countries could borrow from the trust on terms appropriate to their level of development. The newly industrializing countries would pay commercial rates, while low-income countries would pay less—a subsidy that richer members of the international community should be persuaded to cover. If some of the proposals for international fees or taxes prove to be acceptable to the international community, a pool of resources would become available for such subsidized recycling of market funds.

Fifth, the Bank must recognize that the days of ever-expanding lending for big physical infrastructure projects—roads, ports, power stations—are largely over. The private sector is beginning to take over these investments. The major sectors still needing investments by domestic governments or multilateral organizations are the social sectors. For the World Bank, as for other donors, human development programmes must constitute the new allocation priority.

One final observation. The founders of the Bretton Woods institutions and the United Nations were neither inhibited nor timid 50 years ago. When bombs were still raining on London, John Maynard Keynes was preparing the blueprint for the Bretton Woods institutions. When Europe was still at war, Jean Monnet was dreaming about a European Economic Community. When the dust of war still had not begun to settle, the Marshall Plan for the reconstruction of Europe was taking shape. When hostility among nations was still simmering, the hopeful design of a United Nations was being approved by the leaders of the world, led by President Truman.

Little of this intellectual ferment is evident these days despite unprecedented changes—from the fall of the Berlin Wall to the end of apartheid in South Africa. The unthinkable is already becoming the commonplace. And yet in shaping global economic governance, the sources of creativity are curiously passive. It is time to begin designing global institutions for the 21st century.

Chapter 15

A New 20:20 Global Compact for Basic Social Services

> *"Have some wine," the March Hare said in an encouraging tone.*
> *Alice looked all round the table, but there was nothing on it but*
> *tea. "I don't see any wine," she remarked.*
> *"There isn't any," said the March Hare.*
> *"Then it wasn't very civil of you to offer it," said Alice angrily.*
>
> — Alice in Wonderland

*H*uman Development Report 1991 reached a startling conclusion: "the lack of political commitment, not of financial resources, is often the real cause of human neglect." The report demonstrated the considerable potential for restructuring priorities in national budgets and in aid allocations. It estimated that as much as $50 billion a year could be released to provide basic social services for all—by cutting military expenditures, by privatizing inefficient public enterprises and by correcting wrong development priorities. It also estimated, on the basis of partial data, that bilateral and multilateral donors were earmarking only a small fraction of their aid budgets for human priority concerns.

The report introduced some innovative ratios for estimating the impact of budgets on human development. These ratios, called human priority expenditure ratios, measured the existing expenditure in the budgets on human priority concerns—such as basic education, primary health care, water supply, family planning services and nutrition programmes. The basic idea was to find out what was actually being spent to overcome the worst forms of human deprivation and to compare these allocations across countries and donors.

The data on national and aid budgets, though inadequate, allowed certain rough estimates. On average, 13% of developing country budgets and 7% of bilateral aid budgets were earmarked for human priority concerns. The report suggested 20% as a desirable target.

The 20:20 proposal

The essential feature of the 20:20 proposal, as presented in *Human Development Report 1994* and further refined in interagency consultations in the UN system, is that the developing countries should earmark at least 20% of their national budgets—and donor nations 20% of their aid budgets—for human development priority concerns. Human development priority areas are defined to include primary health care, basic education, rural and peri-urban water supply, essential family planning services and nutrition programmes for the most deprived groups in society.

If implemented, the 20:20 proposal would likely make available $30 billion to $40 billion annually in additional resources for human priority expenditures. Such an additional investment would be sufficient to implement the following global compact for human development over the next ten years (1995–2005):

• Everyone will gain access to basic education.

• Everyone will gain access to primary health care facilities and to safe drinking water.

• All children will be immunized, and most childhood diseases eliminated.

• Maternal mortality rates will be halved.

• All willing couples will have access to family planning services, and the groundwork will be laid for stabilizing the world's population by 2015.

• Severe malnutrition will be eliminated, and moderate malnutrition halved.

• The worst forms of human deprivation will be eliminated through the provision of certain basic social services.

Although the proposal does not deal with many aspects of global poverty—particularly with employment and income generation—it does contain certain attractive features. For example, it would:

• Help slow population growth by focusing on universal female education, primary health care and other elements of an essential human development programme needed to create the underlying conditions for declining fertility.

• Improve the prospects for global human security downstream by eliminating upstream the global spread of many dangerous diseases. For example, AIDS cost $240 billion during the 1980s: preventive health care would have cost only a fraction of that.

• Improve the global environment by addressing some of the worst aspects of the pollution of poverty—polluted water, unknown diseases, galloping population growth.

- Improve human capital and its competitiveness, and thereby widen the access of poor people to market opportunities, at home and abroad.

The proposal is a concrete response to many global targets that the international community has endorsed in recent world conferences and summits—Alma Ata, Bucharest, Jomtien, Children's Summit, Earth Summit, to name a few. What the 20:20 proposal does is to take some of these agreed targets and put them in a concrete time frame, with proper costing of the global targets and a realistic plan for their financing. Some critics may lament that their favourite programme has not made it into the suggested composition of the 20:20 compact. And some reshaping of the proposal will certainly be necessary (discussed below). But what is needed now is a practical judgement on whether it is better to negotiate full funding for a few definable goals or to argue for a large, less easily manageable agenda that has been attempted many times before without much success.

For the donors, the 20:20 proposal offers a realistic chance to move from rhetoric to action on some of their global pledges. The donors can demonstrate to sceptical publics and reluctant legislatures that much can be achieved by refocusing aid funds in the next decade. The prospect for universal coverage of basic education, primary health care, safe drinking water and essential family planning services is exciting—though only a first step towards eliminating global poverty.

It has always been difficult to show tangible benefits from aid programmes: the 20:20 proposal offers that tangible demonstration over a manageable period. Better allocations of existing aid funds can become the best argument for an increase in their level. The skill lies in convincing the donor community that better allocations of existing resources are no substitute for urgently needed additional funds. Nor should the proposal ever be presented as putting a cap on total assistance or as being concerned only with the reallocation of assistance. If the 20:20 proposal is used as a substitute for attaining the 0.7% aid target—rather than as the best argument for better targeted assistance and for additional assistance—it will die.

The 20:20 proposal is based on the principle of shared responsibility between poor and rich nations. Of the additional investment in human priority goals, about one-fourth would be generated by the donors and three-fourths by the developing countries. From an unnecessary North-South confrontation, the world can move towards shared global compacts—not only in human priority expenditure but in many other areas.

Challenges to the proposal

The above analysis recapitulates the underlying rationale of the 20:20 proposal. More important, however, is to deal with some of the key challenges to this proposal and to develop a strategy for constructively and effectively addressing various criticisms and suggestions. Some of the important issues, in no particular order:

- The definition of human priority expenditure is too narrow. It focuses on only a few basic services. Global poverty requires an attack on a much broader front.

- The 20:20 proposal identifies only "top-down" global targets. Needed are national targets defined through a participatory process.

- Social sectors need more effective spending, not more money. In particular, foreign-exchange-intensive spending by donors may distort domestic priorities, which require much recurrent financing and national expertise.

- A mere reallocation exercise may liberate the donors from pressures that must be maintained for reaching the aid target of 0.7% of GNP.

- The human priority expenditure averages for both donors and developing countries may be misleading, because they are based on inadequate and partial data.

- What about countries already above the average—or far below? Is 20:20 a straitjacket—or only a sense of direction?

- What attraction is there in this proposal for countries that have already provided most of the basic services to their people—as in Latin America?

All these issues require careful consideration. Without violating the essence of the 20:20 proposal, much can be done to improve its appeal to many diverse constituencies.

Reshaping the 20:20 proposal

The great attraction of the 20:20 proposal—and its great weakness—is its simplicity. But simplicity is a virtue only so long as it does not become simplistic. Any attempt to reshape the proposal needs to preserve its essential features and yet present it as only one step in a comprehensive attack on global poverty. Several key modifications may be desirable in the further evolution and presentation of the 20:20 proposal—to obtain a broader political consensus.

Broadened definition

To the human development priority areas, two aspects should be added. First is national capacity building in the five subsectors of basic health, basic education, water supply and sanitation, nutrition programmes and family planning services. Second is credit for the poor, to open opportunities for self-employment and sustainable livelihoods. The resource implications of these additions are small and can be accommodated within the 20:20 proposal since the overall numbers still remain to be worked out more precisely.

Extending credit to the poor (through Grameen Bank–type programmes) does not require subsidization, and thus adding this item to the proposal will not require increased budgetary resources. In fact, the Grameen Bank supplies credit at an interest rate five percentage points higher than the market rate, mostly to poor rural women, and its recovery rate is above 95%. A failure to include credit for sustainable livelihood would mean that empowerment and employment aspects would be left out of the proposal, and developing countries might allege that it is taking them back to the basic needs concept they have so often criticized. For this reason, *Human Development Report 1994* added credit for the poor to its elaboration of the 20:20 proposal.

Total package

The 20:20 proposal is only one element in the package for overcoming the worst aspects of human deprivation, not the total package. This proposal is only one step in what ought to be a much more comprehensive strategy for poverty reduction—and, beyond that, for sustainable human development. Restructuring the remaining 80:80 towards the three key objectives of poverty reduction, productive employment and social integration is as important as the focus on the 20:20.

Some elements of that broader strategy can be summarized to keep the proposal in the proper perspective. And a more comprehensive package of action programmes, with the 20:20 proposal as one part, should be agreed on by the global community. Some suggestions:

- A 3% annual reduction in military spending by all nations and an agreement to allocate a substantial portion of the peace dividend to the objective of poverty reduction.
- An agreement to phase out over three years all foreign military bases, military assistance, sophisticated arms shipments (particularly to potential trouble spots) and subsidies to arms exporters.
- An agreement to supplement the 20:20 compact in the future by an "empowerment package" that would focus on sustainable livelihoods, accelerated growth and empowerment of people—covering many other aspects of global poverty besides the worst human deprivation.

- An agreement to start considering more innovative sources of funding to finance the expanding development needs of the future—including the Tobin tax, the environmental permits and the proposals for taxing such global "bads" as arms trade and global emissions.

- A clear declaration by the donors that the 20:20 compact is not a substitute for attaining the 0.7% aid target but the best argument for more efficient and better targeted assistance and the best case for additional funds.

- An agreement to broaden the concept of development cooperation to include international flows of trade, technology, investment and labour and to develop a new reporting and monitoring system for this purpose.

- An understanding to strengthen the development role of the United Nations, including by establishing an Economic Security Council.

Obviously, it will not be possible to agree on all these proposals. But recognizing that the 20:20 compact is only a first step in the international struggle against global poverty will certainly help.

Additional aid

The main point is that the 20:20 proposal is one element in a total package, not the total package itself. To ensure that reallocation of aid funds is not seen as a substitute for additional aid, or even used to reduce aid to other sectors, the following safeguards should be built into the presentation of the 20:20 proposal. The additional funds for the provision of basic services (about $6 billion a year) should come not at the expense of aid to other sectors, but by squeezing military assistance and subsidies to military exporters. In parallel, the developing countries would be expected to reduce their military expenditures, the losses of their inefficient public enterprises and their lower-priority budgetary expenditures—to find more resources for human priority spending.

The pressure for the 0.7% aid target should not be relaxed. An agreement on a firm timetable for reaching this target is still elusive, but the target's inclusion in the 20:20 package is absolutely vital to keep things in perspective. At the same time, developing countries must recognize that better use of existing aid resources is no crime: in fact, it can be a prelude to additional resources. If the 20:20 compact is endorsed, and the 0.7% ODA target reiterated, that by itself would reassure developing countries that the battle for additional resources is not being given up. Instead, it can be fought on many new and innovative fronts.

Refining the estimates

A careful exercise should be carried out to refine the basic estimates and convert an idea into a negotiating proposal:

• Rework the total additional resource requirements and the additional requirements for each basic service. The estimates in *Human Development Report 1994* are:

Basic education	$5–6 billion
Primary health and nutrition	$5–7 billion
Family planning	$10–12 billion
Water supply and sanitation	$10–15 billion
Total for priority human agenda	$30–40 billion

These estimates require much further work.

• Rework the human development priority ratios for aid donors. The OECD Creditor Reporting System is inadequate because it includes only bilateral project assistance and excludes any sectoral breakdown of multilateral assistance, non-project assistance or technical cooperation. So ratios based on its data are only a partial reflection of the human priority spending by donors. Such ratios naturally irritate donors that give much more of their assistance through multilateral and non-project channels. They should be getting more credit for this type of assistance because much more of it ends up supporting poverty reduction programmes and enhancing human development.

• Rework the human development priority ratios for developing countries to include not just spending by central government but that at all other levels (provincial governments, local bodies, NGOs, the private sector), which sometimes gets left out in data reporting systems.

These exercises will also bring out clearly where developing countries and donors stand relative to the 20:20 standard and what strategy to recommend if they are either above or far below it. The 20:20 proposal should be used to create pressure for a change in the right direction: an average ratio should never be presented as a precise goal for each nation. A new aid reporting system and a new country budgeting system are also needed to ensure greater transparency and better monitoring. It will be necessary to work closely with the DAC on the first and with the World Bank and the IMF on the second, since they now report only central government budget expenditure.

Followup institutional arrangements

To ensure ownership and commitment, each country must prepare its own targets for basic social services for all in the light of its situation and stage of development. These targets will necessarily vary, and the proposed average ratio of 20% should not be regarded as a straitjacket. Nor should the concept of basic priority services be interpreted in the same way in all countries. In any such proposal, to respond to the differing requirements of different countries, considerable flexibility of interpretation must be maintained if a broad consensus is to be obtained on its implementation.

One of the key areas to be negotiated is the institutional followup for the 20:20 proposal. In fact, UNDP is the only multisectoral agency in a position to negotiate, manage and monitor such a 20:20 compact, though the detailed implementation could rest with the concerned agencies in the UN system and with bilateral and multilateral donors.

Conclusion

There is much controversy over the 20:20 proposal. The developing countries fear that the proposal might be seen as establishing a cap on official development assistance or as imposing new conditionality on the spending of existing funds. So, it is important to overcome this fear in formulating and implementing the proposal. The task of overcoming the worst aspects of human deprivation in the next decade is far too important to be sacrificed on the altar of unnecessary controversy. And if total consensus on this proposal proves elusive, one final option is still available: why not adopt a 20:20 compact for Sub-Saharan Africa, since this region needs it most and has endorsed the basic proposal? Although the 20:20 proposal was endorsed by the world leaders participating in the Social Summit, it has not been accepted as a binding international commitment. It has been made voluntary, between consenting nations. We need to generate public pressure to ensure that developing countries and the donor community implement the spirit of the 20:20 proposal. If they are not willing to earmark even one-fifth of their budgets to overcome the worst human deprivations, what credibility can we give to their rhetoric for poverty reduction?

Chapter 16

An Economic Security Council

> *Said the mouse to the cur,*
> *"Such a trial dear Sir,*
> *With no jury or judge,*
> *Would be wasting our breath."*
>
> *"I'll be judge, I'll be jury,"*
> *Said cunning old Fury;*
> *"I'll try the whole cause,*
> *And condemn you to death."*
>
> — Alice in Wonderland

The global agenda is changing fast. Instead of a preoccupation with East-West cold war and nuclear security, there is finally a rising concern with many issues of human security.

While economic and social issues are rising to the top of the global agenda, there paradoxically are no global institutions of economic governance to handle these issues effectively and regularly. Chapter 14 showed how institutions of global economic governance have weakened exactly when global interdependence has increased. A serious vacuum in global economic management is being filled through ad hoc improvisations.

In this situation, the establishment of an Economic Security Council within the United Nations has become imperative. And, after 50 years of experimentation with the UN and Bretton Woods systems, this may be the most revolutionary and indispensable innovation for the 21st century. It is necessary that the council be created not through stealth but through a thorough understanding of the role of global economic governance, an area in strong need of leadership. It is also essential that the council enjoy a clear and comprehensive mandate for decision-making in agreed areas of social and economic governance.

Present forums

Some argue that a new forum such as the Economic Security Council would be impossible to establish because it would require a change in the UN Charter and political will of heroic proportions. As a substitute for the council, they recommend strengthening the present forums or gradually enlarging their roles. Such advice, though well meant, misses the point—because bureaucratic skill can never replace political will. If political will is lacking, it is lacking just as much for giving a more meaningful role to the present forums. Often, a courageous step helps focus the collective human mind, while minor adjustments in arrangements go unnoticed and have little impact. That was the thinking behind the global economic governance structure erected in the 1940s.

The idea of enlarging the role of the present forums is quite pervasive, however, and cannot be dismissed lightly. It must be dealt with effectively before turning to a new Economic Security Council.

Several forums perform the role of global economic governance, in one form or another, often with overlapping mandates.

Group of Seven
The most powerful forum for global economic management is the Group of Seven industrial countries, consisting of some of the largest economies in the world—the United States, Japan, Germany, France, the United Kingdom, Canada and Italy. Their annual summits, with quiet bureaucratic coordination throughout the year, normally set the tone for global financial and monetary policy.

The forum has two major problems. The first is its limited country coverage. All the developing countries and the former socialist bloc are left out. Even some among the ten largest economies in the world (in dollars adjusted for purchasing power parity) are not members of the G-7: China, India, Brazil and Russia. The G-7 membership represents only 12% of the world's population. While the G-7 has tried to co-opt Russia and the European Union by inviting their representatives to its annual summits, this is more a cosmetic gesture than one of any real significance. Nor can it make up for the absence of the developing world. Any further co-option, such as inviting a few powerful developing nations, will hardly be meaningful—unless the G-7 allows equality of rights in decision-making, approaching the format of the Economic Security Council.

A second problem with the G-7 is its policy focus. The issues that the G-7 normally considers fall within a narrow range of macroeconomic management, particularly in the monetary and financial fields. It neither considers nor makes any far-reaching decisions on some of the most urgent problems confronting the global community: population growth, environmental degradation, drug trafficking, refugee flows, food security, child survival, women's empowerment, human development. Instead, the G-7 has deliberately interpreted its mandate more narrowly—confining it to monetary and financial issues, where it can exercise greater clout. But even that is challenged by the emergence of many new centres of financial wealth in the developing world.

The G-7 can continue to play a useful role in coordinating the policy frameworks of some of the most powerful industrial nations. But its mandate to step beyond this role to address larger issues of global governance will be increasingly challenged in the 21st century. The broader issues of human security require a wider international consensus and the willing consent of many nations.

Development and interim committees

The guiding committees of the World Bank and the IMF represent some of the world's most powerful policy-makers—normally the finance ministers or central bank governors of around 24 countries, representing various constituencies. The committees meet at least once (and often twice) a year to review the global economic situation and to make some major decisions on the policy directions and operations of the the World Bank and the IMF.

While these committees are a fairly important part of global economic governance, they suffer from even more flaws than the G-7. They do not enjoy the power and the clout of the G-7, and their agendas are more narrowly focused on issues of concern to the World Bank and the IMF. Developing countries may be represented in these forums—and assisted by the professional work of their own G-24—but their voices and influence are fairly limited. So, despite a significant role in specialized areas, the committees are not in a position to address the larger issues of human security. Nor would they ever be trusted with such a mandate.

The Economic and Social Council

The Economic and Social Council (ECOSOC) was set up within the United Nations to deliberate many of the socio-economic issues now at the top of the global agenda. Two questions are often asked: Has ECOSOC ever played such a role? And could it be revived to play a more effective role in the future? Unfortunately, the answer to both questions is a resounding no.

Many things went wrong with the workings of ECOSOC right from the start. Industrial countries never trusted its one-country, one-vote governance structure. They preferred to take important economic issues to their own forums (the G-7 in recent years) or to the multilateral institutions they dominated (the World Bank and the IMF). With 54 members, ECOSOC became an unwieldy forum for any serious decision-making. It lacked a professional secretariat to distil attractive policy options and present them to the international community. And it quickly degenerated into talk sessions—with much noise and no action. Its annual sessions, lasting over a month, became pointless exercises dominated by lengthy monologues. After some time, even the ministers from developing countries, let alone those from the more powerful industrial nations, lost interest in attending ECOSOC sessions.

An influential segment in the United Nations has argued for reviving ECOSOC by giving it more effective powers. Some well-meaning observers suggest that a gradual evolution of the proposed Economic Security Council could best be secured by first setting up a small executive committee of ECOSOC (or by expanding its present bureau) for ministerial-level consultations and decisions. Although such proposals are attractive on paper, there is little chance that they will succeed, for there are always many hurdles in tinkering with existing forums. Developing countries are unlikely to accept a more limited ECOSOC. Moreover, old traditions die hard. Each time an innovation is tried, many bureaucrats will undermine it in the name of established practice. Trying to convert useless talkathons into streamlined decision-making is like trying to turn a tortoise into a swan.

But there is a more important reason for opting for a new Economic Security Council rather than a refurbished ECOSOC. Strengthening institutions of global economic governance requires tremendous political leadership and courage. Why waste the political capital on retooling an old jalopy when a new car can be designed to fit new needs? Those who believe that ECOSOC can be made effective but that it would be impossible to set up a new council are guilty of self-serving errors in reasoning. It normally is far more difficult to get policy-makers to focus on restructuring old forums than it is to convince them that new realities require new institutional responses—as evidenced by experiments over the past 50 years with the present institutions of global governance. The proposal for an Economic Security Council offers the opportunity to design a new framework that can serve the interests of all nations and all important constituencies.

Summits and UN conferences
Another ad hoc improvisation for global governance, fairly popular over the past two decades, is holding periodic international conferences or

summits, often under the UN umbrella. Such events have been organized on many diverse topics: population, women, children, education,
health, the environment. These events have greatly increased global
awareness of these issues, and some of the summits and conferences
have been extraordinarily successful, such as the Children's Summit,
the Earth Summit and the Population Conference. But few have had a
lasting impact, led to more financial support or resulted in effective
implementation mechanisms. Increasingly, the tendency is to rush to a
summit—as a substitute for a carefully considered solution to global
problems or even as homage to the egos of the international entrepreneurs who organize such summits. The summits are seldom a substitute for a durable, global decision-making mechanism for nations to
meet and debate their problems, reach consensus and create sensible
systems for implementation, often through an uneasy process of compromise.

Why an Economic Security Council?

The foregoing discussion exposes the limits of today's forums of global
economic governance. But why a new Economic Security Council? And
why would such a forum be acceptable to industrial or developing
nations?

The need for an Economic Security Council rests squarely on the
new imperatives of global human security (chapter 9). Global issues
such as poverty, narcotics control, population growth, ecological security, international migration and the travel of deadly diseases (AIDS)
cannot be resolved by a single nation acting alone. They require collective action by many nations. And they are the issues that will shape the
global agenda in the years ahead. Macroeconomic coordination, particularly monetary and financial, will continue to be needed. But it will be
less effective in a world that is politically and socially unstable—where
the security of individuals in one nation is threatened by what happens
to the security of individuals in another.

This development was anticipated at the birth of the United Nations
50 years ago. No less an authority than the US Secretary of State, in a
report in 1945 to the US President on the establishment of the United
Nations, stated his firm conviction that:

*The battle of peace has to be fought on two fronts. The first is the
security front where victory spells freedom from fear. The second is
the economic and social front where victory means freedom from
want. Only victory on both fronts can assure the world of an endur-*

ing peace. . . . No provisions that can be written into the Charter will enable the Security Council to make the world secure from war if men and women have no security in their homes and their jobs.

It is refreshing to review this perspective in the light of the actual developments over the past five decades. The onset of the cold war, immediately after the birth of the United Nations, got the United Nations constantly embroiled in conflicts between nations. Almost all of these conflicts were on the soil of the Third World, where the two superpowers fought the cold war by proxy. Nuclear weapons had made conflict on the soil of the industrial nations too risky.

The United Nations developed and perfected many of its peace-keeping techniques during this period. Whenever conflict broke out between nations, the first order of business was to arrange a cease-fire, separate the combatants, even organize zones of peace, and initiate a dispute settlement mechanism. Security Council powers were often invoked (under chapter VII) to impose embargoes against the aggressor nation, particularly on arms shipments and on some forms of trade (such as the embargo on oil shipments from Iraq). Conventions and treaties covered all phases of war between nations: prohibiting biological warfare, censuring bombardment of civilians, ensuring humane treatment of prisoners of war under the Geneva Convention.

Most of the real action in the past 50 years was in the Security Council, even though the council was paralysed at times by the rivalries among the superpowers. The rest of the UN system merely limped along, with inadequate resources and weak performance in socio-economic fields. The first pillar of security—national security—consumed most of the attention in UN corridors. The second pillar—socio-economic security—was largely ignored. Two factors contributed to this neglect: the UN missions were often staffed by foreign offices, and the United Nations was a mechanism for governments, not people. Most of the economic action moved to the Bretton Woods institutions—which enjoyed greater confidence from the donors. Even technical assistance, which was supposed to be the exclusive preserve of the UN agencies, was largely (75%) taken over by the World Bank and the bilateral donors.

The end of the cold war caught the United Nations off guard—unable and unwilling to adjust to the new realities. It has not yet recognized that most conflicts are now within nations, not between them—as many as 79 of 82 in the past three years. It has not yet adjusted to the fact that 90% of the casualties in these conflicts are civilians, not soldiers.

Nor has it accepted that these people-centred conflicts require a new concept of people-centred security. But the Secretary-General of the United Nations, Boutros Boutros-Ghali, made an eloquent reference to the issue of human security in a speech (22 August 1994) to the Preparatory Committee of the World Summit for Social Development:

The Summit is a time to respond to the new imperatives of human security all over the globe. . . . Human security can no longer be considered as an exclusively national concern. It is a global imperative. . . . The United Nations can no longer fight the battles of tomorrow with the weapons of yesterday.

The recent interventions by the United Nations in trouble spots around the world—Somalia, Rwanda, Bosnia—betray this lack of adjustment to the new realities. Soldiers in blue berets are being sent to countries that cry out for socio-economic reforms. External intervention is being organized, hastily and thoughtlessly, in situations that can be handled only through domestic action, however long it may take and whatever the cost. After all, who are the combatants in Somalia or Rwanda? Whom are the embargoes meant to punish? Whom are the UN soldiers dispatched to separate? When people fight within a nation, it is a radically different situation than when nations fight. Yet the United Nations is applying to these new situations the same methods of peacekeeping that it applied to conflicts between nations. Neither its concepts nor its operations have changed. As a result, the United Nations ended up spending more than $4 billion on its peacekeeping operations in 1993, more than it had spent on such operations in the preceding 48 years. And what results does it have to show for these operations?

It is time for the United Nations to adjust to the new imperatives of global human security. That requires at least the following five steps:

• An early warning system to forecast "potential Somalias".

• A reinterpretation of chapter VII to define circumstances and modalities through which the United Nations can intervene in internal crises.

• A permanent peace corps to give assistance to countries in tackling their socio-economic problems upstream.

• A significant enlargement of the development role of the UN system.

• An apex body, such as the proposed Economic Security Council, to consider the nature of global human security crises and make prompt decisions to resolve them.

The threats to global human security not only come from internal conflicts within nations—whether civil wars, ethnic conflicts, explosions of poverty and unemployment. They also emerge from what can best be described as "shared global crises". All nations have an increasing stake in the resolution of these crises. The case for a new Economic Security Council rests on the premise that all nations—North and South—have a major interest in attending to these crises.

Narcotics trade. The drug trade is estimated at around $500 billion a year, with $85 billion in drug profits laundered through financial markets each year. No viable solution is possible unless all nations collaborate in controlling the demand for and supply of narcotic drugs and jointly police the laundering of the huge financial gains from drug trade. Any effective plan must include alternative production and employment opportunities in the supplying countries, relevant information and education in the consuming countries and stricter monitoring of financial markets.

HIV/AIDS. HIV/AIDS already has cost the international community more than $240 billion in research, curative measures and lost productivity in the past decade. Any viable plan to control the international spread of this deadly disease will require upstream investment in preventive health care and downstream investment in containment, cure and research. An upstream investment of $10 billion to $20 billion in preventive health care and sex education probably could have avoided most of this financial cost—and much of the tremendous loss of human lives.

Global pollution. Pollution—another global threat that carries no national labels and stops at no national frontiers—can be checked only through collective international action. This is not only true of global warming, ozone depletion, biodiversity loss, the pollution of oceans and the depletion of soil, water and forest resources. It is also true of the pollution of poverty—the accumulation of national despair that disrupts all global channels. Besides treaties and charters, what is urgently needed is to enforce the principle that polluting nations must pay at the international level just as polluters are being obliged to pay within nations. That may require tradable permits for environmental emissions, a tax on the consumption of fossil fuels or other means of pricing the environment. But no step towards enforcing the "polluter pays" principle can be taken unless nations meet, discuss and reach a consensus in an established forum.

International terrorism. Modern communications enable terrorists to ply their grisly trade across international borders. Between 1975 and 1992, there were an average of 500 international terrorist attacks a year.

The peak was in 1987, with 672 attacks. No nation, no building, no individual is safe from the threat of such international terrorism. And containing this emerging threat to human security requires the willing cooperation of all nations.

International migration pressures. International migration has increased significantly. At least 35 million people from the South have taken up residence in the North in the past three decades, with around one million more joining them every year. The number of illegal international migrants is estimated at 15 million to 30 million. And there are around 19 million refugees worldwide and nearly 20 million internally displaced persons within the developing countries. No national walls can contain these migration flows unless all nations cooperate and unless attention is paid to the fundamental underlying causes of deepening poverty and unchecked population growth.

These are selected instances of emerging global threats that kill no less certainly than do the occasional wars—and perhaps far more regularly and on a much larger scale. They pose a persistent threat to human security, in both rich nations and poor. They demand a new concept of global human security—and require the establishment of an Economic Security Council.

Mandate of an Economic Security Council
In at least four areas, an Economic Security Council could fill critical gaps in the system of global economic governance.

First, the Economic Security Council could provide leadership in tackling the shared global economic crises. This role of the council will be of particular interest to rich nations, because they are a shrinking minority in a fast-expanding global population and can no longer protect their people exclusively through their own efforts. They need the cooperation of the majority of the world's people. The developing countries' incentive to cooperate will be increased global attention to their poverty problem—attention that an Economic Security Council could bring, since many of these global crises cannot be resolved without attacking the root causes of deepening poverty in the developing world.

Often, these issues are dealt with by different UN specialized agencies in isolation, without an adequate mandate or enough resources or necessary followup. The council would be a logical replacement of today's ad hoc and ineffective arrangements. It could provide continuous attention to these issues, professional analysis of issues taken together, strategic policy options to the global community, adequate financial resources and followup actions and monitoring systems.

Second, an Economic Security Council could help establish an early warning system and the modalities for global assistance in internal conflicts. The present Security Council, wholly inappropriate for this task, should confine its role to peacekeeping operations for conflicts between nations. For conflicts within nations, an entirely different system should be evolved through the Economic Security Council.

Preventive diplomacy requires an advance warning system about what is to be prevented and when. There is an urgent need for the United Nations to consult the best expertise in the world and to evolve a comprehensive early warning system. *Human Development Report 1994* mentions five quantitative indicators for an early warning system for human security: income and job security, food security, human rights violations, ethnic and other conflicts and the ratio of military to social spending. This is a useful start, but a lot more professional work is required. The Economic Security Council secretariat will need to monitor the situation in potential trouble spots around the globe and alert the council members about where and when international action is warranted. The United Nations now reaches Somalias and Rwandas when it is already too late and when its intervention often compromises its own credibility.

New guidelines must be prepared on where the United Nations should intervene, with what objectives, and for how long. UN intervention can be helpful mainly in preventive development, before situations deteriorate. What the United Nations needs to send countries is real development rather than soldiers, and it needs to do this far enough upstream to prevent the eruption of an internal explosion. The international community must recognize that it cannot police internal conflicts—it can hope only to prevent them.

Some developing countries worry that human security might be interpreted as providing a new excuse for UN intervention in domestic crises. This anxiety stems from a misunderstanding, for it is the present system that is needlessly interventionist—with a handful of powerful nations in the Security Council deciding where to intervene and how, and with soldiers sent to police socio-economic conflicts between people or between ethnic groups. It would be far less interventionist to send development, rather than soldiers, to poor lands. And it would be best to design some agreed rules of the game—in place of the present ad hoc system—and to make decisions in an Economic Security Council that could represent developing countries far more adequately than the present Security Council.

Third, the proposed Economic Security Council would be responsible for strengthening the UN development system. Several structural reforms are in order, each requiring tremendous political courage and continuous dialogue.

- The existing dispersed, underfinanced and uncoordinated UN development funds and agencies should be integrated into a single UN Development Authority. Such an authority would command sufficient resources, disbursing grants of more than $5 billion a year (more than the IDA) and having a major impact on the development of poor nations.

- An adequate resource base must be developed for multilateral initiatives, preferably through international taxes or fees. Many proposals are on the global agenda—a Tobin tax on speculative movements of international foreign exchange, a tax on fossil fuels, tradable permits for global emissions, a tax on arms shipments—each requiring continuous dialogue at the highest political level.

- The UN development programmes should be brought together under a single human development umbrella—with a common development message and consolidated country missions and development strategies. Today's proliferation of field offices, development reports and turf battles must come to some merciful end, in the interest of both recipients and donors.

- The UN development system must be based more on professionalism and less on political influence, both in the selection of staff and in the analysis of country development issues.

These are far-reaching reforms. They cannot be made through periodic reviews of the UN system, at which the UN bureaucracy excels. International bureaucrats, however brilliant, often deliver only cosmetic changes. Nor can these reforms come through a restructured ECOSOC. To arrive at a consensus on such fundamental reforms, we need a political forum—such as the proposed Economic Security Council—to discuss all policy options continuously and to lay new groundwork, step by step, for the emergence of an effective UN development system.

Fourth, the Economic Security Council will also have to establish its mandate in policy leadership on macroeconomic management, which will be more difficult and more vigorously resisted. Many of the present forums—such as the G-7 and the Bretton Woods institutions—will be unwilling to concede this role to the council. A pragmatic solution is to build sound credentials over time, by concentrating on the first three mandates described above and by gradually winning the confidence of both industrial and developing nations. One point should be made clear. The case for an Economic Security Council is sometimes argued exclusively in terms of its macroeconomic role: in aid and trade, debt issues, monetary stability, global economic growth. That is a mistake. There is a distinct role for the council, one that does not require it to challenge the role of existing forums. Once the Economic Security Council is established and proves its effectiveness in managing many issues of global human security, it would be only a matter of time before the compulsions for a more democratic global economic governance attract many issues of macroeconomic management to such a forum.

Composition of the Economic Security Council

When the present Security Council came into existence in 1945, the world looked much different. There were only 51 members of the United Nations, not the 184 of today. A few superpowers watched benignly over the birth of the United Nations, while many in the rest of the world remained silent bystanders.

The world has since changed. Japan and Germany emerged with two of the most powerful economies. Developing countries have won their freedom. Some Arab states have acquired enormous financial wealth through oil. The Russian empire has broken up. The dominant economic influence of the United States has waned, with its output falling from 50% of global output in 1945 to around 20% today.

The composition of a new Economic Security Council can reflect this new balance of economic and political power. The new balance of power could be reflected through a restructuring of the existing Security Council as well, but that is not likely to happen. The permanent members are not going to surrender their seats or their veto powers. Nor are most nations—particularly the developing countries—likely to agree to the induction of more permanent members with the same veto power. It is best to start afresh and to reflect in the new council a more balanced representation of the world's nations and to abandon the concept of veto power for single nations.

Several considerations to guide the composition of the proposed council:

- It should provide a balanced representation of the world of today.
- It should be kept small and manageable.
- It should include as permanent members countries that either are the most populous or have the largest real economies so that their economic influence is recognized and respected.
- The permanent members should enjoy no individual veto power.

To reassure both rich and poor nations that their interests will be protected, it should be agreed that each decision will require a simple majority of the representatives of both industrial and developing nations.

• All important geographical regions or political constituencies (such as the European Union or the island economies) should be able to elect a representative, on a rotating basis, to reflect their interests.

Several general formulas can be suggested for meeting these criteria. It is unnecessary to be more specific at this stage. One basis for choosing permanent members could be to include those countries with the largest economies (in PPP dollars): the United States, Japan, China, Germany, France, the Russian Federation, India, Italy, the United Kingdom and Brazil. A second could be to include the most populous nations: China, India, the United States, Indonesia, Brazil, the Russian Federation, Pakistan, Japan, Bangladesh and Nigeria. A third formula could be to include the largest powers in each region: China in East Asia, India in South Asia, Ethiopia in East Africa, Nigeria in West Africa, Egypt in the Arab States, Brazil in Latin American and the Caribbean, Germany in Western Europe, Poland in Eastern Europe, the Russian Federation in the Commonwealth of Independent States (CIS) nations and the United States in North America. These permanent members would be joined by other, rotating members representing various geographical regions and political constituencies. During negotiations on the council's composition, there will be much hard bargaining and many uneasy compromises. It is neither necessary to anticipate these negotiations nor wise to pre-empt them.

Operations of the council
The proposed Economic Security Council can function well only if it is backed by a competent professional secretariat. The council members must be continuously presented with relevant policy options. Such a secretariat must function under a top development leader, perhaps a Deputy Secretary-General, second in power and influence only to the Secretary-General.

The council must meet regularly—more frequently than the political Security Council. The rotating members could send their top-level economic ministers to New York for the duration of their membership, while the permanent members would have to find a second ambassador with impressive economic credentials. Important meetings of the council could be held at the finance or development minister level or even at the summit level.

The council must be supported by a clear source of funding. Because advice without resources rarely goes far, work on global revenue sources or international taxation should be undertaken by the Economic Security Council at a fairly early stage so that its decisions or recommendations can be backed by financial clout.

The council would be an apex body supervising the policy direction of all multilateral institutions, including the Bretton Woods system and UN development agencies. And it would decide whether ECOSOC should stay in its present form or be restructured. There may be some virtue in establishing ECOSOC as a universal body, abolishing the present Second Committee (for economic matters) and the Third Committee (for social matters) of the General Assembly and using discussions in ECOSOC as a sounding board for the decisions referred to the Economic Security Council.

Some argue that it may not be possible to change the UN Charter and establish a new Economic Security Council on these lines. But it would be a fallacy to seek marginal remedies through a restructured ECOSOC or through changes in the role and composition of the existing Security Council. If political will is weak, none of these marginal devices will work. And if political will is strong, why not pick up one of the greatest challenges in redesigning global economic governance?

Chapter 17

A New Global Vision

"In that direction," the Cat said, waving its right paw round, "lives a Hatter: and in that direction," waving the other paw, "lives a March Hare. Visit either if you like: they're both mad."

"But I don't want to go among mad people," Alice remarked.

"Oh, you can't help that," said the Cat: "we're all mad here. I'm mad. You're mad."

"How do you know I'm mad?" said Alice.

"You must be," said the Cat, "or you wouldn't have come here."

— Alice in Wonderland

*I*t is only appropriate to conclude this book with the global vision so often repeated by Barbara Ward. In 1966, in her book *Spaceship Earth,* Barbara wrote: "Our physical unity has gone far ahead of our moral unity."[1] That is one of those seminal statements characteristic of Barbara, who could summarize the dilemmas of an entire age in one simple, pithy sentence. It also is a theme that dominated her world of ideas and that was at the heart of her constant search for social equity, for human justice, for reduced gaps between the rich and the poor, for a planetary bargain for our planetary survival.

Barbara Ward worried about the visible disparity between the growing physical unity of our planet and the increasing bankruptcy of our development concepts and processes. She commented freely and courageously on "the gaps in power, the gaps in wealth, the gaps in ideology which hold the nations apart [and which] also make up the abyss into which mankind can fall to annihilation."[2] As early as 1962, she wrote in her book *The Rich Nations and the Poor Nations:* "The gap between the rich and the poor has become inevitably the most tragic and urgent problem of our day." She returned to this theme again and again. But to her, the answers were not technological, they were moral. In an age conditioned by moral cynicism, she had the courage to remind us of our moral commitments. About 30 years ago, she wrote with a growing sense of anguish but also with great moral courage:

It has required great vision, great holiness, great wisdom to keep
alive and vivid the sense of the unity of man. It is precisely the
saints, the poets, the philosophers, and the great men of science
who have borne witness to the underlying unity which daily life
has denied. But now the distances are abolished. It is at least pos-
sible that our new technological resources, properly deployed, will
conquer ancient shortage. Can we not at such a time realize the
moral unity of our human experience and make it the basis of a
patriotism for the world itself? [3]

We live today in a period of unprecedented technological progress.
When we were celebrating in 1927 the remarkable feat of Charles
Lindbergh's flying across the Atlantic in 33 hours, little did we realize
that in a few decades we would be traveling the same distance in one-
tenth that time in a Concorde. Whoever thought that the remote corners
of the world would be linked by telephone and fax, that $1 trillion would
move through global financial markets every 24 hours, that human productivity would expand world output sevenfold in the past five decades?
Our technological advance has been breathless, yet almost taken for
granted.

Our moral concepts and our institutional responsibility, by contrast,
have lagged sadly behind.

• We live in a world where there is enough food for everyone, yet
we waste it rather than feed the 800 million people who go hungry every
night.

• We live in a world where so many children are denied their very
childhood, yet societies often choose to spend much more on arms than
on the education and health of their children.

• We live in a world where poor nations can easily find the financial
resources for air-conditioned jeeps for their military generals, yet fail to
find the resources for even windowless schoolrooms for their children.

• We live in a world where, when children cry for milk in the
middle of the night, their military generals are out shopping for tanks.

• We live in a world where just one poor nation last year spent a
sum on new jetfighters and warships that could instead have financed
the entire cost of basic education for all its children, *and* primary health
care and safe drinking water for all its people, *and* family planning services for all its willing couples. Just one year's purchases of military
hardware! And then that country complained bitterly that its foreign aid
allocation was too low to finance its social programmes!

There is a missing moral core in our technological advance. In rich nations and poor, the moral foundations of economic growth are often lacking. And we are too embarrassed even to mention morality any more. The technocrats tell us to be more technocratic. The professionals remind us to be more scientific in our analysis. We are told that technology and morality often do not mix. We are reminded to focus on the economy, not on the society.

Too often, our concepts have become self-serving and elitist. We speak with great awe about the globalization of prosperity. We conveniently forget the much more disturbing globalization of poverty. We miss having Barbara in our midst to keep reminding us that "our physical unity has gone far ahead of our moral unity."

What is wrong with such a picture? After all, in the past societies lived with great disparities in their midst and with much greater burdens of crushing poverty—and perhaps they always will. Why this moral outrage?

I raised this question with Barbara Ward one afternoon in the autumn of 1976. I had journeyed to Sussex to visit her in her modest but gracious home, overlooking the downs of the English countryside. It was a sublime day, with the half-warm sun bathing the surrounding hills, and we were sitting on a settee by the window. I asked Barbara whether a capitalist or a socialist ideology held the key to this human dilemma.

Barbara was looking pale. Cancer was consuming her body, though her spirits were still high and her will was strong. She thought for a long time and then said: "The basic premise of socialism is that man is motivated by non-materialistic idealism. How romantic but how untrue! The basic premise of capitalism is that man is motivated by selfish greed. How sordid but how true!" Then she paused for some time before adding: "No, my friend, don't look for a solution in these ideologies. The ultimate solution will lie in a new humanism—people realizing that they can only survive together or not survive at all. Without morality, there will be much violence. Without morality, societies will perish."

She turned to this theme again when I asked her to write a foreword for my book *The Poverty Curtain*.[4] She was gracious enough to respond immediately, though I felt guilty about taxing her frail energies. She graphically hinted at this coming violence in her foreword:

As the 1970s advance, there is an undefinable but deepening sense of a profound change in human affairs. Those who have profited from earlier arrangements are fearful and their fear can go on to violence and aggression. Those who suffered before are hopeful but their hope, if too long deferred, can also turn to violence. So this is a time of growing unsteadiness in the world's understanding of itself. . . . But whether it is fear or hope that stirs the depths, profound movements are at work in planetary politics, movements as vast—and perhaps as irreversible—as, say, a geological adjustment of continental plates.

Barbara went on to give a brilliant analysis that placed the demand for equality of opportunities between the rich and the poor in its long-term, historical perspective. She presented both a more hopeful scenario and a more pessimistic one—what she called the "second route"—and then she concluded:

We are therefore still set for the second route of indifference to planetary need, of belief in automatic processes, of reliance upon mechanisms which do not and cannot, of themselves, secure the public good. And at the end of that route lies deepening anarchy, a widening breakdown of order and—and who knows how soon?—the terrorist with the plutonium bomb.

We have entered a new age of violence in this past decade—with rising street crime, with a weakening social fabric, with moral decay in the midst of enormous economic growth, with several nations facing the threat of social disintegration, with more conflicts within nations than between nations—and I often go back in my mind to that lingering afternoon in the autumn of 1976 and realize again how prophetic and perceptive Barbara always was.

Barbara desperately wanted to be proved wrong in her pessimism. She clung to her hope for humanity till the very end. In her last book, *Progress for a Small Planet,* in 1979, she reaffirmed that hope and the deep faith in human rationality that she always held:[5]

The first micro-organism must have seemed minute enough in the wash of the primitive oceans. Yet it had within it, the seed of life. Let us at least be bold enough to hope and, where we can, begin to act.

Were she alive today, I think Barbara Ward would be optimistic. The democratic forces of change would present her with the ultimate triumph of the human spirit—about which she sang so lyrically throughout her life.

Towards the end of her life, Barbara turned to the emerging compulsions of the physical environment as her ultimate hope for human sanity. In her last book, she posed a question:

> *If we were to depend solely upon the record of our political history, we could well doubt whether any widening of understanding and solidarity to a planetary level was even conceivable. . . . Why should we hope for anything different today?*

And then she answered her question and found some hope in "the irreversible geophysical unity of our shared and single planet." "We cannot change it," she said. "It envelops us, provides for us, sustains us. Our only choice is to preserve it in cooperative ventures or to end it and ourselves in a common ruin."

Today, we can reassure ourselves that much more than a shared physical environment is beginning to bring us together in common bonds of human security. The imperatives of human survival are changing fast. And there is a great opportunity to construct a new edifice of human civilization in the 21st century—based on equality of opportunity and on the centrality of human beings.

Human security is an idea whose time has come. As Barbara Ward kept reminding us: "Ideas are the prime movers of history. Revolutions usually begin with ideas."

I thus conclude this book on a note of hope. We are at an exciting juncture in our human journey. People now stand at the centre of development. They are taking command of their own destiny in one country after another. Many nations are beginning to recognize that their real security lies in investing in their people rather than in arms. The traditional North-South divide is giving way to a more mature partnership.

In this milieu, we can sing of the dawning of a new human age, guided by a new vision of human progress—the central theme of this book. At least, such a human vision should be our guiding star—and our sincere endeavour. For human destiny is a choice, not a chance.

Notes

1. New York: Columbia University Press, 1966.
2. Barbara Ward, *The Rich Nations and the Poor Nations,* New York: W.W. Norton, 1962.
3. Ibid.
4. New York: Columbia University Press, 1976.
5. London: Earthscan, 1979.

Part 3

An Epilogue:
Reflections Through the
Looking-Glass

An Epilogue: Reflections Through the Looking-Glass

> "I can't believe that!" said Alice.
>
> "Can't you?" the Queen said in a pitying tone. "Try again: draw a long breath, and shut your eyes."
>
> Alice laughed. "There's no use trying", she said: "one can't believe impossible things."
>
> "I daresay you haven't had much practice," said the Queen. "When I was your age, I always did it for half-an-hour a day. Why, sometimes I've believed as many as six impossible things before breakfast."
>
> — Through the Looking-Glass

The draft of the first edition of this book was completed in mid-1994 and published in 1995. Four years have elapsed since then. The concept and measurement of human development have evolved a great deal in the meanwhile and what started as a mere idea ten years ago seems to have become by now an irresistible intellectual force. This epilogue traces the story of this fascinating evolution.

Human Development Reports (1995–98)

Perhaps the place to start is the continuing analysis of human development policy issues in UNDP's annual *Human Development Reports*. The first edition of this book ended with the coverage of the new theme of human security in the 1994 *Human Development Report* (See pages 39–43). Four new *Human Development Reports* have emerged since then, each focusing on a specific policy issue pertaining to human development, considerably adding to our understanding of the key areas that deserve attention of international and national policy-makers.

The 1995 *Human Development Report* focused on exploring the gender dimension in human development. It reached the not too startling conclusion that "human development, if not engendered, is endangered". The real contribution of the report was in documenting that women's capabilities were expanding quite fast—particularly in terms of spectacular improvements in education and health—but their opportunites still remained limited, leading to a great deal of wasted human potential and rising frustration. Two new measures were developed. The Gender-related Development Index (GDI) captured gender inequality in human capabilities, particularly in education, health and basic purchasing power. The Gender Empowerment Measure (GEM) reflected inequalities in certain key areas of political and economic participation and decision making, particularly the stark gender disparities in representation in the workforce, in parliaments, among administrators and managers, among professional and technical workers, and in the share of total earned income.

The contrast between women's capabilites and opportunities emerged as one of the most powerful stories of the report. For example, female rates of adult literacy and combined school enrolment in the developing world had increased twice as fast as male rates between 1970 and 1990. Yet women still occupied only 10% of parliamentary seats, only 6% of cabinet positions, less than a seventh of top administrative and managerial positions, and often less than one-quarter of the share in total earned income. Increased capabilites were getting frustrated in the market place and in male-dominated political systems and social structures. It was time to open the door to more opportunities for women, through changed laws and bolder policies, so that the entire human potential of society could be used productively, not only a part of it.

Another startling breakthrough in the 1995 report was the preliminary documentation of the economic contribution of women to national income accounts which was either not being registered at all or registered very inadequately. This consisted of women's household work and social activities which, if not performed, would have to be paid for. The results derived from time-use data from a sample of 31 countries were quite dramatic. It appeared that women worked longer hours than men in nearly every country. On the whole, they contributed more than half of the global economic output but received less than one-fourth of the total monetary reward. This was simply because roughly two-thirds of men's time was spent in paid activities in the market, while two-thirds of women's time was spent in the household in activities which were vital but not formally paid for. As such, as much as $ 11 trillion of women's work was simply not counted in national or global income accounts. And since the monetary value of this work was not counted, it appeared as if women did not count at all in cultures where increasingly materialistic values were prevailing now. The report rightly recommended that new "satellite" national income accounts should be prepared, fully reflecting the economic contribution of women, so that all societies begin to realize that women are the "principal breadwinners in a society" and there is fundamental revision in present property rights, divorce settlements, collateral for bank credit and in many other market economic transactions where women's role is presently marginalized.

The 1995 report on gender inequalities had a very profound impact on the deliberations of the Beijing World Conference on Women in Septemeber 1995 and led to many concrete initiatives, including preparation of new national accounts by several countries to document women's economic contribution.

The 1996 *Human Development Report* took up the theme of a link between economic growth and human development. It reached the conclusion that, in the long run, economic growth and human development definitely move together—but there is no automatic link between the two. There can be a major break between economic growth and human development in the short run, leading to many unfortunate situations where production can increase while human lives are more deprived. The experience of Brazil and Pakistan illustrated such a disturbing delink. On the other hand, several countries, such as Costa Rica, Sri Lanka and Botswana had achieved fairly high levels of human development even at comparatively low levels of per capita income. The skill lay in translating the benefits of growth into the lives of the people through deliberate policy actions.

The report rightly concluded that the structure and quality of growth demand even more attention than its quantity. Unless determined policy efforts are made, economic growth can become "jobless" (expansion of output without expansion of jobs), or "ruthless" (where the fruits of growth mostly benefit the rich), or "voiceless" (where growth in the economy has not been accompanied by an expansion of democracy or empowerment), or "rootless" (which causes people's cultural identity to wither), or even "futureless" (where the present generation squanders resources, particularly natural environmental capital, needed by future generations). Thus economic growth is a wild horse: it needs to be trained to serve the real interests of society. If the horse misbehaves in some societies, leading to deprivation of many human lives rather than their enrichment, then the fault is not that of the horse but of the skill of the rider. Economic growth is essential in poor societies—but even more important is its structure and its distribution.

One of the more disturbing conclusions of the report was that economic growth had failed in about 100 countries for much of the last 15 years, reducing the income of 1.6 billion people (more than a quarter of the world's population). In 70 of these countries, average incomes in 1996 were lower than in 1980—and in 43 countries, even lower than in 1970. In other words, while global output expanded at a spectacular pace in the last two decades, it had failed to benefit all. More than a quarter of humanity had sunk even deeper into poverty and despair, illustrating quite dramatically the uneven distribution of global and national economic growth.

How to continuously link economic growth and human development, how to keep restoring the broken links, was, therefore, the central theme of the report. It reminded policy-makers that such a link is neither automatic nor can be taken for granted, that economic growth does not often trickle down to the poor unless the playing fields of life are made more even through deliberate policy action, especially by building up the human capabilities of the entire population and opening doors to more equal sharing of opportunities in the market place.

The 1997 *Human Development Report* turned its policy attention to the much discussed and familiar issue of poverty, but it came out with some interesting new insights. For one thing, it evolved a new concept of human poverty which was much broader than the old, traditional concept of income poverty. It argued that poverty is a multi-dimensional concept. It is more than a lack of income. It, in fact, embraces a denial of many opportunities of life. The most basic human choices are to lead a long and healthy life, to be educated, and to achieve a certain level of material well-being. Other choices include access to job opportunies, political and social freedom, community participation and a clean physical environment. The denial of these basic human choices diminishes the opportunities that are available for betterment of human lives. It is this very denial that makes and keeps people poor.

What is critical for our understanding, therefore, is poverty of opportunity, not poverty of income. Poverty of income is often the result of existing power structures, poverty of opportunity is often their cause. This is why the World Bank's much used measure of absolute poverty (proportion of people subsisting on less than $ 1 a day of income in real Purchasing Power Parity dollars) is so misleading. It draws our attention to the symptoms, not to the real causes, of poverty. A much broader, multi-dimensional, measure of poverty is needed.

In its search for such a measure of poverty, however, the report was less successful. It chose some of the right indicators to reflect human deprivation—for example, population not expected to survive to age 40 as showing "survival deprivation" and adult illiteracy rate as reflecting deprivation in education and knowledge. Where it missed out inexplicably was in capturing income deprivaiton as still an important component of human deprivation. It can be convincingly argued that income should not be the only dimension in which poverty should be measured. But it will be absurd to argue that it is not important at all—which is what the new Human Poverty Index (HPI) seems to imply. Instead, this index uses three indicators to reflect deprivation in "economic provisioning": population without access to safe water, population without access to health services, and underweight children under age 5. All these three indicators link up more with survival deprivation than with economic deprivation. The omission of income from the HPI is also curious for two other reasons. First, a modified concept of income is already included in the estimates of the Human Development Index (HDI): HPI is, after all, only a reverse image of HDI. Second, when income is excluded in such an arbitrary fashion, HPI virtually becomes a social indicator, needing to be used in tandem with income poverty estimates in order to obtain an overall understanding of human deprivation. One of the virtues of various human development indices developed so far (HDI, GDI, GEM), as noted earlier in this book, has been that they have combined social and economic dimensions, not separated them. It is encouraging that the 1998 *Human Development Report* has corrected this flaw in the calculation of HPI of industrial countries by including the proportion of people whose disposable personal income is less than 50% of the median income, leaving them unable to achieve the standard of living necessary to avoid economic hardships and to participate in the life of the communtiy. At least, income deprivation has come back into the HPI for industrial countries though this deficiency has still to be remedied in the case of estimates given for developing countries in the latest 1998 report.

Besides broadening the concept of poverty, the main contribution of the 1997 report lies in arguing convincingly that poverty reduction strategies are manageable and that they have been attempted successfully by several countries. China, Tunisia, the Republic of Korea, Malaysia, Indonesia, Singapore, Morocco and several states in India—about 14 countries and states with a total population of over 1.6 billion—have managed to halve the proportion of their people living below the national income poverty line in less than 20 years. Ten more countries, with almost another billion people, have reduced the proportion of their people in income poverty by a quarter or more. What is more significant is that poverty of opportunity is getting reduced at a more rapid rate as there have been spectacular advances in the spread of education and health facilities to previously deprived populations.

Poverty is, therefore, not a permanent affliction: it is reversible. But it cannot be treated as a mere flu, it is more like a body cancer. We cannot leave intact the model of development that produces persistent poverty and then wistfully hope that we can take care of poverty downstream through limited income transfers or through discrete poverty reduction programmes. If the poor lack education, if they lack critical assets (particularly land), if they lack financial credits since formal credit institutions do not bank on them, if they are socially excluded and politically marginalized, then a few technocratic programmes downstream are not the real answer. The answer lies in a fundamental change in the very model of development so that human capabilities are built up and human opportunities enlarged. In other words, the real answer lies in a major transition from traditional economic growth models to genuine models of human development where people become the real agents and beneficiaries of economic growth and no longer remain an abstract residual of inhuman development processes.

The 1998 *Human Development Report* deals with the link of present consumption standards with future human development levels. It reaches two major conclusions. First, while there has been unprecedented increase in total consumption in the 20th century, it has been badly distributed. The poorest 20% of the world's population has been left out of this consumption explosion. The evidence of under-consumption is everywhere: three-fifths of people in the developing world lack elementary sanitation; a third have no access to safe water; a quarter do not have adequate housing; a fifth do not have access to primary health care; and over a billion people are deprived of basic consumption needs. Gross under-consumption coexists with obscene over-consumption, making our planet a highly unstable place.

Second, the existing link between consumption patterns and human development levels can be greatly improved. It is often breaking down because of misleading advertisements, inadequate education and information, uneven income distribution, and underprovision of basic social services by the state so that we often witness the dilemma first highlighted by John Galbraith in the *Affluent Society* (1958) of public squalor amidst private affluence—that is explosion of private consumption goods and scarcity of good public services of education, health, housing, transport and environmental improvement.

It is in defining action programmes that the report is on less sure footing. Subsidies and taxes can certainly help adjust consumption patterns, but generally such fiscal incentives have been perverse so far in many societies, with, for example, generous subsidies for energy consumption leading to its wasteful use. Regulating misleading advertisements and generating more positive education campaigns and information flows may well be a sensible option, but shrill criticism immediately arises about information and thought control and loud appeals are raised against curtailment of human freedom. What is more, the notion of "consumer sovereignty" has become such a fetish by now that many free marketeers are unable to understand or accept that consumers' so-called sovereign rights are being violated everyday in the market by misleading advertisements (where profit greed overcomes consumer need), by inadequate income (resulting in denial of even basic needs for many), and by "external diseconomies" (where consumption of some consumers adversely affects the consumption of other consumers, i.e. through indirect smoking, or generation of pollution, or over-use of various harmful substances). Some desperate reformers have resorted to moral denunciations of present patterns of materialistic consumption and stirring appeals for a return to a more austere society—but this has not halted the relentless explosion of consumption nor reduced widening consumption disparities between the rich and the poor. It is sobering to think that the delink between consumption and human development may have grown larger, not smaller, over time, despite the spread of more information and knowledge (witness the alarming spread of drugs, alcohol, smoking, and many other consumption habits which are injurious to human capabilities—despite plenty of public warnings). How to adjust today's consumption patterns to advance tomorrow's human development levels still remains a question mark.

So, where do we end up in this evolution of ideas in the *Human Development Reports*? Many policy themes have been explored so far, and several more are likely to be analysed in future reports. What this has done is to build up steadily a body of useful knowledge about many policy areas in human development. Furthermore, this analysis has been backed up by a great deal of practical country experience of what has actually worked, or what has failed, and why. This is an invaluable part of our learning process, and it is certainly of great use for busy policy-makers who can benefit from the actual experience of other countries. There is no substitute, however, but to descend from the global level of dialogue to the national and regional levels and to see how human development ideas can actually be put into practice. This is the theme to which we now turn.

National and Regional Perspectives

Ever since the first *Human Development Report* appeared in 1990, national policy makers have begun to respond to the challenge of putting their people at the centre of development by preparing their own national human development reports. The first such reports were prepared in 1992, by Bangladesh, Cameroon, Pakistan and the Philippines, with some technical assistance from UNDP consultants. By now, 108 countries have published national human development reports, some (like Bangladesh) each year, with a total of over 210 such reports. The geographical spread has been wide, covering all regions of the developing world: 33 countries in Sub-Saharan Africa, 17 in Asia and the Pacific, 29 in Eastern Europe and the CIS, 18 in Latin America and the Carribbean, and 11 in the Arab states. This is indeed very impressive coverage at the practical, national level of an idea which was still wandering in search of leadership only a decade ago.

The coverage of human development policy issues in these national reports has, however, been quite uneven—ranging from a discussion of a few selected social policy issues to a more comprehensive blueprint for new patterns of development, from analysis of social sector programmes to coverage of all social and economic policy parameters, from a disaggregated analysis of a few deprived regions to a comprehensive survey of the basic needs of all the people. Most reports are being prepared by national governments (often their planning commissions), with assistance from their own intellectual think-tanks and normally from the UNDP. These reports have generally been used so far by national policy-making authorities to sharpen awareness of key deficiencies in people–centred strategies, to build nation-wide consensus on human development issues, to highlight national concerns about certain important areas of policy, to enlist the support of the civil society, as well as to mobilize external support for important programmes in building human capital. Some of the most interesting and informative work has been done when some countries have disaggregated their national human development indicators by geographical region, or province, or urban and rural areas, or ethnic origin. The disturbing contrasts in the human development levels of various groups of society have often shocked national policy-makers into some remedial actions.

There is great potential in the regular preparation of these national human development reports so long as they became a serious basis of policy action, not yet one more annual ritual or a passing fad. Their real potential still remains unexploited in many countries, as well as by the UNDP which has often initiated these national efforts and provided much needed technical expertise and relevant policy experience from other countries. The real challenge is to convert many of these reports from analytical exercises into active blueprints for national policy action.

At the same time as there has been a virtual explosion of national human development reports, some reports have also appeared to cover an entire region or sub-region. Four such regional efforts have been made so far: in Africa, South Asia, the Pacific Islands, and Europe and the CIS. The most comprehensive and far-reaching intellectual effort has been the emergence of annual reports on *Human Development in South Asia*, which are being produced since 1997 by an independent policy think-tank, the Human Development Centre in Islamabad.[1] These reports have raised some extremely important issues for the future of South Asia and have illustrated how civil societies can be mobilized, as well as national policy-makers made uncomfortable and the international community sensitized, around issues of human development.

South Asia Perspective
The South Asian reports have provided a much needed and missing dimension to the development debate in the region. South Asia contains nearly one-fourth of humanity and has enormous

development potential. But many opportunities for a vital break-through have been missed in the last 50 years, as there has been poor investment in human capital, as investment in arms has often taken precedence over investment in people (particularly in India and Pakistan), as bureaucratic economic controls have triumphed over the forces of economic liberation, and as elitist power structures have pre-empted the patronage of the state in their own favour rather than in favour of their people. Many of these countries illustrate examples of anti-human development models and strategies, as already analysed in Chapter 7 of this book. In addition, there are such curtains of intellectual isolation in the region that they hardly get to know about each other or learn from each other.

In this intecllectual milieu, the emergence of the first report on *Human Development in South Asia* in April 1997 was a "rude awakening" for many national policy-makers and for the interna-tional community. The overall message of the report was unmis-takable and shocking. South Asia had by then emerged as the poorest, the most illiterate, the most malnourished and the most gender-insensitive region in the world.

The report exploded the popular myth that it was Sub-Saharan Africa that was lagging behind all other regions of the world in human development. That was true three decades ago but no longer. This dubious distinction now belonged to South Asia. South Asia's averge per capita income of $ 309 was much below $ 555 for Sub-Saharan Africa and $ 970 for all developing coun-tries. South Asia's literacy rate of 48% lagged behind the 55% already achieved in Sub-Saharan Africa and 77% in the rest of the developing world. Two-thirds of the children in South Asia were underweight compared to about one-half in Sub-Saharan Africa.

In a global context, the scale of human deprivation in South Asia was simply mind-boggling. Nearly one-half of the world's illiterates and 40% of the world's poor lived in South Asia. Out of a total population of 1.2 billion, around 500 million people were in the category of the absolute poor, surviving on less than one US dollar a day. More than one-half of adults were illiterate, and over one-fourth of the total population did not have access to even a simple daily necessity like safe drinking water.

The burden of this human deprivation naturally fell more heavily on children and women. About 85 million children in South Asia had never seen the inside of a school. An estimated 134 million children lost their very childhoods, working long hours in inhuman conditions, many working for an average wage of only 8 US cents a day. Half of the world's malnourished children lived in South Asia. Birth in South Asia carried the prospect of denied opportunities at every step, rather than the promise of new hopes and new dawns.

The situation of women was even more shocking. South Asia had emerged as the only region in the world where men outnumbered women. While there were 106 women to 100 men in the rest of the world, since biologically women outlive men, in South Asia the ratio was exactly the reverse: only 94 women to 100 men. About 74 million women were simply "missing" in South Asia—the unfortunate victims of social and economic neglect from cradle to grave. Adult female literacy was only one-half of male literacy. Female literacy rate was only 36% in South Asia compared to an average of 55% in the developing world. South Asia had the lowest ratio of female administrators and managers—only 3% compared to 20% in Latin America. And such indices of gender disparity persisted in a region where four out of seven countries (namely, Bangladesh, India, Pakistan and Sri Lanka) could boast of female head of government at present or in the recent past. Obviously, there were two different societies, two different cultures, two different worlds among the women of South Asia—a small minority which was highly educated, brilliant and articulate, and a large majority which was repressed and disempowered, and which carried the inhuman burden of centuries.

The many shocking statistics and disturbing graphs given in the 1997 South Asia report were sufficient to shatter the complacency of policy-makers in South Asia and the relatively detached attitude of the international community. They began to realize that if South Asia slowly disintegrated, it would not only be a catastrophe for its teeming millions, it would be a global tragedy as well. The scale of this human tragedy will far exceed anything witnessed in Somalia, Rwanda or Burundi in the past. The recent introduction of a nuclear dimension has only served to highlight this choice between potential catastrophe and yet unlimited development potential of the hard-working people of South Asia.

The report highlighted the potential of South Asia by comparing its development experience with that of the East Asian industrializing tigers over the last four decades. The countries of South and East Asia had started at roughly the same per capita income level in 1960. By now, the per capita income of East Asian economies was about 27 times higher. These East Asian high-performing economies included South Korea, Singapore, Hong Kong, Indonesia, Malaysia and Thailand. In recent years, during the 1980s and 1990s, China had achieved an annual growth rate in its per capita income which was about five times what was being experienced in South Asia.

Why was there such divergence between the development experience of East Asia (including China) and that of the SAARC region? Many explanations had been offered (including vastly contrasting philosophies of economic liberalization), but there was at least one explanation on which all analysts were in complete consensus: the central role of education, skills and technology in the accelerated growth of East Asia. The contrast between South and East Asia was quite sobering. The average adult literacy rate in East Asia was over twice as high (at 98%) as in South Asia. What was even more worrisome for global competition was the low level of technical education in South Asia. Less than 2% of South Asian secondary school children enrolled for technical and scientific education compared to 20% in East Asia. The East Asian high-performing economies were spending over 10 times as much on education per person as did South Asia. Obviously, South Asia was simply not ready, or adequately positioned, to enter the intense global competition of the 21st century.

For this reason, the 1998 report on *Human Development in South Asia* chose to focus on the challenge of education in this region. It outlined concrete strategies as to how South Asia could emerge as the next economic frontier in the 21st century by investing liberally in basic education for all and in relevant technical skills, and by focusing on more pro-poor economic growth paradigms.

The development challenge for South Asia is a formidable one. It raises some intriguing possibilities in the context of global experience, particularly the more recent development experience in Asia itself.

Three great development waves have swept over Asia in the last five decades. The first wave started in Japan in the 1940s and 1950s when Japan combined its cheap labour with education and technical skills and rapidly took over global markets in the export of low and medium technology consumer goods. A recent World Bank study concluded that 85% of the wealth of Japan consists of human and social capital. The very success of Japan and its rising economic prosperity and real wages obliged it later on to move to higher technology production and to capital goods exports.

Then came the second wave as low-income East Asian societies stepped into this growing void in the 1960s and 1970s, following the same simple but brilliant model where low wages become a powerful engine of competition and growth as they are combined with an educated and skilled labour force and open economies.

The third wave emerged in China in the 1980s and 1990s and continues unabated, based on similar human development models as followed by Japan and East Asian Industrializing tigers in the past.

An intriguing question remains; will the fourth great wave of development touch the shores of South Asia? Can South Asia become the next economic frontier in the 21st century? Or will it miss the opportunity once again, as it has done so often in the last 50 years?

The model for accelerated development is both available and inviting. It is based on four pillars: skilled human capital, high savings and investment, open economies, and good governance. The most critical element in such a development model is a liberal investment in basic education and technical skills. This converts the poverty of a country from liability into an asset as low wages are combined with technical skills to conquer global markets. Globalization thus turns into an opportunity, not a threat, since poor economies are able to leapfrog several decades of development by taking advantage of expanding global markets.

This is the lesson to be drawn from the first three waves of Asian development, despite the recent financial problems of East Asia. East Asia is like a well-built, speedy car which has developed a flat tyre, and this tyre is likely to be fixed fairly soon. South Asia is still a bicycle economy, and absence of a puncture is no cause for celebration. The real challenge is to convert a bicycle economy into a car economy.

It appears that South Asia is simply not ready for this challenge. At present, one in two adults is illiterate. One in three children is out of school. Two in five children drop out of primary school before completing their studies. Girls spend only one-third as much time in schools as boys. Only one in fifty secondary school age children enrol in technical and vocational programmes—and then they generally emerge with technologies of the past, not of the future.

The quality of education is poor. South Asia has only two-thirds of the teachers actually needed; one-third of the teachers are untrained; only 31% at primary level are females; about 40% of teachers are absent from schools, collecting only their salary cheques and then doing other jobs, as society pays them even less than domestic servants. It is certainly a very disturbing picture.

As the 1998 report on *Human Development in South Asia* pointed out in shocking detail, South Asia—the proud inheritor of great civilizations, and the unique blend of many religions and cultures—has simply frittered away much of its development potential by failing to invest in human development.

In this context, the contrast between investment in arms and investment in people could not have been more shocking, particularly in India and Pakistan. Both countries have together spent $ 70 billion on defence during 1990–96 compared to only $ 12 billion on education. They have six times more soldiers than doctors. They have been purchasing twice as many arms from the global arms bazaar as Saudi Arabia does, which is about 25 times richer with its oil wealth. While the global community has reduced its total military expenditure by a quarter since 1987, after the end of the cold war, India and Pakistan are the only two principal exceptions where military spending has been going up by about 5% a year. Basic social agendas await as arms accumulate. Modern nuclear weapons are parked in their bunkers while hungry people are parked on their city pavements.

It is in this disturbing overall framework that the report outlined a practical plan of action to place all the children of South Asia in primary schools within the next five years and to create relevant modern technological skills for its emerging generations. The cost is indeed modest, especially if all non-formal channels for imparting basic education are also used. A mere 0.3% of the combined income of these societies can finance the recurring cost of this educational challenge—or around 1% if capital costs are also included. Considering the payoff, it could be one of the most handsome bargains in history. It could be financed by just freezing military expenditures at their current level for the next five years, or by privatizing some high-cost domestic debts through the rapid privatization of public assets, or by setting much more rational priorities in development budgets. Financial resources are not the real issue: it is the political will.

The central message of the 1998 report on *Human Development in South Asia* has acquired even greater significance in the context of unfolding events in India and Pakistan in the recent period (this is being written in June 1998 in the aftermath of nuclear tests by both countries). The sooner the two countries turn from a nuclear arms race to a human development race, the better it is for the future prosperity of their people. In the last analysis, nuclear lavas may make great international theatre but they do not fill empty stomachs. Nor have desperately poor nations ever graduated into great super-powers, except by building the development potential of their people It is socio-economic lavas that drown out nations; nuclear lavas never rescue them. The two South Asian reports have tried to shake up the conscience of policy-makers and civil society in the region by both pointing to the danger of these emerging socio-economic lavas as well as by beckoning South Asia to the much greater challenge of becoming the most promising economic frontier of the 21st century.

It appears that the message is sinking in, even at the global level. For a long time, South Asia had gone off the radar screen of the western nations. It was quietly assumed that focus of development assistance and international political attention should be on Sub-Saharan Africa, which was the "poorest" region and where several countries had begun to disintegrate. The articulate, brilliant spokespersons for South Asia were quite successful in hiding the dire poverty and vast human deprivation of their people, both from themselves and from the world.

This perception is beginning to change—and one modestly hopes that the South Asian reports have made some contribution to the new discovery of South Asia by the international community. Of course, recent nuclear explosions have helped draw international attention, though it should have been there from the beginning if the shocking portrait of human deprivation in South Asia had been prepared and projected much earlier. So far, South Asia has received little financial support or political policy attention from powerful industrial nations. While Sub-Saharan Africa has received around $ 30 per capita per annum of official development assistance, the much poorer South Asian region has received an average of only $ 5. Whereas debt relief schemes are being designed for many other regions, particularly Africa, there have been no serious proposals for debt rescheduling in the more heavily indebted region of South Asia. On the political front, South Asia has not received even a fraction of the political interest or capital that powerful nations have invested in the settlement of political disputes in the Middle East, Bosnia or Northern Ireland.

The situation may be about to change. But, in the last analysis, the challenge of human development must be tackled by South Asian societies themselves. It is not a responsibility of the outside world. This is the central theme that comes through the disturbing analysis in the reports on *Human Development in South Asia*.

Policy Impact

After all this evolution of human development ideas and policy practices, where do we stand today? And in which direction should we go?

It appears that the challenge of putting people at the centre of development has had significant impact in at least four areas. First, there has been widespread intellectual acceptance that the real goal of all development efforts must be to enrich human lives, not just to raise income. All human choices are increasingly talked about—not only basic choices of education and health but also cultural development, community participation, environmental improvement, political freedom and broader human rights. Gone are the days when the prosperity of a society was identified only with the measure and growth of its GNP. Human development indicators are beginning to take center stage, as they reflect the real wealth of a nation.

Sometimes the recognition has been genuine and enthusiastic that economic growth is merely a means: it is human development which is the real end. Sometimes it has been more grudging, as in the case of the World Bank which initially regarded the central messages of the *Human Development Reports* as exaggerated and overblown. But this conservative citadel of economic growth has come a long way in the last few years. The most befitting tribute paid by the World Bank to the emergence of human development paradigms was in a path-breaking study in 1995 which concluded that as much as two-thirds of the total wealth of nations consisted of human and social capital, while natural capital contributed 20% and physical capital only 16%. It was a remarkably candid admission that all major physical investments that the World Bank lending programmes had traditionally financed (e.g. roads, airports, power stations, telecommunications, buildings, machinery, and much other physical infrastructure) had contributed less than one-sixth to the wealth of nations. It was human capital and institutions of good governance which were decisive for an economic breakthrough. The World Bank has recently followed up this insight by sharply accelerating its lending in the human development fields as well as by focusing on more development research and policy analysis in this area.

Second, several global policy initiatives have been influenced by the ideas of the *Human Development Reports*. Sometimes the impact has been swift and spectacular; sometimes, more slow and indirect. For instance, one of the central proposals of these reports (first floated in the 1991 *Human Development Report* and then

elaborated and refined in the 1994 *Human Development Report*)
that more priority should be given by national and aid budgets to
human priority concerns of primary education, basic health care,
adequate nutrition for the severely malnourished, safe drinking
water and essential family planning services by earmarking at
least 20% of budgetary resources for these tasks, was an idea
which became the rallying cry in the World Summit on Social
Development in 1995 and was largely endorsed. The *Washington
Post* wrote at the time to pay a fairly generous tribute: "The most
promising [proposal at the Social Summit] was the '20/20' plan
conceived by Pakistan's Haq, in which donors would direct 20
percent of their foreign aid programs to meet basic human needs
and receiving countries would commit 20% of their budgets to the
same goal." Another idea where implementation followed quickly
on the heels of its launching in the 1992 *Human Development
Report* was the proposal to establish a new international NGO,
Honesty International, to monitor the rapid spread of corruption
and to expose corrupt governments and multinationals. A new
NGO, Transparency International, was set up through private
initiative only a year later in Berlin and it is already having a major
impact by monitoring and exposing corrupt practices at both
global and national levels.

In many cases, however, the policy impact has been more
indirect by changing the overall environment in which policies are
formulated. Here the influence of human development reports and
the policy themes that they have explored has been quite extensive. The persistent and courageous analysis in these reports on
investment in arms versus investment in people, and their constant highlighting of military–social spending ratios in many poor
developing countries, have greatly sensitized thinking at the
national and global levels about possible and beneficial trade-offs.
In fact, many donors (including the World Bank, IMF, Japan,
Germany and several others) are now insisting that they will
monitor these military–social spending ratios very carefully in
allocating their external assistance funds. The seminal idea of
human security, floated in the 1994 *Human Development Report*,
has had far-reaching influence in convincing policy-makers that
most conflicts are now becoming people centred, not soldier
centred or territory centred, that it is increasingly the security of
people which is under threat all over the world—from the spread
of drugs, pollution, HIV/AIDS, poverty, terrorism and human
despair—and it is time that we give some thought to critical issues
of human security, not constantly be obsessed by territorial

security alone. Another instance is the analysis of gender disparities in the 1995 *Human Development Report* which, as already noted, greatly influenced deliberations and policy action programmes in the Beijing World Conference on Women in 1995.

There are many other ideas and proposals that the *Human Development Reports* formulated and projected which have found a firm place on the global agenda even though they are still far from implementation: for example, establishment of a new Economic or Human Security Council to deal with major threats to human security; a new framework of global development cooperation to fit the new realities of the post-cold war world; setting up of a Global Demilitarization Fund to capture the emerging peace dividend for human development objectives; introduction of the "Tobin Tax" on foreign currency hurricanes across nations to reduce their present volatility and unpredictability; a concrete plan of action to halve world poverty over the next decade; concrete proposals for restructuring of UN and Bretton Woods institutions in the 21st century; and many more seminal and professionally well worked out ideas. The main contribution is that these ideas are already becoming a part of the agenda of global dialogue: there is always a long time period between the grudging acceptance of new ideas and their eventual implementation.

Third, human development ideas are now beginning to be pursued at a practical level in national strategies. As noted earlier, over 100 countries have already prepared their own national human development reports. Many more are getting ready to do so. This is just a start to creating a process of national awareness, conscience-raising and consensus-building. The real task lies ahead for many nations, particularly as they realize that human development paradigms do not only mean more accelerated investment in education and health (which certainly may be necessary) but they are a blueprint for radical transformation of the entire society, where playing fields are levelled and equal opportunities created for all the people, whether it takes land reforms, progressive taxation, redistribution of income, or social safety nets for the poor and the marginalized. Many national reports have so far stayed on the softer issues of human development, without getting deeply into much tougher economic and structural decisions that their societies face.

Fourth, the real impact of human development ideas and these reports has emerged at the civil society level. It appears that people were ready—in fact, waiting—to embrace the new paradigm.

There was almost an outpouring of relief that development was being discussed for once not in terms of abstract financial numbers but in more familiar and acceptable human terms. These were concepts and statistics people could touch and grasp, rather than from which they would withdraw in puzzled amusement.

It is this widespread acceptance of human development ideas by civil society which has given them their real vigour and momentum. The annual circulation of *Human Development Report*, has exploded to over 100,000 copies in 14 languages, with a major dissemination of reports on *Human Development in South Asia* and national reports as well. Media reaction has been enthusiastic and sustained, and modern communication break-throughs are ensuring that the central issues of human develop-ment are kept before policy-makers all the time till they are sufficiently shocked and embarrassed into doing something con-crete about them. This is a vital contribution, since most funda-mental societal changes these days are arising out of people's initiatives, not from governments.

Future Horizons

In the world of ideas, evolution never stops. Indeed, stagnant ideas die quickly and are overtaken by other more vital concerns. It is critical, therefore, that the intellectual evolution in the human development area be stimulated further. There are at least three directions in which this needs to be done.

First, it is time that the human development ideas should graduate out of the confines of global regional and national reports and become a new and vibrant school of thought. These reports should continue, of course, as they have already made pioneering contributions to unleashing new ideas and certainly can enrich them further. But a vigorous intellectual movement has to extend far beyond annual report writing. It must spread to all institutions of learning, think-tanks, and intellectual circles. It must be a part of the intellectual discourse all the time. It should be debated, criticized, brutalized, and evolved further in many directions. That is why it is necessary today to establish human development as a distinct discipline in university education, to set up special chairs and schools of human development, to encourage the emergence of more human development centres all over the world for pioneering ever more thinking and research in these areas—both analytically and empirically.[2]

Such an intellectual evolution is all the more necessary since there is great danger that human development may become yet one more fad—more honoured as a fashion than accepted as a blueprint for a fundamental restructuring of society. Even after fairly vigorous debate over the last decade, it is simply amazing how many misconceptions prevail about the basic concept of human development—even on the part of sympathetic advocates. Often, the concept is confused with human resource development; or just investment in education, health or some other social sectors; or simply made synonymous with human capital (an intellectual trap the World Bank normally slides into). Yet this is a narrow and dangerously simplistic interpretation. Of course, human development strategies do enjoin more investment in building human capabilities—and investments in education, health and other social sectors are an essential part of that strategy. But it is only one part of the total picture. Human beings are not merely fodder for the production machine: they are also its owners and its beneficiaries. It would be a supreme irony to regard people as the real end of all development and then to treat them merely as the means. The profound insight in human development para-digms is that all processes (economic, political and social) must now be judged by only one criterion: what do they actually mean for the people? Do people participate in these processes and influence them meaningfully? Do they benefit from them? Are these processes sustainable in terms of their future needs? Are people still the masters of development processes or have they become their unwitting slaves? Is development continuing to enlarge all their choices? Mere processes have dominated people's lives for so long that it is a radical reversal of perspectives. A people-centred development perspective is the heart of human development paradigms—not just investment in human resources, or concern with human welfare. Vital though these concerns are, the human development perspective is a much broader one. Yet considerable intellectual confusion still invades this field. And that is why the human development concept needs to be debated even more vigorously in academic circles, particularly in univer-sities.

Second, the measurement of human development has come a long way since it was first introduced in the form of the HDI in 1990 (see chapter 4). The HDI measure is being extensively used now to judge the progress of nations. Further evolution has taken place in adding a dimension of gender equality (in the form of GDI and GEM: see chapter 4) and in developing a multi-dimensional measure of poverty (HPI). But the evolution remains incomplete and must go much further.

It is true that the attraction of the HDI lies in its being simple and composite so that it can be easily compiled, used and understood. But some vital dimensions are still missing. For one thing, indices of political freedom must be added (see chapter 5). It is obvious that to be healthy and educated in a prison carries a very different significance than to enjoy those attributes in political freedom. Human development indicators of adult literacy or life expectancy in an authoritarian or democratic regime naturally cannot be given the same value. Again, the environmental dimension is important and must be incorporated to show whether human development levels are sustainable. If feasible, we need to develop a distinct component to reflect cultural development, though this is likely to pose difficult problems of measurement. The basic point is not to complicate the exercise, but to continue to evolve it further. Of course, detailed indicators of human development will always be far more extensive than can be squeezed into a single composite index, and the basic concept of human development will always be far richer than any single measure can ever hope to capture. But that should not inhibit further efforts to improve the measurement of human development.

Third, more concrete policy action needs to be organized to advance human development levels all over the world. One institutional dilemma at present is that no one is quite certain at national or global levels where precisely the policy responsibility lies for formulating and implementing human development policies and programmes. Some developing countries have established human resource development ministries, which may be needed in any case to coordinate the implementation of social sector programmes but which should not be confused with the implementation of human development strategies. Ideally, the design and implementation of such strategies must be the chief responsibility of planning commissions and finance ministries since they must replace, broaden and deepen existing economic growth models. Curiously, in many developing countries which are professing to adopt new human development models, planning and finance ministries normally formulate economic growth plans for macro discussion with the World Bank and the IMF while social sector ministries design various "human resource development" programmes for a discussion with UN agencies and Bretton Woods institutions for funding. Such a confusion at the policy and institutional level is naturally not very helpful for advancing concrete policy action within developing countries.

At the global level, the situation is even more confusing. Despite their professions to the contrary, the World Bank and the IMF are still fully committed to the defence of traditional economic growth models, though they are quite willing to add the qualitative dimension and equity considerations downstream. This is generally a half-hearted compromise: their overall faith in the supremacy of growth forces seldom weakens. Within the UN system, the human development concern is still interpreted in narrow sectoral terms by individual UN agencies dealing with education (UNESCO), health (WHO), population (UNFPA), children (UNICEF), and others. There is no over-arching responsibility for human development strategies, though it properly belongs to the United Nations Development Programme (UNDP) and the UNDP has indeed been making a spirited bid to take over both intellectual and operational leadership for such a global role. Unfortunately, because of the absence of a single, integrated Human Development Agency within the UN system, because of the differing mandates of various UN sector agencies (which jealously guard their turf), and because of the relative indifference of Bretton Woods institutions to the macro framework of human development paradigms, a yawning gap still remains at the international level in supporting, guiding and monitoring global human development compacts or national strategies.

Some Personal Reflections

This brings me to the conclusion of this retrospective on the evolution of human development ideas over the last decade. But let me add some personal reflections.

I have found nothing more fascinating than the birth and evolution of new ideas. Reflecting on this about two decades ago, I outlined three stages for the evolution of a new idea (*The Poverty Curtain*, Columbia, .1976) which are worth recapitulating:

> *The first stage is characterized by organized resistance. As new ideas begin to challenge the supremacy of the old, all the wrath and scorn is heaped upon the heads of those who have the audacity to think differently...*
>
> *The second stage can generally be described as widespread and uncritical acceptance of new ideas. At some point, there is a sudden realization that the time for a new idea has arrived and all those who had opposed it thus far hurry over to adopt it as their own. Their advocacy becomes even more passionate than those of the pioneers, and they take great pains to prove that they discovered the idea in the first place....*

It is the third stage which is generally the most rewarding—a critical evaluation of ideas and their practical implementation...

It is my own belief that we are now graduating out of the second stage into the third on ideas of human development. This is likely to be the most challenging stage—and potentially the most rewarding.

Often, pay-off from investment in ideas is grossly underestimated. National planning authorities and international financial institutions do not think twice while investing billions of dollars in machinery, buildings and physical infrastructure: they generally have a nervous fit investing a few million dollars in the generation of new ideas. When the UNDP showed the courage, foresight and leadership to invest just a million dollars in the production of *Human Development Reports* 10 years ago, it managed to change the nature and character of development dialogue worldwide and to exercise a decisive influence in shaping new development strategies. This investment constituted only one-tenth of 1% of the UNDP's total resources each year. It is fascinating, though quite disturbing at the same time that the intellectual software of development gets so little attention while the hardware of development claims the bulk of funds.

One final thought. Throughout the time I have been associated with the production of *Human Development Reports*, I have realized that what endeared them to civil society was their raw courage, their ability to state facts professionally but honestly, their refusal to make any intellectual compromises with institutional constraints. Not a single year went by without some governments demanding a stoppage of these reports, as they felt uncomfortable with their basic messages. But they did not succeed because many more forces wanted that the truth be told, and told quite bluntly. I have come to realize that in the intellectual world, often it is courage that is lacking, not wisdom.

So let me conclude these reflections with my favourite lines from Robert Frost:

> *Two roads diverged in the wood and I—*
> *I took the one less travelled by,*
> *And that has made all the difference.*

Human development has been that "less travelled" road. It is certainly the more challenging one. And the only viable option for humanity in future.

Notes

1. By late 1995, I had returned from UNDP after founding, authoring and launching the annual *Human Development Reports* (1990–95), and set up the Human Development Centre in Islamabad, Pakistan, to produce annual reports on *Human Development in South Asia* (1997 and 1998 reports have appeared so far).

2. A significant development in this context will be the publication in 1999 of a new *Journal of Human Development* through the joint initiative of the UNDP and the Human Development Centre in Islamabad, with the aim of "stimulating intellectual ferment in the human development field and advancing the subject into a new school of thought".

Human Development Profile of Nations

"Can you do Addition?" the White Queen asked. "What's one and one and one and one and one and one and one and one and one and one?"

"I don't know," said Alice. "I lost count."

— Through the Looking Glass

The data in the following tables have been derived from the UNDP's *Human Development Reports* for 1990–98 (New York: Oxford University Press) and from UNDP data bases.

In the tables, the following signs have been used:
.. Data not available.
(.) Less than half the unit shown.
T Total

Table 1 Basic indicators of human development in industrial countries

HDI rank	Human development index 1995	Life expectancy at birth (years) 1995	Mean years of schooling 1992	GNP per capita (US$) 1995	Real GDP per capita (PPP$) 1995	Average annual GNP growth rate (%) 1980–95	Unemployment rate (%) 1996	Annual rate of inflation (%) 1995
1 Canada	0.961	79.1	12.2	19,380	21,916	2.4	9.7	2.9
2 France	0.946	78.7	12.0	24,990	21,176	1.9	12.1	1.7
3 Norway	0.943	77.6	12.1	31,250	22,427	2.9	4.9	2.4
4 Iceland	0.942	79.2	9.2	24,950	21,064	2.0	3.7	2.9
5 Finland	0.942	76.4	10.9	20,580	18,547	1.6	16.1	3.1
6 USA	0.942	76.4	12.4	26,980	26,977	2.5	5.4	2.5
7 Netherlands	0.942	77.5	11.1	24,000	19,876	2.2	6.4	2.1
8 Japan	0.941	79.9	10.8	39,640	21,930	3.1	3.4	-0.6
9 New Zealand	0.939	76.6	10.7	14,340	17,267	2.0	6.1	-1.7
10 Sweden	0.937	78.4	11.4	23,750	19,297	1.1	8.0	3.9
11 Spain	0.936	77.7	6.9	13,580	14,789	2.4	22.2	4.7
12 Belgium	0.933	76.9	11.2	24,710	21,548	1.8	9.5	2.1
13 Austria	0.933	76.7	11.4	26,890	21,322	2.1	5.3	2.2
14 United Kingdom	0.933	76.8	11.7	18,700	19,302	2.1	8.2	2.8
15 Australia	0.932	78.2	12.0	18,720	19,632	2.9	8.5	0.0
16 Ireland	0.931	76.4	8.9	14,710	17,590	3.4	11.9	1.2
17 Switzerland	0.930	78.2	11.6	40,630	24,881	1.4	3.8	0.3
18 Denmark	0.928	75.3	11.0	29,890	21,983	1.9	6.8	1.5
19 Germany	0.925	76.4	11.6	27,510	20,370	..	9.0	..
20 Greece	0.924	77.9	7.0	8,210	11,636	..	..	9.0
21 Italy	0.923	78.0	7.5	19,020	20,174	1.8	12.2	4.7
23 Israel	0.914	77.5	10.2	15,920	16,699	4.8	..	9.6
26 Luxembourg	0.900	76.1	10.5	41,210	34,004	2.7	3.3	2.1
27 Malta	0.900	76.5	6.1	..	13,316	..	..	..
33 Portugal	0.893	74.8	6.4	9,740	12,674	2.5	7.5	3.8
37 Slovenia	0.886	73.2	..	8,200	10,594	..	13.9	..
39 Czech Rep.	0.883	72.4	9.2	3,870	9,775	..	3.9	9.1
42 Slovakia	0.875	70.9	..	2,950	7,320	..	12.6	9.0
47 Hungary	0.857	68.9	9.8	4,120	6,793	0.1	9.8	24.1
52 Poland	0.850	71.1	8.2	2,790	5,442	0.9	12.2	27.4
67 Bulgaria	0.789	71.2	7.0	1,330	4,604	0.2	12.5	50.5
68 Belarus	0.783	69.3	7.0	2,070	4,398	..	3.8	646.5
72 Russian Fed.	0.769	65.5	9.0	2,240	4,531	-2.9	3.5	190.8
74 Romania	0.767	69.6	7.1	1,480	4,431	-0.5	7.8	35.5
76 Croatia	0.759	71.6	..	3,250	3,972	..	..	..
77 Estonia	0.758	69.2	9.0	2,860	4,062	..	2.2	34.5
79 Lithuania	0.750	70.2	9.0	1,900	3,843	..	7.1	37.2
80 Macedonia, FYR	0.749	71.9	..	860	4,058	..	..	..
92 Latvia	0.704	68.0	9.0	2,270	3,273	-2.5	7.0	23.9
93 Kazakstan	0.695	67.5	5.0	1,330	3,037	..	3.5	161.0

Table 1 Basic indicators of human development in industrial countries (Cont.)

HDI rank	Human develop-ment index 1995	Life expectancy at birth (years) 1995	Mean years of schooling 1992	GNP per capita (US $) 1995	Real GDP per capita (PPP $) 1995	Average annual GNP growth rate (%) 1980–95	Unem-ployment rate (%) 1996	Annual rate of inflation (%) 1995
99 Armenia	0.674	70.9	5.0	730	2,208	−4.4	9.1	161.2
102 Ukraine	0.665	68.5	6.0	1,630	2,361	..	..	412.0
103 Turkmenistan	0.660	64.9	5.0	920	2,345	..	..	919.5
104 Uzbekistan	0.659	67.5	5.0	970	2,376	..	0.4	369.3
105 Albania	0.656	70.6	6.2	670	2,853	..	..	10.3
108 Georgia	0.633	73.2	5.0	440	1,389	−8.8	..	163.4
109 Kyrgyzstan	0.633	67.9	5.0	700	1,927	..	4.4	38.5
110 Azerbaijan	0.623	71.1	5.0	480	1,463	..	1.0	609.5
113 Moldova, Rep. of	0.610	67.8	6.0	920	1,547	..	1.5	..
118 Tajikistan	0.575	66.9	5.0	340	943	..	2.5	226.9
Aggregates								
Industrial	0.911	74.2	10.0	18,158	16,337	2.2	8.1	9.1
Eastern Europe and CIS	0.76[a]	68.1[a]	8.8	2,125	4,203[a]	..	..	170.8
OECD	0.96[b]	75.4[b]	11.1	20,152	18,621[b]	2.5	7.1	3.1
European Union	..	77.2[c]	..	20,460	18,575[c]	2.0	11.5	3.1
Nordic countries	0.936[d]	77.1[d]	11.3	24,036	19,451[d]	1.8	8.9	2.8
World	0.771	63.5	5.2	4,797	5,984	2.6	..	12.1

a,b,c and d pertain to the year 1994.

REFLECTIONS ON HUMAN DEVELOPMENT

Table 2 Basic indicators of human development in developing countries

HDI rank		Human develop-ment index 1995	Life expectancy at birth (years) 1995	Adult literacy rate (%) 1995	Average annual GNP growth rate (%) 1980–95	GNP per capita (US$) 1995	Real GDP per capita (PPS $) 1995	GNP per capita annual growth rate (%) 1995
22	Cyprus	0.914	77.2	94	...	..	13,379	..
24	Hong Kong, China	0.909	79.0	92	6.2	22,990	22,950	4.8
25	Barbados	0.909	76.0	97	1.6	6,560	11,306	1.2
28	Singapore	0.896	77.1	91	7.9	26,730	22,604	6.0
29	Antigua and Barbuda	0.895	75.0	95	..	..	9,131	..
30	Bahamas	0.894	73.1	98	1.8	11,940	15,738	−0.1
31	Korea, Rep. of	0.893	71.7	98	8.7	9,700	11,594	7.5
32	Chile	0.893	75.1	95	4.9	4,160	9,930	3.2
34	Brunei Darussalam	0.889	75.1	88	..	25,160	31,165	..
35	Costa Rica	0.889	76.6	95	3.4	2,610	5,969	0.7
36	Argentina	0.887	72.6	96	1.0	8,030	8,498	−0.4
38	Uruguay	0.884	72.7	97	..	5,170	6,854	−0.6
40	Trinidad and Tobago	0.879	73.1	98	0.4	3,770	9,437	−1.5
41	Dominica	0.879	73.0	94	4.2	2,990	6,424	·4.3
43	Bahrain	0.872	72.2	85	1.2	7,840	16,751	−2.4
44	Fiji	0.869	72.1	92	1.9	2,440	6,159	0.6
45	Panama	0.868	73.4	91	2.1	2,750	6,258	0.1
46	Venezuela	0.860	72.3	91	1.4	3,020	8,090	−1.1
48	United Arab Emirates	0.857	74.4	79	0.3	17,400	18,008	−5.3
49	Mexico	0.854	72.1	90	1.2	3,320	6,769	−0.9
50	Saint Kitts and Nevis	0.854	69.0	90	4.3	5,170	10,150	4.9
51	Grenada	0.851	72.0	98	3.2	2,980	5,425	3.0
53	Colombia	0.849	70.3	91	3.5	1,910	6,347	1.6
54	Kuwait	0.848	75.4	79	0.3	17,390	23,848	−1.5
55	Saint Vincent	0.845	72.0	82	5.4	2,280	5,969	4.5
56	Seychelles	0.845	72.0	88	3.3	6,620	7,697	2.3
57	Qatar	0.841	71.1	79	1.4	11,600	19,772	−7.9
58	Saint Lucia	0.838	71.0	82	..	3,370	6,530	..
59	Thailand	0.838	69.5	94	7.9	2,740	7,742	6.3
60	Mauritius	0.834	70.9	83	5.7	3,380	13,294	4.6
61	Malaysia	0.833	71.4	84	6.7	3,890	9,572	4.0
62	Brazil	0.809	66.6	83	1.4	3,640	5,928	−0.4
63	Belize	0.807	74.2	70	4.4	2,630	5,623	1.7
64	Libyan Arab Jamahiriya	0.805	64.3	76	..	..	6,309	..
65	Suriname	0.796	70.9	93	4.4	880	4,862	3.4
66	Lebanon	0.796	69.3	92	..	2,660	4,977	..
69	Turkey	0.782	68.5	82	4.5	2,780	5,516	· 2.3
70	Saudi Arabia	0.778	70.7	63	0.6	7,040	8,516	−4.0
71	Oman	0.771	70.3	59	8.6	4,820	9,383	3.7

Table 2 Basic indicators of human development in developing countries (Cont.)

HDI rank		Human develop- ment index 1995	Life expectancy at birth (years) 1995	Adult literacy rate (%) 1995	Average annual GNP growth rate (%) 1980–95	GNP per capita (US$) 1995	Real GDP per capita (PPS$) 1995	GNP per capita annual growth rate (%) 1995
73	Ecuador	0.767	69.5	90	2.4	1,390	4,602	−0.1
75	Korea, Dem. People's Rep. of	0.766	71.6	95	..	..	4,058	..
78	Iran, Islamic Rep. of	0.758	68.5	69	3.1	..	5,480	−0.2
81	Syrian Arab Rep.	0.749	68.1	71	3.4	1,120	5,374	0.1
82	Algeria	0.746	68.1	62	1.8	1,600	5,618	−0.9
83	Tunisia	0.744	68.7	67	3.6	1,820	5,261	1.2
84	Jamaica	0.735	74.1	85	2.6	1,510	3,801	1.4
85	Cuba	0.729	75.7	96	..	..	3,100	..
86	Peru	0.729	67.7	89	1.4	2,310	3,940	−0.8
87	Jordan	0.729	68.9	87	..	1,510	4,187	..
88	Dominican Rep.	0.720	70.3	82	3.2	1,460	3,923	1.1
89	South Africa	0.717	64.1	82	1.3	3,160	4,334	−1.0
90	Sri Lanka	0.716	72.5	90	4.6	700	3,408	3.2
91	Paraguay	0.707	69.1	92	2.9	1,690	3,583	0 0
94	Samoa (Western)	0.694	68.4	98	..	1,120	2,948	..
95	Maldives	0.683	63.3	93	..	990	3,540	..
96	Indonesia	0.679	64.0	84	6.8	980	3,971	4.9
97	Botswana	0.678	51.7	70	8.8	3,020	5,611	5.4
98	Philippines	0.677	67.4	95	2.1	1,050	2,762	−0.3
100	Guyana	0.670	63.5	98	−1.0	590	3,205	−1.7
101	Mongolia	0.669	64.8	83	..	310	3,916	..
106	China	0.650	69.2	82	10.1	620	2,935	8.6
107	Namibia	0.644	55.8	76	..	2,000	4,054	..
111	Guatemala	0.615	66.1	65	1.6	1,340	3,682	−1.3
112	Egypt	0.612	64.8	51	4.3	790	3,829	1.9
114	El Salvador	0.604	69.4	72	1.9	1,610	2,610	0.5
115	Swaziland	0.597	58.8	77	4.2	1,170	2,954	1.0
116	Bolivia	0.593	60.5	83	1.7	800	2,617	−0.5
117	Cape Verde	0.591	65.7	72	4.8	960	2,612	2.9
119	Honduras	0.572	68.8	73	2.7	600	1,977	−0.5
120	Gabon	0.568	54.5	63	−1.5	3,490	3,766	−4.3
121	Sao Tome and Principe	0.563	69.0	75	−1.6	350	1,744	−3.7
122	Viet Nam	0.563	66.4	94	..	240	1,236	..
123	Solomon Islands	0.560	71.1	62	6.7	910	2,230	3.4
124	Vanuatu	0.559	66.3	64	..	1,200	2,507	..
125	Morocco	0.557	65.7	44	2.8	1,110	3,477	0.7

REFLECTIONS ON HUMAN DEVELOPMENT

HDI rank		Human develop-ment index 1995	Life expectancy at birth (years) 1995	Adult literacy rate (%) 1995	Average annual GNP growth rate (%) 1980-95	GNP per capita (US$) 1995	Real GDP per capita (PPS$) 1995	GNP per capita annual growth rate (%) 1995
126	Nicaragua	0.547	67.5	66	-0.8	380	1,837	-3.7
127	Iraq	0.538	58.5	58	..	..	3,170	..
128	Congo				2.5	680		-0.6
129	Papua New Guinea	0.507	56.8	72	3.4	1,160	2,500	2.7
130	Zimbabwe	0.507	48.9	85	2.8	540	2,135	-0.2
131	Myanmar	0.481	58.9	83	..	..	1,130	..
132	Cameroon	0.481	55.3	63	1.5	650	2,355	-1.3
133	Ghana	0.473	57.0	65	2.8	390	2,032	-0.3
134	Lesotho	0.469	58.1	71	3.4	770	1,290	0.9
135	Equatorial Guinea	0.465	49.0	79	..	380	1,712	..
136	Lao People's Dem. Rep.	0.465	52.2	57	..	350	2,571	..
137	Kenya	0.463	53.8	78	3.2	280	1,438	0.0
138	Pakistan	0.453	62.8	38	5.8	460	2,209	2.7
139	India	0.451	61.6	52	5.3	340	1,422	3.2
140	Cambodia	0.422	52.9	65	..	270	1,110	..
141	Comoros	0.411	56.5	57	2.0	470	1,317	-0.7
142	Nigeria	0.391	51.4	57	2.3	260	1,270	-0.8
143	Congo, Dem. Rep. of	0.383	52.4	77	-2.7	120	355	-5.8
144	Togo	0.380	50.5	52	0.5	310	1,167	-2.4
145	Benin	0.378	54.4	37	3.4	370	1,800	0.3
146	Zambia	0.378	42.7	78	0.6	400	986	-2.4
147	Bangladesh	0.371	56.9	38	4.5	240	1,382	2.2
148	Côte d' Ivoire	0.368	51.8	40	0.1	660	1,731	-3.4
149	Mauritania	0.361	52.5	38	2.3	460	1,622	-0.2
150	Tanzania, U. Rep. of	0.358	50.6	68	..	120	636	..
151	Yemen	0.356	56.7	38	..	260	856	..
152	Nepal	0.351	55.9	28	4.9	200	1,145	2.2
153	Madagascar	0.348	57.6	46	-0.1	230	673	-3.0
154	Central African Rep.	0.347	48.4	60	0.8	340	1,092	-1.5
155	Bhutan	0.347	52.0	42	7.3	420	1,382	4.8
156	Angola	0.344	47.4	42	..	410	1,839	..
157	Sudan	0.347	52.2	46	..	..	1,110	..
158	Senegal	0.342	50.3	33	2.9	600	1,815	0.1
159	Haiti	0.340	54.6	45	-2.1	250	917	-4.0
160	Uganda	0.340	40.5	62	..	240	1,483	..
161	Malawi	0.334	41.0	56	2.4	170	773	-0.7
162	Djibouti	0.324	49.2	46	..	..	1,300	..
163	Chad	0.316	47.2	48	4.9	180	1,172	2.4
164	Guinea-Bissau	0.295	43.4	55	4.6	250	811	2.7

Table 2 Basic indicators of human development in developing countries (Cont.)

HDI rank		Human development index 1995	Life expectancy at birth (years) 1995	Adult literacy rate (%) 1995	Average annual GNP growth rate (%) 1980–95	GNP per capita (US$) 1995	Real GDP per capita (PPS$) 1995	GNP per capita annual growth rate (%) 1995
165	Gambia	0.291	46.0	39	2.5	320	948	−1.2
166	Mozambique	0.281	46.3	40	1.1	80	959	−0.8
167	Guinea	0.277	45.5	36	..	550	1,139	..
168	Eritrea	0.275	50.2	25	..	..	983	..
169	Ethiopia	0.249	48.7	36	..	100	455	..
170	Burundi	0.241	44.5	35	2.6	160	637	−0.2
171	Mali	0.236	47.0	31	2.0	250	565	−0.7
172	Rwanda	0.231	28.2	61	−2.3	180	552	−3.7
173	Burkina-Faso	0.219	46.3	19	3.5	230	784	0.8
174	Niger	0.207	47.5	14	−0.7	220	765	−3.9
175	Sierra Leone	0.183	34.7	31	−0.3	180	625	−2.0
	Aggregates							
	All developing countries	0.586	62.1	70	4.1	1,140	3,065	2.1
	Sub-Saharan Africa	0.384	50.4	57	1.6	514	1,397	−1.3
	South Asia	0.461	61.8	51	4.6	346	1,724	2.3
	East Asia	0.676	69.3	82	9.3	1,055	3,359	7.8
	South-East Asia and Pacific	0.684	64.7	87	6.3	1,407	3,852	4.3
	Latin America and the Carribean	0.831	69.2	87	1.6	3,313	5,982	−0.4
	Arab States	0.636	63.5	56	1.5	2,162	4,454	−1.2
	Least developed countries	0.342	50.9	49	2.1	215	1,003	−0.5
	Industrial countries	0.911	74.2	99	2.2	18,158	16,337	1.7
	World	0.771	63.5	78	2.6	5,022	5,984	0.9

Table 3 Selected indicators of human progress in industrial countries

HDI rank		Tertiary students (per 100,000 people) 1995	Scientists and technicians (per 1,000 people) 1990–96	Doctors (per 100,000 people) around 1993	Televisions (per 100 people) 1995	Telephones (per 100 people) 1995	Internet users (per 1,000,000 people) 1995	Book titles published (per 100,000 people) 1992–94
1	Canada	6,865	4	221	65	60	41,208	76
2	France	3,786	5	280	58	60	8,612	78
3	Norway	3,994	5	..	56	60	64,073	159
4	Iceland	2,756	4	..	45	60	111,940	537
5	Finland	4,171	5	269	52	60	138,998	247
6	USA	5,398	4	245	78	60	38,006	20
7	Netherlands	3,769	4	..	50	50	38,810	222
8	Japan	3,190	7	177	62	50	7,188	28
9	New Zealand	4,603	3	210	51	50	50,106	..
10	Sweden	2,936	7	299	48	70	50,968	158
11	Spain	3,992	2	400	49	40	3,826	112
12	Belgium	3,337	4	365	46	50	9,877	..
13	Austria	2,983	2	327	50	50	18,624	100
14	United Kingdom	3,380	3	164	61	50	25,627	164
15	Australia	5,401	4	..	64	50	55,389	61
16	Ireland	3,545	2	167	38	40	11,155	..
17	Switzerland	2,067	..	301	46	60	35,511	217
18	Denmark	3,255	5	283	54	60	38,256	230
19	Germany	2,631	4	319	55	50	18,322	87
20	Greece	2,841	1	387	44	50	7,643	..
21	Italy	3,170	2	..	44	40	5,233	57
23	Israel	3,598	..	459	30	40	53,486	86
26	Luxembourg	..	..	213	59	60	15,931	169
27	Malta	1,773	0	250	45	50	2,285	115
33	Portugal	3,209	1	291	33	40	9,072	68
37	Slovenia	2,489	4	219	37	30	28,629	151
39	Czech Rep.	1,908	2	293	41	20	21,285	91
42	Slovakia	1,715	3	325	22	20	5,217	65
47	Hungary	1,777	2	337	44	20	10,770	100
52	Poland	2,220	2	..	41	20	6,475	28
67	Bulgaria	2,942	3	333	36	30	1,193	69
68	Belarus	3,031	3	379	27	20	21	32
72	Russian Fed.	3,004	4	380	38	20	1,494	20
74	Romania	1,483	2	176	20	10	749	18
76	Croatia	1,917	3	201	23	30	5,024	59
77	Estonia	2,670	3	312	41	30	26,954	152
79	Lithuania	2,023	1	399	36	30	..	77
80	Macedonia, FYR	1,372	2	219	17	20	378	31
92	Latvia	1,737	2	303	47	30	..	65
93	Kazakstan	2,807	..	360	28	10	108	7

Table 3 Selected indicators of human progress in industrial countries (Cont.)

HDI rank		Tertiary students (per 100,000 people) 1995	Scientists and technicians (per 1,000 people) 1990–96	Doctors (per 100,000 people) arround 1993	Tele- visions (per 100 people) 1995	Tele- phones (per 100 people) 1995	Internet users (per 1,000,000 people) 1995	Book titles published (per 100,000 people) 1992–94
99	Armenia	4,709	..	312	24	20	451	6
102	Ukraine	2,977	4	429	23	20	427	10
103	Turkmenistan	1,889	..	353	22	10	..	14
104	Uzbekistan	3,392	2	335	18	10	15	6
105	Albania	902	..	141	9	(.)	96	..
108	Georgia	2,845	..	436	22	10	112	6
109	Kyrgyzstan	1,115	1	310	24	10	..	7
110	Azerbaijan	1,593	..	390	21	10	21	5
113	Moldova, Rep. of	1,976	2	356	30	10	35	18
118	Tajikistan	1,870	1	210	26	10	..	4
	Aggregates							
	Industrial	3,645	4	287	52	40	17,854	52
	Eastern Europe and CIS	2,643	3	354	32	20	2,630	25
	OECD	3,717	3	224	54	50	19,780	61
	European Union	3,299	4	291	52	50	17,109	108
	Nordic countries	3,463	6	287	51	60	70,208	197
	World	1,451	1	122	23	10[a]	4,834	18

a: ITU (International Telecommunication Union)

REFLECTIONS ON HUMAN DEVELOPMENT

Table 4 Selected indicators of human progress in developing countries

HDI rank		Mean years of schooling (age 25+) 1992	Enrolment ratio for all levels (% age 6–23) 1996	Daily calorie supply per capita 1995	Population with access to health services (%) 1990–96	Population with access to safe water (%) 1990–96	Radios (per 1,000 people) 1995	Daily newspapers (copies per 1,000 people) 1995
22	Cyprus	7.0	..	3,676	..	..	309	101
24	Hong Kong, China	7.2	72	3,187	99[a]	..	668	735
25	Barbados	9.4	76	3,155	..	100	900	157
28	Singapore	4.0	72	..	100[b]	100	601	301
29	Antigua and Barbuda	4.6	..	2,300	..	..	439	91
30	Bahamas	6.2	75	2,458	..	..	735	125
31	Korea, Rep. of	9.3	82	3,159	100	93	1,024	394
32	Chile	7.8	72	2,713	97[c]	95	348	99
34	Brunei Darussalam	5.0	70	2,818	..	..	273	68
35	Costa Rica	5.7	68	2,855	80[d]	96	263	88
36	Argentina	9.2	77	3,097	71	71	676	135
38	Uruguay	8.1	75	2,813	95	..	609	235
40	Trinidad and Tobago	8.4	67	2,550	100	97	505	186
41	Dominica	4.7	..	2,982	..	96	634	..
43	Bahrain	4.3	85		..	..	575	126
44	Fiji	5.1	79	3,015	..	100	612	45
45	Panama	6.8	70	2,462	70	93	228	61
46	Venezuela	6.5	68	..	..	79	458	206
48	United Arab Emirates	5.6	82	3,329	99	95	271	136
49	Mexico	4.9	66	3,116	93	83	263	115
50	Saint Kitts and Nevis	6.0	..	2,156	..	100	668	..
51	Grenada	4.7	..	2,630	..	..	598	..
53	Colombia	7.5	70	2,749	81	85	564	42
54	Kuwait	5.5	..	..	100	..	473	387
55	Saint Vincent	4.6	..	2,397	..	89	670	..
56	Seychelles	4.6	..	2,311	..	..	548	41
57	Qatar	5.8	73	..	..	..	438	146
58	Saint Lucia	3.9	..	2,757	..	..	765	..
59	Thailand	3.9	53	2,247	90	89	189	46
60	Mauritius	4.1	61	2,886	100	98	367	112
61	Malaysia	5.6	62	2,765	..	78	432	139
62	Brazil	4.0	72	2,824	..	76	399	45
63	Belize	4.6	..	2,776	..	89	587	..
64	Libyan Arab Jamahiriya	3.5	..	3,117	95	97	231	13
65	Suriname	4.2	..	2,521	..	..	679	101
66	Lebanon	4.4	75	3,269	94	94	891	110
69	Turkey	3.6	63	3,577	49	49	164	118
70	Saudi Arabia	3.9	56	2,736	95	95	291	58

Table 4 Selected indicators of human progress in developing countries (Cont.)

HDI rank	Mean years of schooling (age 25+) 1992	Enrolment ratio for all levels (% age 6–23) 1996	Daily calorie supply per capita 1995	Population with access to health services (%) 1990–96	Population with access to safe water (%) 1990–96	Radios (per 1,000 people) 1995	Daily newspapers (copies per 1,000 people) 1995
71 Oman	0.9	60	..	82	82	580	29
73 Ecuador	5.6	72	2,420	68	68	332	70
75 Korea, Dem. People's Rep. of	6.0	..	2,282	81	81	136	226
78 Iran, Islamic Rep. of	3.9	68	2,945	90	90	228	17
81 Syrian Arab Rep.	4.2	64	3,295	86	86	264	19
82 Algeria	2.8	66	3,035	78	78	238	51
83 Tunisia	2.1	67	3,173	98	98	200	45
84 Jamaica	5.3	65	2,615	86	86	438	65
85 Cuba	8.0	63	2,277	93	93	351	119
86 Peru	6.5	81	2,147	67	67	259	85
87 Jordan	5.0	..	2,726	98	98	251	47
88 Dominican Rep.	4.3	68	2,308	65	65	176	34
89 South Africa	3.9	..	2,865	99	99	316	31
90 Sri Lanka	7.2	66	2,302	57	57	206	25
91 Paraguay	4.9	62	2,552	60	60	180	41
94 Samoa (Western)	..	..	..	82	82	485	..
95 Maldives	4.5	..	2,211	96	96	118	12
96 Indonesia	4.1	62	2,699	62	62	149	24
97 Botswana	2.5	71	2,140	93	93	131	31
98 Philippines	7.6	78	2,319	84	84	147	62
100 Guyana	5.1	67	2,388	61	61	494	47
101 Mongolia	7.2	52	1,895	40	40	134	81
106 China	5.0	58	2,708	67	67	185	..
107 Namibia	..	..	2,093	57	57	140	100
111 Guatemala	4.1	46	2,298	77	77	71	23
112 Egypt	3.0	69	3,315	87	87	312	43
114 El Salvador	4.2	55	2,571	69	69	459	49
115 Swaziland	3.8	72	2,660	60	60	163	18
116 Bolivia	4.0	66	2,189	63	63	672	67
117 Cape Verde	2.2	64	3,003	51	51	179	..
119 Honduras	4.0	60	2,358	87	87	409	42
120 Gabon	2.6	..	2,443	68	68	181	28
121 São Tomé and Principe	2.3	..	..	82	82	271	..
122 Viet Nam	4.9	55	2,438	43	43	106	8
123 Solomon Islands	1.0	..	2,085	61	61	122	..
124 Vanuatu	3.7	..	2,499	..	87	296	..
125 Morocco	3.0	46	3,140	70	65	226	15

HDI rank		Mean years of schooling (age 25+) 1992	Enrolment ratio for all levels (% age 6–23) 1996	Daily calorie supply per capita 1995	Population with access to health services (%) 1990–96	Population with access to safe water (%) 1990–96	Radios (per 1,000 people) 1995	Daily newspapers (copies per 1,000 people) 1995
126	Nicaragua	4.5	62	2,308	83	61	280	32
127	Iraq	5.0	53	2,266	93	78	224	26
128	Congo	2.1	..	2,083	83	34	116	8
129	Papua New Guinea	1.0	38	2,273	96	28	77	15
130	Zimbabwe	3.1	68	1,961	85	79	89	17
131	Myanmar	2.5	48	2,728	60	60	89	22
132	Cameroon	1.6	46	2,199	80	50	152	6
133	Ghana	3.5	44	2,574	60	65	231	18
134	Lesotho	3.5	56	1,965	80	62	37	7
135	Equatorial Guinea	0.8	64	..	..	95	425	5
136	Lao People's Dem. Rep.	2.9	50	2,105	67	44	129	3
137	Kenya	2.3	55	1,980	77	53	96	17
138	Pakistan	1.9	38	2,471	55	74	92	21
139	India	2.4	56	2,382	85	81	81	..
140	Cambodia	2.0	..	1,996	53	36	112	..
141	Comoros	1.0	39	1,794	..	53	137	..
142	Nigeria	1.2	50	2,497	51	50	197	17
143	Congo, Dem. Rep. of	2.1	38	1,870	26	42	98	3
144	Togo	1.6	50	1,736	..	55	215	2
145	Benin	0.7	35	2,386	18	50	92	1
146	Zambia	2.7	48	1,915	..	27	99	13
147	Bangladesh	2.0	39	2,001	45	97	47	6
148	Côted' Ivoire	1.9	39	2,494	..	42	153	15
149	Mauritania	0.4	36	2,568	63	74	150	1
150	Tanzania, U. Rep. of	2.0	34	2,003	42	38	276	12
151	Yemen	0.9	..	2,013	38	61	43	15
152	Nepal	2.1	55	2,367	..	63	36	7
153	Madagascar	2.2	33	1,996	38	34	192	4
154	Central African Rep.	1.1	37	1,877	52	38	75	1
155	Bhutan	0.3	..	..	65	58	17	..
156	Angola	1.5	31	1,904	..	32	34	11
157	Sudan	0.8	31	2,310	70	50	270	24
158	Senegal	0.9	31	2,365	90	63	120	6
159	Haiti	1.7	..	..	60	37	53	6
160	Uganda	1.1	34	2,249	49	46	117	2
161	Malawi	1.7	67	2,026	35	37	256	3
162	Djibouti	0.4	20	1,827	..	90	80	..
163	Chad	0.3	25	1,917	30	24	248	0

Table 4 Selected indicators of human progress in developing countries (Cont.)

HDI rank		Mean years of schooling (age 25+) 1992	Enrolment ratio for all levels (% age 6–23) 1996	Daily calorie supply per capita 1995	Population with access to health services (%) 1990–96	Population with access to safe water (%) 1990–96	Radios (per 1,000 people) 1995	Daily newspapers (copies per 1,000 people) 1995
164	Guinea-Bissau	0.4	29	2,423	40	59	42	6
165	Gambia	0.6	34	2,122	93	48	164	1
166	Mozambique	1.6	25	1,675	39	63	38	8
167	Guinea	0.9	24	2,150	80	46	44	..
168	Eritrea	..	..	..	..	22	98	..
169	Ethiopia	1.1	18	..	46	25	193	2
170	Burundi	0.4	31	1,741	80	52	68	3
171	Mali	0.4	..	2,137	40	66	46	4
172	Rwanda	1.1	37	2,678	80	..	101	1
173	Burkina-Faso	0.2	20	2,248	90	42	28	1
174	Niger	0.2	15	2,135	99	48	68	0
175	Sierra Leone	0.9	28	1,992	38	34	250	5
	Aggregates							
	All Developing countries	3.9	56	2,569	80	71	175	50
	Sub-Saharan Africa	1.6	39	2,220	53	50	166	11
	South Asia	2.3	53	2,385	78	82	88	15
	East Asia	5.2	59	2,717	88	68	180	362
	South-East Asia and Pacific	4.5	61	2,532	85	65	156	36
	Latin America and the Carribean	5.4	70	2,781	79	77	384	80
	Arab States	3.4	58	2,903	87	79	264	39
	Least developed countries	1.6	36	2,088	49	56	113	8
	Industrial countries	10.0	..	3,157	..	..	455	235
	World	5.2	56	2,700	80	72	236	115

a, b, c and d pertain to the years 1985–95.

Table 5 Selected indicators of human distress in industrial countries

HDI rank		Drug crimes (per 100,000 people) 1980–86	Intentional homicides by men (per 100,000 males) 1985–90	Reported rapes (per 100,000 women age 15–59) 1987–89	Births outside marriage (%) 1985–92	AIDS cases (per 100,000 people) 1996	Youth unemployment (% age 15–24) 1996	Suicides (per 100,000 people) 1989–93	Adults with less than upper-secondary education (as % of 15–64) 1991
1	Canada	225	2.7	23	23	2.7	17.0	27	24
2	France	..	1.4	17	32	6.3	27.0	41	49
3	Norway	116	1.6	20	34	1.2	12.0	29	21
4	Iceland	..	0.6	..	..	1.1	9.0	..	..
5	Finland	..	4.1	19	..	0.4	25.0	56	40
6	USA	234	12.4	118	27	13.8	12.0	25	17
7	Netherlands	38	1.2	26	12	2.4	11.0	21	44
8	Japan	31	0.9	5	1	0.2	7.0	33	33
9	New Zealand	..	2.6	..	25	1.6	12.0	30	..
10	Sweden	..	1.7	43	52	1.5	16.0	32	33
11	Spain	15	1.7	12	10	14.3	42.0	15	78
12	Belgium	40	2.3	..	12	1.5	20.0	..	57
13	Austria	77	1.4	27	22	1.6	5.3	43	33
14	United Kingdom	..	1.6	..	31	2.1	15.0	..	35
15	Australia	..	2.5	44	16	3.1	15.0	25	44
16	Ireland	..	1.2	..	18	1.4	18.0	20	60
17	Switzerland	129	1.1	18	6	4.4	5.0	1	19
18	Denmark	176	1.4	35	47	3.0	10.0	45	39
19	Germany	..	1.2	26	15	1.4	8.0	32	18
20	Greece	..	1.2	..	3	2.0	28.0	8	..
21	Italy	6	2.5	4	7	8.6	34.0	16	72
22	Israel	25	0.5	4	1	0.7	..	15	..
26	Luxembourg	..	1.6	..	13	2.9	9.0	..	..
27	Malta	..	0.6	2	1	1.1	..	..	..
33	Portugal	13	2.3	5	16	7.3	17.0	15	93
37	Slovenia	..	..	..	..	0.4	..	..	..
39	Czech Rep.	..	1.3	12	..	0.2	7.0	38	27
42	Slovakia	..	..	..	..	..	..	..	..
47	Hungary	..	3.5	31	9	0.5	18.0	73	..
52	Poland	..	2.5	19	5	0.3	..	30	..
67	Bulgaria	..	4.0	21	12	0.1	..	35	..
68	Belarus	..	..	..	8	..	..	59	..
72	Russian Fed.	..	9.0	..	14	(.)	..	79	..
74	Romania	..	..	..	..	2.4	..	..	..
76	Croatia	..	..	..	..	0.4	..	..	..
77	Estonia	..	..	..	25	0.5	..	79	..
79	Lithuania	..	..	..	7	0.1	..	88	..
80	Macedonia, FYR	..	..	.	..	0.1	..	..	..

Table 5 Selected indicators of human distress in industrial countries (Cont.)

HDI rank	Drug crimes (per 100,000 people) 1980–86	Intentional homicides by men (per 100,000 males) 1985–90	Reported rapes (per 100,000 women age 15–59) 1987–89	Births outside marriage (%) 1985–92	AIDS cases (per 100,000 people) 1996	Youth unemployment (% age 15–24) 1996	Suicides (per 100,000 people) 1989–93	Adults with less than upper-secondary education (as % of 15–64) 1991
92 Latvia	..	..	..	..	0.2	..	89	..
93 Kazakstan	..	..	..	..	(.)	..	47	..
99 Armenia	..	..	..	..	0.2	..	5	..
102 Ukraine	..	..	..	11	0.3	..	47	..
103 Turkmenistan	..	..	..	..	..	..	..	..
104 Uzbekistan	..	..	..	..	..	..	12	..
105 Albania	..	..	..	..	(.)	..	3	..
108 Georgia	..	..	..	..	..	..	..	..
109 Kyrgyzstan	..	..	..	..	..	..	..	..
110 Azerbaijan	..	..	..	..	(.)	..	..	..
113 Moldova, Rep. of	..	..	..	10	(.)	..	..	..
118 Tajikistan	..	..	..	..	..	..	6	..
Aggregates								
Industrial	..	5.4	48	17	5.0	..	36	..
Eastern Europe and CIS	..	..	..	13	0.3	..	57	..
OECD	..	4.8	51	20	5.7	14.0	28	34
European Union	..	1.7	17	19	5.0	22.0	27	47
Nordic countries	..	2.1	32	46	1.5	15.0	39	34
World	..	..	..	..	3.9	..	..	..

Table 6 Selected indicators of human distress in developing countries

HDI rank	Infant mortality rate (per 1,000 live births) 1996	Underweight children (as % of children under five) 1990–97	Children not in primary school (%) 1993–95	People in poverty $1 a day (PPP$) 1989–94	Income share of lowest 40% of households (%) 1981–93	Refugees by country of asylum (thousands) 1995
22 Cyprus	9	..	3	..	..	0.1
24 Hong Kong, China	5[a]	..	9	..	16.2	1.5
25 Barbados	11	..	22	..	..	..
28 Singapore	4	..	1	..	15.0	0.0
29 Antigua and Barbuda	..	..	..	..	..	..
30 Bahamas	19	..	..	..	..	..
31 Korea, Rep. of	6	..	7	..	19.7	..
32 Chile	11	1	13	15	10.2	0.3
34 Brunei Darussalam	9	..	9	..	..	..
35 Costa Rica	13	2	8	19	13.1	24.2
36 Argentina	22	..	5	..	..	12.0
38 Uruguay	20	7	5	..	..	0.1
40 Trinidad and Tobago	15	7	11	..	..	..
41 Dominica	..	..	..	..	..	..
43 Bahrain	18	..	0	..	..	..
44 Fiji	20	..	1	12	..	..
45 Panama	18	7	9	26	8.3	0.9
46 Venezuela	24	6	12	12	14.3	11.2
48 United Arab Emirates	15	..	17	..	..	0.4
49 Mexico	27	14	0	15	11.9	39.6
50 Saint Kitts and Nevis	..	..	..	..	..	..
51 Grenada	..	..	..	..	..	..
53 Colombia	26	8	15	7	11.2	5.5
54 Kuwait	13	..	39	..	..	30.0
55 Saint Vincent	..	..	..	..	..	..
56 Seychelles	..	..	..	..	..	..
57 Qatar	17	..	20	..	..	..
58 Saint Lucia	..	..	..	..	..	..
59 Thailand	31	26	..	(.)	15.5	101.4
60 Mauritius	20	16	..	..	..	..
61 Malaysia	11	23	..	6	12.9	0.2
62 Brazil	44	6	10	29	7.0	2.0
63 Belize	36	..	1	..	..	8.7
64 Libyan Arab Jamahiriya	50	..	3	..	..	3.3
65 Suriname	25	..	..	..	..	(.)
66 Lebanon	33	..	..	..	..	348.3
69 Turkey	41	10	6	..	..	9.9
70 Saudi Arabia	25	..	38	..	..	13.3
71 Oman	15	..	29	..	..	..
73 Ecuador	31	17	..	..	30	14.5

Table 6 Selected indicators of human distress in developing countries (Cont.)

HDI rank		Infant mortality rate (per 1,000 live births) 1996	Underweight children (as % of children under five) 1990–97	Children not in primary school (%) 1993–95	People in poverty $1 a day (PPP$) 1989–94	Income share of lowest 40% of households (%) 1981–93	Refugees by country of asylum (thousands) 1995
75	Korea, Dem. People's Rep. of	23	..	..	..	..	..
78	Iran, Islamic Rep. of	33	16	3	..	..	2,024.5
81	Syrian Arab Rep.	28	13	9	..	..	374.3
82	Algeria	34	13	5	2.0	17.9	206.8
83	Tunisia	28	9	3	4.0	16.3	0.1
84	Jamaica	10	10	0	5.0	15.9	2.0
85	Cuba	10	..	4	..	..	1.8
86	Peru	45	8	13	49.0	14.1	0.7
87	Jordan	21	9	11	3.0	16.8	1,288.9
88	Dominican Rep.	45	6	19	20.0	12.1	1.0
89	South Africa	50	..	4	24.0	9.1	91.8
90	Sri Lanka	17	38	..	4.0	22.0	0.0
91	Paraguay	28	4	11	..	..	0.1
94	Samoa (Western)	42	..	..	..	..	..
95	Maldives	54	..	..	..	..	..
96	Indonesia	47	11	3	15.0	20.8	0.0
97	Botswana	40	..	4	35.0	10.5	0.3
98	Philippines	32	30	0	28.0	16.6	0.1
100	Guyana	60	..	..	..	..	..
101	Mongolia	55	..	25	..	..	..
106	China	38	16	1	29.0	17.4	288.3
107	Namibia	60	..	8	..	..	1.4
111	Guatemala	43	27	42	53.0	7.9	1.5
112	Egypt	57	15	11	8.0	..	7.7
114	El Salvador	34	11	21	..	..	0.2
115	Swaziland	68	..	5	..	..	0.5
116	Bolivia	71	8	9	7.0	15.3	0.7
117	Cape Verde	54	..	0	..	..	..
119	Honduras	29	18	10	47.0	8.7	0.1
120	Gabon	87	..	..	..	..	0.8
121	São Tomé and Principe	..	..	..	..	..	..
122	Viet Nam	33	45	..	..	19.2	(.)
123	Solomon Islands	24	..	..	..	..	..
124	Vanuatu	41	..	26	..	..	..
125	Morocco	64	9	28	1.0	17.1	0.4
126	Nicaragua	44	12	14	44.0	12.2	0.6
127	Iraq	94	12	21	..	..	123.3

REFLECTIONS ON HUMAN DEVELOPMENT

HDI rank		Infant mortality rate (per 1,000 live births) 1996	Underweight children (as % of children under five) 1990–97	Children not in primary school (%) 1993–95	People in poverty $1 a day (PPP$) 1989–94	Income share of lowest 40% of households (%) 1981–93	Refugees by country of asylum (thousands) 1995
128	Congo	81	24	..	..	..	15.0
129	Papua New Guinea	79	35	..	..	..	9.5
130	Zimbabwe	49	16	0	41.0	10.3	0.3
131	Myanmar	105	43	..	..	..	..
132	Cameroon	63	14	24	..	..	45.9
133	Ghana	70	27	..	..	18.3	89.2
134	Lesotho	96	16	35	50.0	9.3	(.)
135	Equatorial Guinea	111	..	..	..	..	..
136	Lao People's Dem. Rep.	102	..	32	..	..	..
137	Kenya	61	23	9	50.0	10.1	239.5
138	Pakistan	95	38	..	12.0	21.3	867.6
139	India	73	53	..	53.0	21.3	274.1
140	Cambodia	108	..	..	..	..	0.0
141	Comoros	83	..	47	..	..	..
142	Nigeria	114	36	..	29.0	15.2	8.1
143	Congo, Dem. Rep. of	128	..	..	..	..	15.0
144	Togo	78	19	22	..	..	11.0
145	Benin	84	..	48	..	..	23.5
146	Zambia	112	28	25	85.0	15.2	130.6
147	Bangladesh	83	56	38	29.0	22.9	51.1
148	Côte d' Ivoire	90	24	48	18.0	18.0	297.9
149	Mauritania	124	23	44	31.0	14.2	40.4
150	Tanzania, U. Rep. of	93	27	52	16.0	8.1	829.7
151	Yemen	78	39	..	..	..	40.3
152	Nepal	82	..	..	53.0	22.0	124.8
153	Madagascar	100	34	..	72.0	..	(.)
154	Central African Rep.	103	..	42	..	..	33.8
155	Bhutan	90	..	..	..	..	..
156	Angola	170	..	..	..	..	10.9
157	Sudan	73	..	..	..	..	558.2
158	Senegal	74	22	46	54.0	10.5	68.6
159	Haiti	94	28	74	..	..	..
160	Uganda	88	26	..	50.0	20.6	229.3
161	Malawi	137	30	0	..	..	1.0
162	Djibouti	112	..	68	..	..	25.7
163	Chad	92	..	..	..	..	0.1
164	Guinea-Bissau	132	..	44	87.0	8.6	15.3
165	Gambia	78	..	45	..	..	7.2
166	Mozambique	133	..	61	..	..	0.1

Table 6 Selected indicators of human distress in developing countries (Cont.)

HDI rank		Infant mortality rate (per 1,000 live births) 1996	Underweight children (as % of children under five) 1990–97	Children not in primary school (%) 1993–95	People in poverty $1 a day (PPP$) 1989–94	Income share of lowest 40% of households (%) 1981–93	Refugees by country of asylum (thousands) 1995
167	Guinea	130	..	63	26.0	..	633.0
168	Eritrea	78	..	69	..	..	1.1
169	Ethiopia	113	48	..	34.0	21.3	393.5
170	Burundi	106	37	48	..	..	142.7
171	Mali	134	27	75	..	..	15.6
172	Rwanda	105	29	24	46.0	22.8	7.8
173	Burkina-Faso	82	30	71	..	..	29.5
174	Niger	191	36	77	61.0	..	22.6
175	Sierra Leone	164	29	..	..	..	4.7
	Aggregates						
	All developing countries	65	29	9	32.0	..	8,581.7
	Sub-Saharan Africa	105	30	37	39.0	..	3,692.0
	South Asia	74	50	..	43.0	..	3,624.0
	East Asia	37	16	1	26.0	..	297.0
	South-East Asia and Pacific	48	25	..	14.0	..	157.2
	Latin America and the Carribean	35	10	13	24.0	..	88.4
	Arab States	55	17	15	4.0	..	834.9
	Least developed countries	106	41	45	..	..	3,449.6
	Industrial countries	13	..	5	..	..	3,889.8
	World	59	29	8	..	..	12,471.5

a pertains to 1994.

Table 7 Critical gender disparities in industrial countries

HDI rank	Gap in mean years of schooling 1992	Gap in university full-time equivalent enrolment 1991	Gap in earned income share 1995	Gap in administrators and managers 1992–96	Gap in professional and technical workers 1992–96	Gap in economic activity rate 1995	Parliamentary seats occupied by women (as % of total) 1996
1 Canada	97	119	61	73	128	80	19
2 France	102	116	64	10	71	76	6
3 Norway	98	121	74	44	141	82	39
4 Iceland	102	..	72	35	116	83	25
5 Finland	98	97	72	33	167	86	34
6 USA	102	111	68	75	111	80	11
7 Netherlands	104	74	52	26	79	65	28
8 Japan	98	..	52	10	76	66	8
9 New Zealand	104	101	63	51	97	77	29
10 Sweden	100	91	81	64	181	90	40
11 Spain	93	109	42	47	76	54	20
12 Belgium	100	76	51	23	102	65	15
13 Austria	90	80	51	31	86	65	25
14 United Kingdom	102	110	60	49	82	73	8
15 Australia	98	107	67	76	34	74	21
16 Ireland	102	90	37	31	84	49	14
17 Switzerland	93	63	48	39	33	65	20
18 Denmark	98	110	72	31	97	84	33
19 Germany	91	68	53	37	97	69	26
20 Greece	89	107	47	28	79	55	6
21 Italy	99	95	45	116	22	57	10
22 Israel	83	98	49	25	114	65	8
26 Luxembourg	95	..	40	9	61	56	20
27 Malta	92	..	27	..	..	35	6
33 Portugal	76	..	52	48	101	71	13
37 Slovenia	..	..	65	39	111	81	8
39 Czech Rep.	88	80	64	31	118	86	..
42 Slovakia	..	..	69	38	135	87	15
47 Hungary	102	77	63	47	159	74	11
52 Poland	93	..	64	52	162	81	13
67 Bulgaria	84	..	70	..	..	89	13
68 Belarus	..	..	71	..	..	84	..
72 Russian Fed.	..	..	70	..	..	83	8
74 Romania	89	80	60	37	124	78	6
76 Croatia	..	..	58	..	..	72	7
77 Estonia	..	..	72	60	208	85	13
79 Lithuania	..	..	69	..	..	83	18
80 Macedonia, FYR	..	..	52	..	..	..	3
92 Latvia	..	..	79	58	209	85	9
93 Kazakstan	..	..	65	..	..	82	11

Table 7 Critical gender disparities in industrial countries (Cont.)

HDI rank	Gap in mean years of schooling 1992	Gap in university full-time equivalent enrolment 1991	Gap in earned income share 1995	Gap in administrators and managers 1992–96	Gap in professional and technical workers 1992–96	Gap in economic activity rate 1995	Parliamentary seats occupied by women (as % of total) 1996
99 Armenia	..	..	69	..	..	87	6
102 Ukraine	..	..	74	..	..	81	4
103 Turkmenistan	..	..	62	..	..	81	18
104 Uzbekistan	..	..	64	..	..	84	6
105 Albania	71	..	52	..	..	72	12
108 Georgia	..	..	65	22	72	79	7
109 Kyrgyzstan	..	..	66	..	..	84	5
110 Azerbaijan	..	..	58	..	..	75	12
113 Moldova, Rep. of	..	..	71	..	..	86	5
118 Tajikistan	..	..	58	..	..	76	3
Aggregates							
Industrial	95		57	58	100	75	4
Eastern Europe and CIS	..	..	65	..	..	82 ·	8
OECD	98	103	..	56	93	69	13
European Union	96	96	53	50	89	67	16
Nordic countries	99	102	76	36	127	86	37
World	74	..	47	..	..	68	13

Note: Gaps are expressed in relation to male average, which is indexed to equal 100. The smaller the figure the bigger the gap, the closer the figure to 100 the smaller the gap, and a figure above 100 indicates that the female average is higher.

Reflections on Human Development

Table 8 Critical gender disparities in developing countries

HDI rank	Gap in primary enrolment ratio 1995	Gap in literacy rate 1995	Gap in economic activity rate 1995	Gap in earned income share 1995	Maternal mortality rate (per 100,000 live births) 1990	Female administrators and managers (%) 1992-96	Female professional and technical workers (%) 1992-96	Parliamentary seats occupied by women (as % of total) 1996
22 Cyprus	..	93	62	39	..	10	41	5
24 Hong Kong, China	..	92	58	34	7	20	38	..
25 Barbados	95	99	88	66	..	39	51	18
28 Singapore	99	90	64	47	10	20	41	3
29 Antigua and Barbuda	100	..	..	..	..	..	..	11
30 Bahamas	99	99	87	65	..	35	51	11
31 Korea, Rep. of	101	97	68	41	130	5	32	3
32 Chile	99	100	47	28	65	20	54	7
34 Brunei Darussalam	99	90	51	38	..	11	35	..
35 Costa Rica	102	100	42	37	60	23	45	16
36 Argentina	89	100	45	28	100	..	..	20
38 Uruguay	100	101	68	51	85	28	64	7
40 Trinidad and Tobago	100	98	49	37	90	40	52	19
41 Dominica	82	..	..	..	..	36	57	9
43 Bahrain	100	89	24	18	..	6	26	..
44 Fiji	100	95	38	28	..	10	45	6
45 Panama	98	99	51	39	55	28	49	10
46 Venezuela	84	98	50	37	120	23	57	6
48 United Arab Emirates	99	101	15	11	26	2	25	0
49 Mexico	100	95	46	35	110	23	40	14
50 Saint Kitts and Nevis	..	..	..	..	..	..	..	13
51 Grenada	100	..	..	..	..	32	53	..
53 Colombia	68	100	60	50	100	31	44	10
54 Kuwait	100	91	45	34	29	5	37	0
55 Saint Vincent	100	..	..	..	..	..	..	10
56 Seychelles	..	..	..	..	..	29	58	27
57 Qatar	78	101	15	11	..	..	..	..
58 Saint Lucia	100	..	..	..	..	..	..	14
59 Thailand	70	95	87	58	200	22	52	7
60 Mauritius	..	90	..	34	120	23	38	8
61 Malaysia	83	88	58	44	80	19	44	10
62 Brazil	102	100	54	41	220	..	63	7
63 Belize	99	100	30	23	..	37	39	11

Table 8 Critical gender disparities in developing countries (Cont.)

HDI rank		Gap in primary enrolment ratio 1995	Gap in literacy rate 1995	Gap in economic activity rate 1995	Gap in earned income share 1995	Maternal mortality rate (per 100,000 live births) 1990	Female administrators and managers (%) 1992–96	Female professional and technical workers (%) 1992–96	Parliamentary seats occupied by women (as % of total) 1996
64	Libyan Arab Jamahiriya	97	72	26	19	220	..	..	..
65	Suriname	96	96	47	35	..	12	62	16
66	Lebanon	94	95	39	29	300	..	..	2
69	Turkey	..	79	57	55	180	10	33	3
70	Saudi Arabia	89	70	15	11	130	..	..	..
71	Oman	96	65	16	12	190	..	..	..
73	Ecuador	91	96	36	23	150	28	47	..
75	Korea, Dem. People's Rep. of	..	100	77	58	70	..	..	..
78	Iran, Islamic Rep. of	93	76	32	23	120	4	33	4
81	Syrian Arab Rep.	91	65	35	25	180	3	37	10
82	Algeria	92	66	32	24	160	6	28	7
83	Tunisia	96	69	44	33	170	13	36	7
84	Jamaica	96	110	86	64	120	..	59	12
85	Cuba	101	99	61	46	95	19	48	23
86	Peru	91	88	42	31	280	26	40	11
87	Jordan	101	85	27	24	150	5	29	3
88	Dominican Rep.	105	100	41	32	110	21	50	10
89	South Africa	..	100	60	45	230	17	47	24
90	Sri Lanka	100	93	55	55	140	16	28	5
91	Paraguay	101	97	41	30	160	23	54	6
94	Samoa (Western)	81	..	..	..	..	12	47	4
95	Maldives	..	100	73	55	..	14	35	6
96	Indonesia	93	87	66	49	650	7	41	13
97	Botswana	..	74	85	64	250	36	61	9
98	Philippines	98	99	59	54	280	33	64	12
100	Guyana	100	99	49	37	..	13	48	20
101	Mongolia	107	87	88	66	65	..	..	8
106	China	98	81	82	62	95	12	45	21
107	Namibia	..	95	68	52	370	21	41	..
111	Guatemala	50	79	36	27	200	32	45	13
112	Egypt	99	61	40	33	170	12	30	2
114	El Salvador	66	95	52	51	300	29	43	11
115	Swaziland	..	97	60	48	..	26	60	8
116	Bolivia	96	84	60	37	650	28	42	6

REFLECTIONS ON HUMAN DEVELOPMENT

HDI rank	Gap in primary enrolment ratio 1995	Gap in literacy rate 1995	Gap in economic activity rate 1995	Gap in earned income share 1995	Maternal mortality rate (per 100,000 live births) 1990	Female administrators and managers (%) 1992–96	Female professional and technical workers (%) 1992–96	Parliamentary seats occupied by women (as % of total) 1996
117 Cape Verde	99	78	64	48	..	23	48	11
119 Honduras	101	100	42	32	220	53	45	8
120 Gabon	..	72	80	59	500	..	..	6
121 São Tomé and Principe	..	..	..	..	..	..	..	7
122 Viet Nam	80	95	97	72	160	..	..	19
123 Solomon Islands	..	100	88	65	..	3	27	2
124 Vanuatu	..	..	..	..	..	13	35	..
125 Morocco	75	55	53	39	610	22	31	1
126 Nicaragua	104	103	51	39	160	..	..	11
127 Iraq	89	64	22	16	310	13	44	..
128 Congo	..	81	77	57	890	6	29	2
129 Papua New Guinea	87	77	72	54	930	..	..	0
130 Zimbabwe	..	88	80	60	570	15	40	15
131 Myanmar	87	88	77	73	580	..	..	..
132 Cameroon	..	69	60	44	550	10	24	12
133 Ghana	..	71	103	16	740	9	36	..
134 Lesotho	118	77	58	44	610	33	57	11
135 Equatorial Guinea	96	76	55	41	..	2	27	9
136 Lao People's Dem. Rep.	87	64	89	66	650	..	..	9
137 Kenya	..	81	85	72	650	..	..	3
138 Pakistan	68	49	36	26	340	4	19	3
139 India	78	58	46	34	570	2	21	7
140 Cambodia	44	66	109	82	900	..	..	6
141 Comoros	66	79	74	54	..	..	..	0
142 Nigeria	78	70	56	43	1000	6	26	..
143 Congo, Dem. Rep. of	..	78	77	57	870	9	17	2
144 Togo	72	55	67	48	640	8	21	1
145 Benin	60	53	93	72	990	..	..	7
146 Zambia	97	83	83	65	940	6	32	10
147 Bangladesh	88	53	73	30	850	5	35	9
148 Côte d' Ivoire	..	60	49	35	810	..	..	8
149 Mauritania	51	53	..	58	930	8	21	1

Table 8 Critical gender disparities in developing countries (Cont.)

HDI rank		Gap in primary enrolment ratio 1995	Gap in literacy rate 1995	Gap in economic activity rate 1995	Gap in earned income share 1995	Maternal mortality rate (per 100,000 live births) 1990	Female administrators and managers (%) 1992–96	Female professional and technical workers (%) 1992–96	Parliamentary seats occupied by women (as % of total) 1996
150	Tanzania, U. Rep. of	..	72	98	90	770	..	..	17
151	Yemen	49	100	39	27	1,400	..	..	1
152	Nepal	58	34	68	50	1,500	..	..	5
153	Madagascar	113	100	81	60	490	..	..	4
154	Central African Rep.	56	76	88	63	700	9	19	4
155	Bhutan	25	50	66	48	1,600	..	..	2
156	Angola	..	52	87	64	1,500	..	..	10
157	Sudan	85	60	40	29	660	2	29	18
158	Senegal	..	54	74	54	1,200	..	..	12
159	Haiti	39	88	76	56	1,000	33	39	3
160	Uganda	91	68	91	68	1,200	..	..	18
161	Malawi	102	58	96	72	560	5	35	6
162	Djibouti	78	..	..	..	..	2	20	0
163	Chad	54	56	80	59	1,500	..	..	17
164	Guinea-Bissau	82	63	67	49	910	..	..	10
165	Gambia	72	47	81	60	1,100	15	24	..
166	Mozambique	77	40	94	72	1,500	11	20	25
167	Guinea	49	44	90	67	1,600	..	..	7
168	Eritrea	89	100	90	52	1,400	17	30	21
169	Ethiopia	29	56	69	50	1,400	11	24	..
170	Burundi	69	46	97	73	1,300	13	30	..
171	Mali	68	59	87	64	1,200	20	19	2
172	Rwanda	106	74	96	70	1,300	8	32	17
173	Burkina-Faso	67	31	87	66	930	14	26	9
174	Niger	36	32	79	59	1,200	8	8	..
175	Sierra Leone	100	40	57	..	1,800	8	32	6
	Aggregates								
	All developing countries	88	78	67	37	490	10	36	12
	Sub-Saharan Africa	79	72	74	52	977	10	28	12
	South Asia	77	58	51	38	551	3	21	7
	East Asia	102	82	86	42	95	11	45	20
	South-East Asia and Pacific	86	91	73	45	449	15	47	12

HDI rank	Gap in primary enrolment ratio 1995	Gap in literacy rate 1995	Gap in economic activity rate 1995	Gap in earned income share 1995	Maternal mortality rate (per 100,000 live births) 1990	Female administrators and managers (%) 1992–96	Female professional and technical workers (%) 1992–96	Parliamentary seats occupied by women (as % of total) 1996
Latin America and the Carribean	93	97	50	41	191	20	50	10
Arab States	91	66	37	20	396	..	..	4
Least developed countries	75	66	76	55	1,041	9	24	9
Industrial countries	..	85	75	60	30	37	50	4
World	..	..	68	47	435	14	39	13

Note: Gaps are expressed in relation to male average, which is indexed to equal 100. The smaller the figure the bigger the gap, the closer the figure to 100 the smaller the gap, and a figure above 100 indicates that the female average is higher. For columns 6 and 7, all regional aggregates, except for industrial countries, pertain to the year 1990.

Table 9 Key policy variables in industrial countries

HDI rank		Social security benefits expenditure (as % of GDP) 1993	ODA (as % of GNP) 1996	Bilateral aid for human priorities (%) 1989-91	Aid to least developed countries (as % of GNP) 1995-96	Ratio of income of highest 20% to lowest 20% 1981-93	CO_2 emissions (share of world total %) 1995	Commercial energy use (oil equivalent) GDP output per kg US$) 1994	Public expenditure on education (as % of GNP) 1996
1	Canada	21.7	0.32	9.0	0.07	7.1	1.9	2.0	7.3
2	France	..	0.48	3.6	0.10	7.5	1.5	4.4	5.9
3	Norway	19.6	0.85	17.9	0.33	5.9	0.3	4.6	8.3
4	Iceland	..	..	..	..	..	..	2.7	5.0
5	Finland	30.5	0.34	8.4	0.09	6.0	0.2	3.0	7.6
6	USA	10.5	0.12	11.3	0.02	8.9	24.1	2.6	5.3
7	Netherlands	..	0.81	13.8	0.23	4.5	0.6	3.7	5.3
8	Japan	11.5	0.20	3.4	0.04	4.3	5.0	6.2	3.8
9	New Zealand	20.2	0.21	..	0.05	8.8	0.1	2.8	6.7
10	Sweden	38.3	0.84	2.9	0.23	4.6	0.2	3.3	8.0
11	Spain	..	0.22	..	0.03	4.4	1.0	3.6	5.0
12	Belgium	..	0.34	..	0.09	4.6	0.5	3.2	5.7
13	Austria	24.5	0.24	6.9	0.04	..	0.3	5.4	5.5
14	United Kingdom	..	0.27	6.6	0.07	9.6	2.4	3.5	5.5
15	Australia	..	0.30	10.5	0.06	9.6	1.3	2.7	5.6
16	Ireland	14.0	0.31	14.9	0.13	8.6	0.1	3.9	6.3
17	Switzerland	19.4	0.34	..	0.10	..	0.2	7.4	5.5
18	Denmark	29.5	1.04	25.0	0.31	7.1	0.2	5.5	8.3
19	Germany	24.7	0.33	2.1	0.07	5.8	3.7	..	4.7
20	Greece	..	..	..	..	..	0.3	2.2	3.7
21	Italy	..	0.20	8.5	0.04	6.0	1.8	5.5	4.9
23	Israel	11.8	..	..	..	6.6	0.2	3.7	6.6
26	Luxembourg	..	0.44	..	0.06	..	..	2.3	..
27	Malta	..	..	..	..	..	..	..	5.2
33	Portugal	9.0	0.21	..	0.15	..	0.2	2.8	5.4
37	Slovenia	..	..	..	..	..	0.1	..	5.8
39	Czech Rep.	11.1	..	..	..	..	0.5	0.8	6.1
42	Slovakia	13.3	..	..	..	..	0.2	0.9	5.1
47	Hungary	17.3	..	..	..	3.2	0.2	1.0	6.6
52	Poland	17.0	..	..	..	3.9	1.5	0.7	4.6
67	Bulgaria	19.8	..	..	..	4.7	0.2	1.1	4.2
68	Belarus	12.0	..	..	..	..	0.3	0.8	5.6
72	Russian Fed.	..	..	..	..	11.4	8.0	0.5	4.1
74	Romania	16.9	..	..	..	..	0.5	0.7	3.2
76	Croatia	..	..	..	..	..	0.1	..	5.3
77	Estonia	..	..	..	..	..	0.1	0.7	6.9
79	Lithuania	..	..	..	..	..	0.1	0.8	6.1
80	Macedonia, FYR	..	..	..	..	..	..	..	5.5

Table 9 Key policy variables in industrial countries (Cont.)

HDI rank	Social security benefits expenditure (as % of GDP) 1993	ODA (as % of GNP) 1996	Bilateral aid for human priorities (%) 1989–91	Aid to least developed countries (as % of GNP) 1995–96	Ratio of income of highest 20% to lowest 20%) 1981–93	CO_2 emissions (share of world total %) 1995	Commercial energy use (oil equivalent) GDP output per kg US$) 1994	Public expenditure on education (as % of GNP) 1996
92 Latvia	..	..	..	..	..	..	1.2	6.3
93 Kazakstan	..	..	..	..	..	1.0	0.3	4.1
99 Armenia	..	..	..	..	..	..	1.4	..
102 Ukraine	..	..	..	..	..	1.9	0.4	7.7
103 Turkmenistan	..	..	..	..	..	0.1	..	..
104 Uzbekistan	..	..	..	..	..	0.4	0.3	9.5
105 Albania	..	..	..	..	..	..	2.4	3.4
108 Georgia	..	..	..	..	..	..	0.7	5.2
109 Kyrgyzstan	..	..	..	..	22.8	..	0.9	6.8
110 Azerbaijan	..	..	..	..	..	0.2	0.2	3.0
113 Moldova, Rep. of	..	..	..	..	..	..	..	6.1
118 Tajikistan	..	..	..	..	..	..	0.5	8.6
Aggregates								
Industrial	..	..	..	..	..	61.5	2.8	5.2
Eastern Europe and CIS	..	..	..	..	..	15.4	0.5	4.9
OECD	14.0	0.25	7.0	0.06	6.8[a]	52.0	3.3	5.1
European Union	..	0.37	9.2	0.09	6.1[b]	13.0	4.1	5.7
Nordic countries	30.8	0.79	8.7	0.24	5.7[c]	0.9	3.9	8.0
World	..	..	..	..	..	..	2.4	4.9

a,b and c pertain to the years 1980–91.

Table 10 Key policy variables in developing countries

HDI rank		Annual population growth rate (%) 1970–95	Contraceptive prevalence rate (%) 1990–95	Public expenditure on education (as % of GNP) 1995	Public expenditure on health (as % of GDP) 1990	Military expenditure (as % of combined education and health expenditure 1990–91	Commercial energy use (oil equivalent GDP output per kg US $) 1994	Total external debt (as % of GNP) 1995
22	Cyprus	0.8	..	4.4	..	17	2.8	..
24	Hong Kong, China	1.8	86	2.8	1.1	10	5.3	..
25	Barbados	0.4	55	7.2	..	5	4.2	..
28	Singapore	1.9	74	3.0	1.1	129	1.6	..
29	Antigua and Barbuda	0.6	53	..	..	..	2.9	..
30	Bahamas	2.0	62	..	..	..	1.5	..
31	Korea, Rep. of	1.4	79	3.7	2.7	60	1.8	..
32	Chile	1.6	..	2.9	3.4	68	2.3	43
34	Brunei Darussalam	3.3	..	..	..	125	1.0	..
35	Costa Rica	2.8	75	4.5	..	5	3.4	43
36	Argentina	1.5	..	4.5	2.5	51	2.7	33
38	Uruguay	0.5	..	2.8	2.5	38	4.6	32
40	Trinidad and Tobago	1.1	53	4.5	..	9	0.7	54
41	Dominica	0.1	50	..	..	..	7.4	..
43	Bahrain	3.8	54	4.8	..	41	0.8	..
44	Fiji	1.7	41	5.4	..	37	3.9	..
45	Panama	2.3	64	5.2	..	34	3.9	101
46	Venezuela	2.9	49	5.2	2.0	33	1.2	49
48	United Arab Emirates	9.6	..	1.8	..	44	..	..
49	Mexico	2.4	53	5.3	1.6	5	1.2	70
50	Saint Kitts and Nevis	−0.5	41	3.3	..	..	7.3	..
51	Grenada	−0.1	54	..	..	..	6.9	..
53	Colombia	2.1	72	3.5	1.8	57	2.1	28
54	Kuwait	3.3	35	5.6	..	88	2.0	..
55	Saint Vincent	1.0	58	..	..	..	8.8	..
56	Seychelles	1.3	..	7.5	..	..	2.9	..
57	Qatar	6.6	32	3.4	..	192	..	..
58	Saint Lucia	1.4	47	9.9	..	..	7.9	..
59	Thailand	2.0	74	4.2	1.1	71	2.2	25
60	Mauritius	1.2	75	4.3	..	4	6.3	46
61	Malaysia	2.5	48	5.3	1.3	38	1.7	43
62	Brazil	2.0	74	..	2.8	23	2.8	24
63	Belize	2.2	47	6.1	..	..	5.1	..
64	Libyan Arab Jamahiriya	4.1	40	..	..	71	..	..
65	Suriname	0.6	..	3.5	..	27	1.1	..

REFLECTIONS ON HUMAN DEVELOPMENT

HDI rank	Annual population growth rate (%) 1970–95	Contraceptive prevalence rate (%) 1990–95	Public expenditure on education (as % of GNP) 1995	Public expenditure on health (as % of GDP) 1990	Military expenditure (as % of combined education and health expenditure) 1990–91	Commercial energy use (oil equivalent GDP output per kg US $) 1994	Total external debt (as % of GNP) 1995
66 Lebanon	0.8	53	2.0	..	..	..	26
69 Turkey	2.2	63	3.4	1.5	87	1.9	44
70 Saudi Arabia	4.7	..	5.5	3.1	151	1.1	..
71 Oman	4.6	9	4.6	..	293	2.4	30
73 Ecuador	2.6	57	3.4	..	26	2.2	84
75 Korea, Dem. People's Rep. of	1.8	62	..	..	..	..	..
78 Iran, Islamic Rep. of	3.6	65	4.0	1.5	38	1.9	..
81 Syrian Arab Rep.	3.3	36	..	0.4	373	1.2	135
82 Algeria	2.9	52	..	5.4	11	2.6	83
83 Tunisia	2.3	60	6.8	3.3	31	2.4	57
84 Jamaica	1.1	62	8.2	..	8	1.5	135
85 Cuba	1.0	70	..	..	125	..	..
86 Peru	2.3	64	3.8	1.9	39	2.7	54
87 Jordan	3.5	35	6.3	1.8	138	1.5	126
88 Dominican Rep.	2.3	64	1.9	2.1	22	2.5	37
89 South Africa	2.5	50	6.8	3.2	41	1.0	..
90 Sri Lanka	1.5	66	3.1	1.8	107	5.1	64
91 Paraguay	2.9	56	2.9	1.2	42	3.5	29
94 Samoa (Western)	0.5	..	..	..	..	..	..
95 Maldives	3.0	..	8.4	..	..	4.8	..
96 Indonesia	2.0	55	..	0.7	49	1.9	57
97 Botswana	3.3	33	9.6	..	22	4.7	16
98 Philippines	2.4	40	2.2	1.0	41	1.9	52
100 Guyana	0.6	31	4.1	..	21	1.5	..
101 Mongolia	2.7	61	5.6	..	..	1.2	62
106 China	1.6	83	2.3	2.1	114	0.7	17
107 Namibia	2.7	29	9.4	..	23	..	..
111 Guatemala	2.9	31	1.7	2.1	31	4.3	22
112 Egypt	2.3	47	5.6	1.0	52	1.2	73
114 El Salvador	1.8	53	2.2	2.6	66	2.7	27
115 Swaziland	2.9	20	8.1	..	11	3.0	..
116 Bolivia	2.3	45	6.6	2.4	57	2.1	91
117 Cape Verde	1.5	..	..	..	..	2.1	..
119 Honduras	3.2	47	3.9	2.9	92	4.4	125
120 Gabon	3.1	..	..	..	51	5.5	122

Table 10 Key policy variables in developing countries (Cont.)

HDI rank		Annual population growth rate (%) 1970–95	Contraceptive prevalence rate (%) 1990–95	Public expenditure on education (as % of GNP) 1995	Public expenditure on health (as % of GDP) 1990	Military expenditure (as % of combined education and health expenditure) 1990–91	Commercial energy use (oil equivalent GDP output per kg US $) 1994	Total external debt (as % of GNP) 1995
121	Saõ Tomé and Principe	2.4	..	..	..	..	2.6	..
122	Viet Nam	2.2	65	2.7	1.1	..	7.5	130
123	Solomon Islands	3.5	..	..	..	..	3.9	..
124	Vanuatu	2.7	..	4.9	..	..	2.9	..
125	Morocco	2.2	50	5.6	0.9	72	2.9	71
126	Nicaragua	2.8	49	..	6.7	97	2.7	590
127	Iraq	3.1	14	..	..	271	..	..
128	Congo	2.9	..	5.9	..	37	2.8	366
129	Papua New Guinea	2.3	..	..	2.8	41	4.8	53
130	Zimbabwe	3.1	48	8.5	3.2	66	1.4	79
131	Myanmar	2.1	17	1.3	..	222	..	..
132	Cameroon	2.8	16	..	1.0	48	6.9	124
133	Ghana	2.8	20	..	1.7	12	4.5	95
134	Lesotho	2.6	23	5.9	..	48	..	45
135	Equatorial Guinea	1.3	..	1.8	..	..	5.2	..
136	Lao People's Dem. Rep.	2.4	19	2.4	1.0	..	9.1	125
137	Kenya	3.5	33	7.4	2.7	24	3.3	98
138	Pakistan	3.0	18	..	1.8	125	1.5	50
139	India	2.1	41	3.5	1.3	65	1.6	28
140	Cambodia	1.5	..	..	..	..	2.4	74
141	Comoros	3.3	21	3.9	3.3	..	11.8	..
142	Nigeria	2.9	6	..	1.2	33	2.2	141
143	Congo, Dem. Rep. of	3.3	8	..	0.8	71	..	..
144	Togo	2.9	12	5.6	2.5	39	6.9	121
145	Benin	2.8	16	3.1	2.8	..	18.0	82
146	Zambia	2.7	25	1.8	2.2	63	1.8	191
147	Bangladesh	2.3	45	2.3	1.4	41	3.1	56
148	Côte d' Ivoire	3.7	11	..	1.7	14	6.8	252
149	Mauritania	2.5	3	5.0	..	40	4.8	243
150	Tanzania, U. Rep. of	3.2	18	..	3.2	77	4.5	207
151	Yemen	3.5	7	7.5	1.5	197	..	155
152	Nepal	2.6	29	2.9	2.2	35	7.3	53
153	Madagascar	3.1	17	..	1.3	37	5.6	142
154	Central African Rep.	2.3	24	..	2.6	33	12.1	..
155	Bhutan	2.1	..	..	..	..	16.9	..

HDI rank	Annual population growth rate (%) 1970–95	Contraceptive prevalence rate (%) 1990–95	Public expenditure on education (as % of GNP) 1995	Public expenditure on health (as % of GDP) 1990	Military expenditure (as % of combined education and health expenditure) 1990–91	Commercial energy use (oil equivalent GDP output per kg US $) 1994	Total external debt (as % of GNP) 1995
156 Angola	2.7	..	..	..	208	7.0	275
157 Sudan	2.7	8	..	0.5	44	12.1	..
158 Senegal	2.8	13	3.6	2.3	33	6.3	82
159 Haiti	1.8	18	..	3.2	30	7.9	40
160 Uganda	2.8	15	..	1.6	18	22.6	64
161 Malawi	3.1	22	5.7	2.9	24	3.4	167
162 Djibouti	5.8	..	..	..	..	..	..
163 Chad	2.2	..	2.2	4.7	74	10.9	81
164 Guinea-Bissau	2.9	..	..	..	..	5.8	354
165 Gambia	3.6	12	5.5	..	11	4.9	..
166 Mozambique	2.5	..	..	4.4	121	3.3	444
167 Guinea	2.6	2	..	2.3	37	6.1	91
168 Eritrea	2.2	5	..	..	..	..	..
169 Ethiopia	2.7	4	4.7	2.3	190	7.0	100
170 Burundi	2.2	9	2.8	1.7	42	8.3	110
171 Mali	2.8	7	2.2	2.8	53	11.5	132
172 Rwanda	1.3	21	..	1.9	25	4.9	89
173 Burkina-Faso	2.7	8	3.6	7.0	30	16.0	55
174 Niger	3.2	4	..	3.4	11	7.4	91
175 Sierra Leone	1.9	..	..	1.7	23	2.4	160
Aggregates							
All Developing countries	2.1	56	3.8	2.0	63	1.5	41
Sub-Saharan Africa	2.8	16	6.3	2.4	44	1.9	121
South Asia[a]	2.3	41	3.6	1.4	61	1.8	35
East Asia[b]	1.8	82	2.7	2.2	85	1.0	17
South-East Asia[c]	2.2	53	..	1.0	66	2.3	50
Latin America and the Carribean[d]	2.3	64	4.5	2.4	29	2.0	38
Arab States[e]	2.8	37	5.1	2.9	108	..	..
Least developed countries	2.6	22	..	1.9	71	5.2	112
Industrial countries	0.7	70	5.2	..	33	2.8	..
World	1.7	58	4.9	2.0	38	2.4	39

a,b,c,d and e pertain to the years 1960–94.

Human Development Indicators
for South Asia

Table 1 Basic human development indicators

	India	Pakistan	Bangladesh	Nepal	Sri Lanka	Bhutan	Maldives	South Asia weighted average	Developing countries
Estimated population (millions) 1995	936	140	120	22	18	1.6	0.25	1238T	4550T
Annual population growth rate (%) 1990–95[a]	1.9	2.9	2.2	2.6	1.3	1.3	3.3	2.0	1.9
Life expectancy at birth (years) 1994	61	62	56	55	72	52	63	61	62
Adult literacy rate (%) 1995	52	38	38	28	90	42	93	49	71
Female literacy rate (%) 1995	38	24	26	14	87	28	93	36	62
Combined first, second, and third, level gross enrolment ratio (%) 1994	56	38	39	55	66	31	71	52	56
Infant mortality rate (per 1,000 live births) 1996	73	95	83	82	17	90	54	77	66
GNP per capita (US$) 1995	340	460	240	200	700	420	990	347	1,090
GNP growth rate (%) 1980–93	5.0	6.1	4.5	4.6	4.6	7.6	n/a	5.0	4.0
GNP per capita annual growth rate (%) 1980–93	3.0	3.1	2.1	2.0	2.7	4.9[b]	7.2	2.9	2.0
Real GDP per capita (PPP$) 1994	1,348	2,154	1,331	1,137	3,277	1,289	2,200	1,461	2,904
Human Development Index 1994[c]	0.446	0.445	0.368	0.347	0.711	0.338	0.611	0.440	0.576
Gender-related Development Index 1994[d]	0.419	0.392	0.339	0.321	0.694	n/a	0.600	0.410	0.555

a: Population figures for 1990 are also taken from UN: Age and Sex Distribution of Population 1992. (Medium variant). The population growth rate has been calculated by using the formula {[(new value/old value)1/n]-1}* 100.

b: Years 1985–95.

c: The Human Development Index (HDI) has three components: life expectancy at birth; educational attainment, comprising adult literacy, with two-thirds weight, and a combined primary, secondary and tertiary enrolment ratio, with one-third weight; and income.

d: The Gender-related Development Index (GDI) adjusts the HDI for gender equality in life expectancy, educational attainment and income.

Source: The above table has been taken from M. Haq, *Human Development in South Asia 1998*, Karachi: Oxford University Press, 1998.

Table 2 Human deprivation profile

	India	Pakistan	Bangladesh	Nepal	Sri Lanka	Bhutan	Maldives	South Asia weighted average	Developing countries
Population in poverty[a] 1995									
• Number (millions)	328	41	55	10	4	n/a	n/a	438	n/a
• As % of total population	35	29	46	45	22	n/a	n/a	35	n/a
Population without access to health services 1995									
• Number (millions)	140	63	66	n/a	1.3	0.60	0.1[b]	271	910
• As % of total population	15	45	55	n/a	7[c]	35	25[d]	22	20
Population without access to safe water 1995									
• Number (millions)	346	56	20	11	7.7	0.7	0.1[e]	442	1,320
• As % of total population	37	40	17	52	43	42[f]	49[g]	36	29
Population without access to sanitation 1995									
• Number (millions)	665	74	62	18	6.7	0.48	0.1	826	2,639
• As % of total population	71	53	52	82	37	30	34	67	58
Illiterate Adults[h] 1995									
• Number (millions)	291	49	45	9	1.2	0.6	0.01	395	851
• As % of total population	48	62	62	72	10	58	7.0	51	29
Illiterate Female Adults[i] 1995									
• Number (millions)	182	28	26	5.4	0.8	0.3	0.005	243	544
• As % of total adult female population	62	76	74	86	13	72	7	64	38
Malnourished children under 5 1995									
• Number (millions)	62	9	11	2	0.7	0.1	0.02	85	174
• As % of total population	53	38	67	49	38	38	39	53	31

Under 5 mortality rate (per 1,000 live births) 1996	111	136	112	116	19	127	76	113	97
Daily calorie supply[k] 1992									
• Quantity	2,395	2,316	2,019	1,957	2,275	n/a	2,624	2,340	2,546
• As % of total requirements	113	103	93	91	100	n/a	87	109	112
People with disabilities									
• Number (millions) 1992	1.80	6.50	0.92	0.63	0.07	n/a	n/a	9.92	n/a
• As % of total population	0.2	4.9	0.8	3.0	0.4	n/a	n/a	0.83	n/a

Note: The data for rows 2, 3, 4 and 7 is the same as observed for the period 1990–95 and 1990–96.
a: Figures for India and Pakistan are for 1993–94 and figures for Sri Lanka are for 1990–91. Population figures for all countries are for the year 1995; a, b, d, and g: Year 1991; c: Years 1985–95; e: Years 1990–96; h and i: calculated by using adult population and adult illiteracy rate; j: Years 1990–97 (moderate and severe underweight); k: the % requirements have been extrapolated from UNDP 1994b and subsequently used to arrive at the quantity figure.

Table 3 Education profile

	India	Pakistan	Bangladesh	Nepal	Sri Lanka	Bhutan	Maldives	South Asia weighted average	Developing countries (excluding South Asia)
Adult literacy rate (%) 1995									
• Male	66	50	49	41	93	56	93	62	80
• Female	38	24	26	14	87	28	93	36	63
• Total	52	38	38	28	90	42	93	49	72
Net primary enrolment (%) 1995									
• Male	98	36	89	80	100	58	100	88	86
• Female	76	25	78	46	100	47	100	69	82
• Total	87	31	84	63	100	53	100	79	84
Combined enrolment (%) 1994									
• Male	63	50	45	68	65	n/a	70	60	60
• Female	47	25	34	42	68	n/a	70	44	52
• Total	56	38	39	55	66	31	71	52	56
Technical education (as % of total secondary) 1988–91	1.6	1.6	0.7	n/a	n/a	n/a	1.0	1.5	n/a
Compulsory education (number of years)	8	5	5	5	11	n/a	n/a	7	7[a]
Educational imbalances									
• Drop-out ratio (%) 1991	37[b]	52	55[c]	48	8	27	7	41	18
• Pupil–teacher ratio 1995	64	38	71	39	28	31	31	60	31
• R&D scientists (per 1,000 people) 1988–95	0.1	0.1	n/a	n/a	0.2	n/a	n/a	0.1	0.3

Out of primary school children (millions) 1995	35	10	4	0.97	n/a	0.13	n/a	50	n/a
Private enrolment 1992 (as a % of total enrolment)									
• Primary level	n/a	13	14	6	2	n/a	53	12	n/a
• Secondary level	n/a	13	90	24	2	n/a	38	46	n/a
Public expenditure on education (as % of GNP)									
• 1960	2.3	1.1	0.6	0.4	3.8	n/a	n/a	2.0	2.5
• 1993/94	3.8	2.7	2.3	2.9	3.2	n/a	8.1	3.5	3.6
Primary school facilities (%)[d]									
• No or inadequate buildings	8	16	62	66	n/a	n/a	n/a	14	n/a
• Without safe drinking water	58	68	30	n/a	n/a	n/a	n/a	57	n/a
• Without latrines	84	70	50	67	n/a	n/a	n/a	80	n/a
• Without electricity	n/a	73	94	85	n/a	n/a	n/a	81	n/a
Culture and communications (per 1,000 people) 1994									
• Daily newspapers[e]	31	21	6	8	25	n/a	12	25	45
• Radios	81	88	47	35	201	17	118	79	184
• TV sets	60	20	10	2	70	n/a	40	50	145
• Telephone lines	11	15	2	4	10	7	48	10	34
• Volumes in public libraries[f]	n/a	n/a	5	n/a	28	n/a	n/a	n/a	n/a

a: Year 1988; b: Year 1993; c: Year 1990; d. Data pertain to the late 1980s and early 1990s; e and f: Year 1992.

Table 4 Health profile

	India	Pakistan	Bangladesh	Nepal	Sri Lanka	Bhutan	Maldives	South Asia weighted average	Developing countries
Population with access to health services (%) 1995	85	55	45	n/a	93	65	75	78	80
Population with access to safe water									
• 1985–87	57	44	46	29	40	n/a	n/a	54	55
• 1995	63	60	83	48	57	58	51	64	71
Population with access to sanitation									
• 1985–87	10	20	6	2	45	n/a	n/a	11	32
• 1995	29	47	48	18	63	70	76	33	42
Population per doctor									
• 1980	2,694	3,500	8,424	30,062	7,172	n/a	30,250[a]	3,875	n/a
• 1993	2,459	1,923	12,884	13,634	6,843	11,111[b]	20,330[c]	3,684	5,767
Population per nurse									
• 1980	4,674	5,870	14,750	7,783	1,262	n/a	570[d]	4,162	n/a
• 1993	3,323	3,300	11,549	2,257	1,745	6,667	600[e]	4,078	4,715
Daily calorie supply per capita 1992	2,395	2,316	2,019	1,957	2,275	n/a	2,624	2,340	2,546
Maternal mortality rate per 100,000 live births 1993	570	340	850	1,500	140	1,600	202[f]	583	384
Women using contraception (%)									
• 1970	12	4	22	1	8	n/a	n/a	12	18
• 1987–94	41	12	47	29	66	19	n/a	38	56
Public expenditure on health (as % of GDP)									
• 1960	0.5	0.3	n/a	0.2	2	n/a	2.4[g]	0.5	0.9
• 1990	1.3	1.8	1.4	2.2	1.8	n/a	5.5[h]	1.4	2.0
Pregnant women aged 15–49 with anaemia (%) 1975–91	88	n/a	58	n/a	n/a	30	n/a	85	n/a

a and d: Year 1970; b: Years 1988–91; c and e: Year 1984; f: Year 1995; g: Year 1982; h: Year 1992.

Table 5 Profile of women and children

	India	Pakistan	Bangladesh	Nepal	Sri Lanka	Bhutan	Maldives	South Asia weighted average	Developing countries
Female population 1995									
• Number (millions)	452	68	58	11	9	0.81	0.12	599	2,237
• As % of male	94	93	94	96	101	99	95	94	97
Adult female literacy (as % of male)									
• 1970	41	35	35	12	80	n/a	n/a	40	n/a
• 1995	58	48	53	34	94	50	100	58	78
Mean years of schooling (female as % of male)									
• 1980	32	25	29	33	79	33	77	32	53
• 1982	34	23	29	31	79	33	76	33	55
Female life expectancy (as % of male)									
• 1970	97	99	97	97	103	104	95	97	103
• 1994	100	103	100	98	107	107	96	100	105
Earned income share (female as % of male) 1994	35	26	30	49	53	n/a	55	34	46
Economic activity rate (age 15+) (female as % of male)									
• 1970	43	11	6	52	37	52	35	37	53
• 1995	50	38	76	68	54	66	77	52	67
Administrators and managers[b] (%) Female 1996	2.3	3.4	5.1	23	17	n/a	14	3.3	10
Share of females in parliament (%) 1996	7	3	9	5	5	2	6	7	12
Gender Development Index (GDI) 1994	0.419	0.392	0.339	0.321	0.694	n/a	0.600	0.410	0.555

Table 5 Profile of women and children (Cont.)

	India	Pakistan	Bangladesh	Nepal	Sri Lanka	Bhutan	Madives	South Asia weighted average	Developing countries
Gender Empowerment Measure (GEM) 1994	0.228	0.189	0.273	n/a	0.307	n/a	0.330	0.229	0.367
Population under 18, 1995									
• Number (millions)	385	71	56	11	6.7	0.8	0.14[a]	531	1827
• As % of total population	41	51	47	50	37	50	56	43	40
Population under 18, 1995									
• Number (millions)	117	24	17	3.6	1.8	0.3	0.05	164	560
• As % of total population	13	17	14	16	10	19	20	14	12
Under 5 mortality rate (per 1,000 live births)									
• 1960	236	226	247	315	130	300	258	236	216
• 1996	111	136	112	116	19	127	76	114	97
Births attended by trained health personnel (%) 1990–96	34	19	14	7	94	15	61	31	54
Child economic activity rate (% age 10–14) 1995	14	18	30	45	2	55	6	17	16
One year olds fully immunized against tuberculosis (%)									
• 1980	14	9	1	43	63	9	8	13	n/a
• 1995–96	96	93	88	73	88	98	98	94	88
One year olds fully immunized against measles (%)									
• 1980	1	3	2	2	0	18	30	1	n/a
• 1995–96	81	78	59	45	86	86	94	78	78
Low birth weight infants (%) 1990–94	33	25	50	26[c]	25	n/a	20	33	18

a: Year 1996; b: Data refer to the latest year; c: Year 1990.

Table 6 Profile on Military Spending

	India	Pakistan	Bangladesh	Nepal	Sri Lanka	Bhutan	Maldives	South Asia weighted average	Developing countries
Defence expenditure (US$ millions), 1993 prices									
• 1985	7,207	2,088	308	22	214	n/a	n/a	9,839	189,727
• 1995	9,360	2,900	400	40	670	n/a	n/a	13,370	162,160
Defence expenditure annual % increase 1985–95	2.6	3.3	2.6	6.2	12	n/a	n/a	3.1	-1.6
Defence expenditure (as % of GNP)									
• 1985	2.5	5.1	1.3	0.7	2.6	n/a	n/a	3.0	7.2
• 1995	2.8	5.2	1.4	0.9	5.3	n/a	n/a	3.4	3.3
Defence expenditure (as % of Central government expenditure)									
• 1985	19.8	30.6	9.4	6.7	1.7	n/a	n/a	21.3	n/a
• 1995	14.5	26.9[a]	17.6[b]	5.9[c]	2.6	n/a	n/a	16.7	n/a
Defence expenditure per capita (US$), 1993 prices									
• 1985	9.4	22	3.1	1.3	14	n/a	n/a	9.9	52
• 1995	10	21	3.3	1.8	37	n/a	n/a	10.8	36
Defence expenditure (as % of education & health expenditure)									
• 1960	68	393	n/a	67	17	n/a	n/a	113	143
• 1990–1	65	125	41	35	107	n/a	n/a	72	60

Table 6 Profile on Military Spending (Cont.)

	India	Pakistan	Bangladesh	Nepal	Sri Lanka	Bhutan	Maldives	South Asia weighted average	Developing countries
Armed forces personnel (no. in thousands)									
• 1985	1,260	484	91	25	22	n/a	n/a	1,882	16,027
• 1995	1,145	590	115	35	37	n/a	n/a	1,922	14,570
• % Increase (85–95)	−9.1	22	26	40	68	n/a	n/a	2.1	−9.1
Number of soldiers 1995									
• per 1,000 population	1.2	4.2	1.0	1.6	2.1	n/a	n/a	1.6	3.2
• per 1,000 doctors[d]	4,000	9,000	6,000	35,000	25,000	n/a	n/a	5,594	18,500
• per 1,000 teachers[e]	300	1,500	300	400	400	n/a	n/a	434	600
Employment in arms 1995 production (000s)	250	50	n/a	n/a	n/a	n/a	n/a	300	4,400
Military holdings[f] 1995 Index (1985=100)	132	154	213	200	1,111	n/a	n/a	147	108
Aggregate number of heavy weapons 1995	7,770	5,400	430	50	300	n/a	n/a	13,950	n/a

a, b, c: Year 1993; d and e: Year 1990; f: Military holdings includes combat aircraft, artillery, ships and tanks that a country possesses.

Table 7 Profile of wealth and poverty

	India	Pakistan	Bangladesh	Nepal	Sri Lanka	Bhutan	Maldives	South Asia weighted average	Developing countries
Total GDP (US$ billions) 1995	324	61	29	4.2	13	0.2[a]	0.2[b]	432	5,393
Real GDP per capita (PPP$) 1994	1,348	2,154	1,331	1,137	3,277	1,289	2,200	1,461	2,904
GNP per capita (US$) 1995	340	460	240	200	700	420	990	347	1,090
Income share:ratio of highest 20% to lowest 20% 1990–96	5.0	4.7	4.0	5.9	4.4	n/a	n/a	4.9	n/a
Population in poverty 1995									
• Number (millions)	328	41	55	10	4	n/a	n/a	438	n/a
• As % of total population	35	29	46	45	22	n/a	n/a	35	n/a
People in poverty (%) 1990									
• Urban	38	20	56	19	15	n/a	n/a	37	n/a
• Rural	49	31	51	43	36	n/a	n/a	47	n/a
Social security benefits expenditure (as % of GDP) 1993	0.3	0.2	n/a	n/a	2.5	n/a	n/a	0.4	n/a
Public expenditure on education and health (as % of GNP) 1990	5.0	4.5	3.7	5.1	5.1	n/a	7	4.8	5.9
Gross domestic investment (as % of GDP) 1994	23	20	14	21	27	n/a	n/a	22	27
Gross domestic savings (as % of GDP) 1994	21	17	8	12	15	7	n/a	19	27
Industry (as % of GDP) 1994	28	25	18	21	25	27	26	27	36

Table 7 Profile of wealth and poverty (Cont.)

	India	Pakistan	Bangladesh	Nepal	Sri Lanka	Bhutan	Maldives	South Asia weighted average	Developing countries
Tax revenue (as % of GNP) 1994	10	13	n/a	8[c]	17	6[d]	n/a	11	14
Exports (as % of GDP) 1994	12	16	12	25	35	28	18	13	26
Debt service ratio (debt service as % of exports of goods and services) 1994	27	35	16	8	9	8[e]	4	27	20
Total net official development assistance received (US$ millions) 1995									
• Quantity	1,738	805	1,269	430	553	73	55	4,923	59,876
• (as % of GNP) 1994	0.6	1.5	4.8	10	48.0	26.8	22.0	1.3	1.4
Total external debt (US$ billions) 1994	99	30	17	2.3	7.8	0.09[f]	0.1	155	1,444

a, b and c: Year 1993; d: Year 1990; e: Year 1991; f: Year 1992.

Table 8 Profile of demography, food security and natural resources

	India	Pakistan	Bangladesh	Nepal	Sri Lanka	Bhutan	Maldives	South Asia weighted average	Developing countries
Population (in millions)									
• 1960	442	50	51	9	10	1	0.1	563T	2,070T
• 1995	936	140	120	22	18	1.6	0.25	1,238T	4,550T
Population (annual growth rate) (%)									
• 1960–70	2.3	2.8	2.6	2.0	2.4	1.8	2.0	2.4	2.5
• 1970–80	2.2	2.6	2.8	2.6	1.7	2.0	2.7	2.3	2.2
• 1980–90	2.1	3.6	2.1	2.6	1.5	2.2	3.2	2.3	2.1
• 1990–95	1.9	2.9	2.2	2.6	1.3	1.3	3.3	2.0	1.9
Population doubling date (at current growth rate) 1994	2,036	2,019	2,037	2,021	2,065	2,020	2,014	2,038	2,036
Crude birth rate (per 1,000)									
• 1960	43	49	47	44	36	42	41	44	42
• 1996	26	37	27	37	18	41	42	28	26
• % decline 1960–96	40	24	43	16	50	2.4	-2.4	36	38
Crude death rate (per 1,000)									
• 1960	21	23	22	26	9	26	21	21	20
• 1996	9	8	10	12	6	14	8	9	9
• % decline 1960–96	57	65	55	54	33	46	62	57	55
Total fertility rate									
• 1960	6.0	7.0	6.7	6.0	5.4	6.0	7.0	6.1	6.0
• 1996	3.2	5.2	3.2	5.1	2.1	5.9	6.8	3.4	3.2
• % decline 1960–95	47	26	52	15	61	2	3	43	47
Total labour force (in millions) 1995	398	46	60	10	8	n/a	n/a	522	2,263

Table 8 Profile of demography, food security and natural resources (Cont.)

	India	Pakistan	Bangladesh	Nepal	Sri Lanka	Bhutan	Maldives	South Asia weighted average	Developing countries
Male labour force (in millions) 1995	271	34	35	6	5	n/a	n/a	351	1,358
Female labour force (in millions) 1995	127	12	25	4	3	n/a	n/a	171	905
% annual growth in labour force									
• 1970–80	1.7	2.7	2.0	1.8	2.3	n/a	n/a	1.8	n/a
• 1980–95	1.9	3.1	2.5	2.4	2.2	n/a	n/a	2.1	2.0
Unemployed/Underemployed labour 1993 (as a % of total)	22[a]	13[b]	12	43[c]	16	6	1	21	n/a
Employed labour force (%)									
• Agriculture (1990–92)	62	47	59	93	49	92	25	60	58
• Industry (1990–92)	11	20	13	1	21	3	32	12	15
• Services (1990–92)	27	33	28	6	30	5	43	29	27
Food production per capita 1993 (1980=100)	123	118	97	114	81	n/a	84	119	123
Food imports per capita 1993 (1980=100)	46	114	86	137	553	n/a	n/a	69	n/a
Food aid (US$, millions) 1992	99	190	240	6	63	3	1	602T	3,130T
Land area (1,000 ha.) 1993	328,759	79,610	14,400	14,080	6,561	4,700	30	448,140T	7,658,208T
As % of land area 1993									
• Forest and woodland	21	4	13	41	32	66	3	19	29
• Arable land	51	26	66	17	14	2	10	45	9
Irrigated land (as % of arable land area) 1994	28	80	34	36	29	30[d]	n/a	38	26
Deforestation (1,000 ha. per year) 1980–89	1,500	9	8	84	58	1	n/a	1,106	866
Reforestation (1,000 ha. per year) 1980–89	138	7	17	4	13	1	n/a	103	797

a: Year 1987–88; b: Year 197; c: Year 1984–5; d: year 1993.

Selected Bibliography

Extensive literature has emerged in recent years on the subject of human development and related policy issues. This bibliography gives a selected list of books and articles.

Adamu, Sam O. 1993. "Disaggregated Human Development Index within Nigeria." Background paper for *Human Development Report 1994*. UNDP, New York.

ADB (Asian Development Bank). 1997. *Emerging Asia: Changes and Challenges*. Manila.

Adelman, Irma, and Sherman Robinson. 1978. *Income Distribution Policy in Developing Countries: A Case Study of Korea*. New York: Oxford University Press.

Adelman, Irma, and Cynthia Taft-Morris. 1973. *Economic Growth and Social Equity in Developing Countries*. Stanford, Calif: Stanford University Press.

Agarwal, Bina. 1994. *A Field of One's Own: Gender and Land Rights in South Asia*. New York: Cambridge University Press.

Ahmad, Yusuf, J., Salah El Serafy and Ernst Lutz, eds. 1989. *Environmental Accounting for Sustainable Development*. Washington, D.C.: World Bank.

Akder, Halis. 1990. "Turkey: Country Profile; Human Development Indices for All Turkish Provinces." Middle East Technical University, Department of Economics, and UNDP, Ankara.

———. 1993. "Disaggregated Human Development Index: A Means to Closing Gaps." Paper presented at seminar on the Uses of the Human Development Index, 17–18 February, UNDP, New York.

Alderman, Harold, Jere Behrman, David Ross, and Richard Sabot. 1996. "Decomposing the Gender Gap in Cognitive Skills in a Poor Rural Economy." *Journal of Human Resources* 31(1): 229-54.

Alderman, Harold, and Paul Gertler. 1989. *The Substitutability of Public and Private Health Care for the Treatment of Children in Pakistan.* Living Standards Measurement Study Working Paper 57. Washington, D.C.: World Bank.

Amjad, Rashid, ed. 1989. *To the Gulf and Back: Studies on the Economic Impact of Asian Labour Migration.* Asian Employment Programme. New Delhi: International Labour Organization.

Anand, Sudhir, and Martin Ravallion. 1993a. "Human Development in Poor Countries: On the Role of Private Incomes and Public Serives." *Journal of Economic Perspectives* 7(1): 133-50.

————. 1993b. "Inequality between and within Nations." Harvard University, Center for Population and Development Studies, Cambridge, Mass.

Anand, Sudhir, and Amartya Sen. 1994a. "Human Development Index: Methodology and Measurement." Human Development Report Office Occasional Paper 12. UNDP, New York.

————. 1994b. "Sustainable Human Development: Concepts and Priorities." Human Development Report Office Occasional Paper 8. UNDP, New York.

————. 1995. "Gender Inequality in Human Development: Theories and Measurement." Human Development Report Office Occasional Paper 19. UNDP, New York.

————. 1997. "Concepts of Human Development and Poverty: A Multidimensional Perspective." Background paper for *Human Development Report 1997.* UNDP, New York.

Ananta, Aris, Salman Taufik and Susanne Yosephine. 1990. "Financial Aspect of Human Development: A Case Study in Indonesia." UNDP, New York.

Appleyard, Reginald T. 1990. "South-North Migration." Summary report by the rapporteur at the Ninth International Organization for Migration Seminar on Migration, 4–6 December, Geneva.

Ashe, Jeffrey, and Christopher E. Cosslett. 1989. *Credit for the Poor.* New York: UNDP.

Atkinson, Anthony B. 1970. "On the Measurement of Inequality." *Journal of Economic Theory*, no. 3: 34–57.

Aturupane, Harsha, Paul Glewwe and Paul Isenman. 1994. "Poverty, Human Development and Growth: An Emerging Consensus?" Paper presented at American Economic Association meeting, 3 January, Boston.

Avramovic, Dragoslav. 1992. "Developing Countries in the International Economic System: Their Problems and Prospects in the Markets for Finance, Commodities, Manufactures and Services." Human Development Report Office Occasional Paper 3. UNDP, New York.

Banuri, Tariq, Shahrukh Rafi Khan and Moazzam Mahmood, eds. 1997. *Just Development: Beyond Adjustment with a Human Face.* Karachi: Oxford University Press.

Bardhan, Pranab K., and T.N. Srinivasan, eds. 1988. *Rural Poverty in South Asia.* New York: Columbia University Press.

Barro, Robert J., and Xavier Salai-i-Martin. 1995. *Economic Growth.* New York: McGraw-Hill.

Bartelmus, Peter. 1990. "Sustainable Development: A Conceptual Framework." DIESA Working Paper Series. United Nations, New York.

Baster, Nancy, ed. 1972. *Measuring Development: The Role and Adequacy of Development Indicators.* London: Frank Cass.

———. 1987. *Malnutrition: What Can Be Done? Lessons from World Bank Experience.* Baltimore and London: Johns Hopkins University Press.

Besley, Timothy, and Ravi Kanbur. 1988. "Food Subsidies and Poverty Alleviation." *Economic Journal*, no. 98: 701–19.

Bhargava, A., and S.R. Osmani. 1996. "Health and Nutrition in Emerging Asia." Background Paper for *Emerging Asia: Changes and Challenges.* Asian Development Bank, Manila.

Bloom, David E., Neil G. Bennet, Ajay S. Mahal and Waseem Noor. 1996. *The Impact of Aids on Human Development.* New Delhi: UNDP.

Botswana, Ministry of Finance and Development Planning, UNDP and UNICEF. 1993. *Planning for People: A Strategy for Accelerated Human Development in Botswana.* Gabarone, Botswana: Ministry of Finance and Development Planning.

Boutros-Ghali, Boutros. 1992. "An Agenda for Peace: Peacemaking and Peace Keeping." Report of the Secretary-General Pursuant to the Statement Adopted by the Summit Meeting of the Security Council, 31 January, United Nations, New York. DPI/1247.

Brundenius, Claes. 1981. "Growth and Equity: The Cuban Experience, 1959–1980." *World Development* 9(11/12): 1083–96.

Bruno, Michael, Martin Ravallion and Lyn Squire. 1996. "Equity and Growth in Developing Countries: Old and New Perspectives on the Policy Issue." Policy Research Working Paper 1563. World Bank, Washington, D.C.

Brundtland, Gro Harlem. 1993. "Population, Environment and Development." The Rafael M. Salas Memorial Lecture, 28 September, United Nations Population Fund, New York.

Carr, Marilyn, Martha Chen, and Renana Jhabvala. 1996. *Speaking Out: Women's Economic Empowerment in South Asia.* London: Intermediate Technology Publications.

Cassen, Robert, and others. 1987. *Does Aid Work?* New York: Oxford University Press.

Caton, Carol L.M. 1990. *Homeless in America.* New York: Oxford University Press.

Cernea, Michael M. 1988. *Nongovernmental Organizations and Local Development.* World Bank Discussion Paper 40. Washington, D.C.

Cernea, Michael M., ed. 1985. *Putting People First: Sociological Variables in Rural Development.* New York: Oxford University Press.

Chambers, Robert. 1997. *Whose Reality Counts? Putting the First Last.* London: Intermediate Technology Publications.

Cheema, G. Shabbir, ed. 1986. *Reaching the Urban Poor: Project Implementation in Developing Countries.* Boulder, Colo.: Westview.

Chenery, Hollis, Montek S. Ahluwalia, C.L.G. Bell, John H. Duloy and Richard Jolly. 1974. *Redistribution with Growth.* London: Oxford University Press.

Chernichovsky, Dov, and Oey Astra Meesook. 1984. *Poverty in Indonesia: A Profile.* World Bank Staff Working Paper 671. Washington, D.C.

Clark, John. 1990. *Democratizing Development: The Role of Voluntary Organizations.* West Hartford, Conn.: Kumarian.

Cohen, C. Desmond. 1989. "Trends in Human Development in the United Kingdom." University of Sussex School of Social Sciences, Brighton, United Kingdom.

———. 1990. "Human Development in Industrial Countries: The UK and the USA." Study prepared for UNDP, New York.

Colclough, Christopher, and Keith Lewin. 1993. *Educating All the Children: Strategies for Primary Schooling in the South.* Oxford: Clarendon.

Commission on Global Governance. 1995. *Our Global Neighbourhood.* New York: Oxford University Press.

Commonwealth Secretariat. 1989. *Engendering Adjustment for the 1990s.* Report of a Commonwealth Expert Group on Women and Structural Adjustment. London.

Cornia, G. Andrea. 1989. "Investing in Human Resources: Health, Nutrition and Development for the 1990s." *Journal of Development Planning,* no. 19: 159–87.

Cornia, G. Andrea, Richard Jolly, and Frances Stewart, eds. 1987. *Adjustment with a Human Face.* 2 vols. Oxford: Clarendon.

Cornia, G. Andrea, and Frances Stewart. 1990. "The Fiscal System, Adjustment and the Poor." Queen Elizabeth House Development Studies Working Paper 29. Oxford University, Oxford.

Cornia, G. Andrea, Rolph van der Hoeven, and Thandika Mkandawire, eds. Forthcoming. *Adjustment, Stagnant Economic Structures and Human Development in Sub-Saharan Africa: Policy Conflicts and Alternatives.* UNICEF Study. London: Macmillan.

Dalal, K.L., ed. 1991. *Human Development: An Indian Perspective.* New Delhi: Vikas for UNDP.

Dasgupta, Partha. 1993. *An Inquiry into Well-Being and Destitution.* New York: Oxford University Press.

Dasgupta, Partha, and Martin Weale. 1992, "On Measuring the Quality of Life." *World Development* 20(1): 119–31.

Deger, Saadet, and Somnath Sen. 1990. *Military Expenditure: The Political Economy of International Security.* New York: Oxford University Press.

Deininger, Klaus, and Lyn Squire. 1996. "A New Data Set Measuring Income Inequality." *The World Bank Economic Review* 10(3): 565–91.

Dell, Sidney. 1990. "Reforming the World Bank for the Tasks of the 1990s." Lecture at the Exim Bank of India, 5 March, Bombay.

Demery, David, and Lionel Demery. 1992. *Adjustment and Equity in Malaysia.* Development Centre Studies. Paris: OECD.

Demery, Lionel, and Tony Addison. 1987. *The Alleviation of Poverty under Structural Adjustment.* Washington, D.C.: World Bank.

Desai, Meghnad. 1989. "Methodological Problems of Measurement of Poverty in Latin America." London School of Economics, Department of Economics, London.

———. 1991. "Human Development: Concept and Measurement." *European Economic Review*, no. 35: 350–57.

———. 1994. "Greening of the HDI?" Background paper for *Human Development Report 1994*. UNDP, New York.

de Soto, Hernando. 1990. *The Other Path*. New York: Perennial Library.

de Valk, P., K.H. Weakwete, eds. 1990. *Decentralising for Participatory Planning*. Aldershot, United Kingdom: Gower.

De Vylder, Stefan. 1995. "Sustainable Human Development and Macroeconomics: Strategic Links and Implications." UNDP Discussion Paper. New York.

Drèze, Jean, and Amartya K. Sen. 1989. *Hunger and Public Action*. Oxford: Clarendon.

———. 1995. *India: Economic Development and Social Opportunity*. New Delhi: Oxford University Press.

———. 1998. *Indian Development: Selected Regional Perspectives*. New Delhi: Oxford University Press.

El-laithy, Heba. 1993. "The Disaggregated Human Development Index for Egypt." Background paper for *Human Development Report 1994*. UNDP, New York.

Emmerij, Louis, ed. 1997. *Economic and Social Development into the XXI Century*. Washington, D.C.: Inter-American Development Bank.

EUROSTAT (Statistical Office of the European Community). 1990. "Inequality and Poverty in Europe." Rapid Reports: Population and Social Conditions 7, Luxembourg.

Faber, Mike, and Stephany Griffith-Jones, eds. 1990. "Approaches to the Third World Debt Reduction." *IDS Bulletin* 21(2).

FAO (Food and Agriculture Organization). 1986. *The Dynamics of Rural Poverty*. Rome.

———. 1988. *Rural Poverty in Latin America and the Carribbean*. Rome.

Fei, John C.H., Gustav Ranis, and Shirley W.Y. Kuo. 1979. *Growth and Equity: The Taiwan Case*. New York: Oxford University Press.

Fields, Gary S. 1980. "A Compendium of Data on Inequality and Poverty for the Developing World." Cornell University, Department of Economics, Ithaca, N.Y.

Folbre, Nancy. 1996. "Engendering Economics: New Perspectives on Women, Work, and Demographic Change." In Michael Bruno and Boris Pleskovic, eds, *Annual World Bank Conference on Development Economics 1995*. Washington, D.C.: World Bank.

Freedom House. 1995. "Freedom in the World." New York.

Genberg, Hans. 1991. "Debt for Health Swaps: A Source for Additional Finance for the Health Sector?" Graduate Institute of International Studies, Geneva.

Gertler, Paul, and Jacques van der Gaag. 1988. *Measuring the Willingness to Pay for Social Services in Developing Countries.* Living Standards Measurement Study Working Paper 45. Washington, D.C.: World Bank.

Ghai, Dharam. 1989. "Participatory Development: Some Perspectivies from Grass-roots Experiences." *Journal of Development Planning,* no. 19: 215–46.

Goodland, Robert, Herman Daly, and Salah El Seragy, eds. 1991. "Environmentally Sustainable Development: Building on Brundtland." Environment Department Working Paper 46. World Bank, Washington, D.C.

Greve, John, and E. Currie. 1990. *Homelessness in Britain.* York: Joseph Rowntree Memorial Turst.

Griffin, Charles C. 1988. *User Charges for Health Care in Principle and Practice.* EDI Seminar Paper 37. Washington, D.C.: World Bank.

Griffin, Keith. 1989. *Alternative Strategies for Economic Development.* London: Macmillian.

———. 1991. "Foreign Aid after the Cold War." *Economic Development and Cultural Change* 22(4): 645–85.

Griffin, Keith, and Azizur Rahman Khan. 1992. "Globalization and the Developing World: An Essay on the International Dimensions of Development in the Post-Cold War Era." Human Development Report Office Occasional Paper 2. UNDP, New York.

Griffin, Keith, and John Knight, eds. 1989. "Human Development in the 1980s and Beyond." *Journal of Development Planning* 19 (special issue).

———. 1990. *Human Development and the International Development Strategy for the 1990s.* London: Macmillan.

Griffith-Johnes, Stephany. 1990a. "Debt Reduction with a Human Face: The IDB and UNICEF Initiative." *Development,* no. 1: 50–53.

———. 1990b. "Debt Relief for Child Development." *IDS Bulietin* 21(2): 78–81.

HABITAT (United Nations Centre for Human Settlements). 1996. *An Urbanized Worlds: Global Report on Human Settlements.* Nairobi.

Haq, Khadija, and Uner Kirdar, eds. 1986. *Human Development: The Neglected Dimension.* North-South Roundtable and UNDP Development Study Programme. Vol. 1. Islamabad.

———. 1987. *Human Development: Adjustment and Growth.* North-South Roundtable and UNDP Development Study Programme. Vol. 2. Islamabad.

———. 1988. *Managing Human Development.* North-South Roundtable and UNDP Development Study Programme. Vol. 3, Islamabad.

———. 1989. *Development for People: Goals and Strategies for the Year 2000.* North-South Roundtable and UNDP Development Study Programme. Vol. 4. Islamabad.

Haq, Mahbub ul. 1976. *The Poverty Curtain: Choices for the Third World.* New York: Columbia University Press.

———. 1993. "Bretton Woods Institutions: The Vision and the Reality." Paper presented at the Bretton Woods Conference, 1–3 September, Bretton Woods, N.H.

Harpham, Trudy, Patrick Vaughan and Susan Rifkin. 1985. *Health and the Urban Poor in Developing Countries.* EPC Publication 5. London: London School of Hygiene and Tropical Medicine.

Henry, Ralph M. 1991. "Trinidad and Tobago: Human Development Indicators." Paper prepared for UNDP. Port of Spain, Trinidad and Tobago.

Hewett, Daniel P. 1991. "Military Expenditures in the Developing World." *Finance and Development* 28(3): 22–25.

Homer-Dixon, Thomas F. 1991. "On the Threshold: Environmental Changes as Causes of Acute Conflict." *International Security* 16 (2): 76–116.

Hossain, Mahabub. 1988. *Credit for Alleviation of Rural Poverty: The Grameen Bank in Bangladesh.* International Food Policy Research Institute Research Report 65. Washington, D.C.

Human Development Centre. 1997. *Human Development in South Asia 1997.* Karachi: Oxford University Press.

———. 1998. *Human Development in South Asia 1998.* Karachi: Oxford University Press.

Humana, Charles, 1986. *The Worlds Guide to Human Rights.* New York: Facts on File.

Husain, Ishrat, and Ishac Diwan, eds. 1989. *Dealing with the Debt Crisis.* Washington, D.C.: World Bank.

ILO (International Labour Organization). 1972. *Employment, Incomes and Equality: A Strategy for Increasing Productive Employment in Kenya.* Geneva.

————. 1988. "Meeting the Social Debt." Programma regional del empleo para America Latina y el Caribe. ILO World Employment Programme, Santiago.

————. 1990. *Employment and Equity: The Challenge of the 1990s*. Programa regional del empleo para America Latina y el Caribe. Santiago: ILO World Employment Programme.

Ines de Neufville, Judith. 1986. "Human Rights Reporting as a Policy Tool: An Examination of the State Department Country Reports." *Human Rights Quarterly*, no. 84: 681–99.

Institute of Strategic and International Studies. 1993. "Disaggregated Human Development Index of Malaysia." Background paper for *Human Development Report 1994*. UNDP, New York.

IPU (Inter-Parliamentary Union). 1997. *Democracy Still in the Making*. Geneva.

Jahan, Selim. 1991. *Female Employment Opportunities and Job Entry Qualifications in Bangladesh*. Dhaka: ILO.

————. 1992. "The US Foreign Aid in the Nineties." *Journal of International and Strategic Studies* (October): 136–59.

Jayawardana, Lal. 1991. *A Global Environmental Compact for Sustainable Development: Resource Requirements and Mechanisms*. Helsinki: World Institute for Development Economics Research.

Jazairy, Idris, Mohiuddin Alamgir, and Theresa Panuccio. 1992. *The State of World Rural Poverty: An Inquiry into Its Causes and Consequences*. International Fund for Agricultural Development. New York: New York University Press.

Kaul, Inge. 1993. "Making the Human Development Concern Operational: A 10-Point Agenda." UNDP, New York.

Kaul, Inge, and Roberto Savio. 1993. "Global Human Security: A New Political Framework for North-South Relations." Society for International Development, Rome and New York.

Kelley, Allen C. 1991. "The Human Development Index: Handle with Care." *Population and Development Review* 17(2): 315–24.

Kennedy, Paul. 1993. *Preparing for the Twenty-First Century*. New York: Random House.

Khan, Akhtar Hameed. 1983. "Orangi Project: A Task Bigger than Colombo." *Pakistan and Gulf Economist* 2(24): 12–18.

Khatib, H. 1993. "The Human Development Index as a Policy and Planning Tool." Paper presented at seminar on the Uses of the Human Development Index, 17–18 February, UNDP, New York.

————. 1994. "*Human Development Report 1990*: Jordan—A Follow-up." Paper prepared for UNDP. Amman.

Kirdar, Uner, and Leonard Silk, eds. 1994. *A World Fit for People.* New York: New York University Press.

———, eds. 1995. *People: From Impoverishment to Empowerment.* New York: New York University Press.

Klugman, Jeni, 1992. "Decentralization: A Survey of Literature." Background paper for *Human Development Report 1993.* UNDP, New York.

Klugman, Jeni, Frances Stewart, and A.H. Helmsing. 1992. "Decentralization in Zimbabwe." Background paper for *Human Development Report 1993.* UNDP New York.

Kynch, Jocelyn, and Amartya K. Sen. 1983. "Indian Women: Wellbeing and Survival." *Cambridge Journal of Economics* 7(3/4): 362–80.

Lal, Deepak, and Hla Myint. 1996. *The Political Economy of Poverty, Equity, and Growth.* Oxford: Clarendon Press.

Lamb, Geoffrey, with Valeriana Kallab, eds. 1992. *Military Expenditure and Economic Development: A Symposium on Research Issues.* World Bank Discussion Paper 185. Washington, D.C.

Latin American and Carribbean Commission on Development and Environment. 1990. *Out Own Agenda.* Inter-American Development Bank and UNDP. Washington, D.C., and New York.

Lewis, John P., and others. 1988. *Strengthening the Poor: What Have We Learned.* U.S. Third World Policy Perspectives 10. Overseas Development Council. New Brunswick, N.J.: Transaction Books.

Lipton, Michael, and Martin Ravallion. 1995. "Poverty and Policy." In Tere Behrman and T.N. Srinivasan, eds, *Handbook of Development Economics.* Vol. 3. Amsterdam: North Holland.

Lipton, Michael, and John Toye. 1990. *Does Aid Work in India?* London: Routledge.

Lisk, Frederick, ed. 1985. *Popular Participation in Planning for Basic Needs.* Aldershot, United Kingdom: Gower.

Lucas, Robert E., Jr. 1990. "Why Doesn't Capital Flow from Rich to Poor Countries?" *American Economic Review* 80(2): 92–96.

Makegetla, Neva Seidman. 1993. "South Africa: Submission on Human Development Index." Background paper for *Human Development Report 1994.* UNDP, New York.

Marsh, Robert M. 1979. "Does Democracy Hinder Development in Latecomer Developing Nations?" *Comparative Social Research,* no. 2: 215–48.

McGranahan, Donald V., and Eduardo Pizarro. 1985. *Measurement and Analysis for Socio-Economic Development.* Geneva: United Nations Research Institute for Social Development.

McNamara, Robert S. 1991. "Reducing Military Expenditures in the Third World." *Finance and Development* 28(3): 26–30.

Meerman, Jacob. 1979. *Public Expenditure in Malaysia: Who Benefits and Why.* New York: Oxford University Press.

Mehrotra, Santosh. 1996. *Education for All: Lessons from High-Achieving Countries.* New York: UNICEF.

Mehrotra, Santosh, and Aung Tun Thet. 1996. "Public Expenditure on Basic Social Services: The Scope for Budget Restructuring in Selected Asian and African Economies." UNICEF Staff Working Paper 14. New York.

Mesa-Lago, Carmelo. 1983. "Social Security and Extreme Poverty in Latin America." *Journal of Development Studies*, no. 12: 83–110.

Milanovic, Branco. 1996. "Income, Inequality, and Poverty during the Transition." Research Paper Series 11. World Bank, Washington, D. C.

Mintcheva-Ivanova, Ianita. 1994. "Human Development and World Competitiveness." Masters thesis. University of New Brunswick. Department of Business Administration, Fredericton, New Brunswick.

Morris, Morris D. 1979. *Measuring the Condition of the World's Poor: The Physical Quality of Life Index.* New York: Pergamon.

Mosley, Paul. 1990. "Innocenti Occasional Paper 5. UNICEF International Child Development Center, Florence.

Mundle, Sudipto. 1995. "Financing Human Resource Development in Advanced Asian Countries: A Report." Asian Development Bank, Manila.

Naoroji, Dadabhai. 1901. *Poverty and UnBritish Rule in India.* New Delhi: Government of India.

Newman, Graeme. 1989. "Report on Crime and the Human Condition." United Nations Centre for Social Development and Humanitarian Affairs, Crime Prevention and Criminal Justice Branch, Vienna.

Nordic UN Project. 1991. *The United Nations in Development: Reform Issues in the Economic and Social Fields—A Nordic Perspective.* Final Report of the Nordic UN Project. Copenhagen.

North-South Roundtable. Forthcoming. *The United Nations and Bretton Woods Institutions: Challenges for the Twenty-first Century.* London: Macmillan.

Nussbaum, Martha, and Amartya K. Sen. 1993. *The Quality of Life.* Oxford: Clarendon.

OECD (Organization for Economic Co-operation and Development).

1986. "Living Conditions in OECD Countries: A Compendium of Social Indicators." OECD Social Policy Studies 3. Paris.

Ogata, Shijuro, Paul Volcker, and others. 1993. "Financing an Effective United Nations: A Report of the Independent Advisory Group on the U.N. Financing." A Project of the Ford Foundation. New York.

Osman, Osman M. 1993. "The Uses of HDI as a Statistical Tool of Policy Planning." Paper presented at seminar on the Uses of the Human Development Index, 17–18 February, UNDP, New York.

Parikh, Kirit S., and R. Sudarshan, eds. 1993. *Human Development and Structural Adjustment.* Madras: Macmillan.

Parker, David, and Eva Jespersen. 1994. "20/20: Mobilizing Resources for Children in the 1990s." UNICEF Staff Working Paper 12. New York.

Patel, Matesh S. 1989. "Eliminating Social Distance between North and South: Cost-Effective Goals for the 1990s." UNICEF Staff Working Paper 5. New York.

Pearce, David W., and Jeremy J. Warford. 1993. *World Without End: Economics, Environment and Sustainable Development.* New York: Oxford University Press.

Pfeffermann, Guy P., and Charles C. Griffin. 1989. *Nutrition and Health Programmes in Latin America: Targeting Social Expenditures.* A World Bank publication in association with the International Centre for Economic Growth. Washington, D.C., and Panama City.

Picciotto, Robert. 1992. "Participatory Development: Myths and Dilemmas." Policy Research Working Paper 930. World Bank, Washington, D.C.

Pinstrup-Andersen, Per. 1988. *Food Subsidies in Developing Countries: Costs, Benefits and Policy Options.* Baltimore: Johns Hopkins University Press.

Potter, Joseph E. 1978. "Demographic Factors and Income Distribution in Latin America." Presented at the International Union for the Scientific Study of Population, 28 August–1 September, Helsinki.

Pronk, Jan, and Mahbub ul Haq. 1992. "Sustainable Development: From Concept to Action." The Hague Report. Ministry of Development Cooperation, The Hague, and UNDP, New York.

Psacharopoulos, George. 1980. "Returns to Education: An Updated International Comparison." In Timothy King, ed., *Education and Income:* World Bank Staff Working Paper 402. Washington, D.C.

————. 1994. "Returns to Investment in Education: A Global Update." *World Development* 22(9): 1325–43.

Psacharopoulos, George, and M. Woodhall. 1985. *Education for Development*. New York: Oxford University Press.

Rahman, Rushidan Islam. 1991. "Poor Women's Access to Economic Gain from Grameen Bank Loans." Working Paper 91/2. Australian National University Research School of Pacific Studies, National Centre for Development Studies, Canberra.

Ranis, Gustav, and Frances Stewart. 1992a. "Decentralization in Chile." Human Development Report Office Occasional Paper 14. UNDP, New York.

————. 1992b. "Decentralization in Indonesia." Background paper for *Human Development Report 1993*. UNDP, New York.

————. 1992c. "Participation and Human Development." Background paper for *Human Development Report 1993*. UNDP, New York.

Ravallion, Martin, and Shaohua Chen. 1996. "What can New Survey Data Tell Us about Recent Changes in Distribution and Poverty?" Policy Research Working Paper 1694. World Bank, Washington, D.C.

Riddell, Roger. 1987. *Foreign Aid Reconsidered*. London: James Currey.

Riddell, Roger, and Mark Robinson. 1992. "The Impact of NGO Poverty Alleviation Projects: Results of the Case Study Evaluations." Working Paper 68. Overseas Development Institute, London.

————. 1993. *Working with the Poor: NGOs and Rural Poverty Alleviation*. London: Overseas Development Institute.

Rogers, Gerry, Charles Gore, and Jose B. Figuerido. 1995. *Social Exclusion: Rhetoric, Reality, Responses*. Geneva: ILO and UNDP.

Ron, Aviva, Brian Abel-Smith and Gionanni Tamburi. 1990. *Health Insurance in Developing Countries: The Social Security Approach*. Geneva: ILO.

Rondinelli, Dennis, John R. Nellis, and G. Shabbir Cheema. 1983. *Decentralization in Developing Countries: A Review of Recent Experience*. World Bank Staff Working Paper 581. Washington, D.C.

Roth, Gabriel. 1989. *The Private Provision of Public Services in Developing Countries*. New York: Oxford University Press.

Rupesinghe, Kumar, and Michiko Kuroda, eds. 1992. *Early Warning and Conflict Resolution*. New York: St. Martin's Press in association with the International Peace Research Institute, Oslo.

Sahota, Gian Singh. 1980. *The Distribution of the Benefits of Public Expenditure in Niegeria.* Washington, D.C.: World Bank.

Saravanamutto, N., and C. Shaw. 1995. *Making Debt Work for Education.* Paris: Association for the Development of African Education.

Schultz, Theodore W. 1980. *Investing in People.* San Francisco: University of California Press.

Sen, Amartya K. 1985. *Commodities and Capabilities.* Amsterdam: North-Holland.

———. 1990. "More than 100 Million Women Are Missing." *New York Review of Books* 37(20): 61–66.

———. 1992. *Inequality Reexamined.* Oxford: Clarendon; and Cambridge, Mass.: Harvard University Press.

Serageldin, Ismail. 1989. *Poverty, Adjustment, and Growth in Africa.* Washington, D.C.: World Bank.

Shiva Kumar, A.K. 1990. "The UNDP's Human Development Index: A Computation for 17 Indian States." Harvard Center for Population Studies, Cambridge, Mass.

Singer, Hans. 1992. "Beyond the Debt Crisis." *Development* 1(1): 35–42.

Singer, Hans, and Stephany Griffith-Jones. 1994. "New Patterns of Macroeconomic Governance." Human Development Report Office Occasional Paper 10. UNDP, New York.

SIPRI (Stockholm International Peace Research Institute). 1994. *SIPRI Yearbook 1994: World Armaments and Disarmament.* Oxford: Oxford University Press.

Sivard, Ruth L. 1989. *World Military and Social Expenditures.* Washington, D.C.: World Priorities.

Snyder, Margaret C. 1995. *Transforming Development: Women, Poverty, and Politics.* London: Intermediate Technology Publications.

Solow, Robert M. 1992. "An Almost Practical Step toward Sustainability." Invited lecture on the occasion of the fortieth anniversary of Resources for the Future, 8 October, Washington, D.C.

The South Commission. 1990. *The Challenge of the South: The Report of the South Commission.* New York: Oxford University Press.

Speth, James Gustave. 1992. "A Post-Rio Compact." *Foreign Policy,* no. 88 (fall): 145–94.

———. 1993. "Towards Sustainable Food Security." Sir John Crawford Memorial Lecture, 25 October, Consultative Group on International Agricultural Research, Washington, D.C.

Spindola, Austregesilo Gomes. 1993. "The Human Development Index and other Development Indicators of Brazil." Background paper for *Human Development Report 1994*. UNDP, New York.

Srinivasan, T. N. 1994. "Human Development: A Paradigm or Reinvention of the Wheel?" Paper presented at American Economic Association meeting, 3 January, Boston.

Standing, Guy. 1992. "Human Development in Eastern and Central Europe." Background paper for *Human Development Report 1993*. UNDP, New York.

Stewart, Frances. 1985. *Basic Needs in Developing Countries*. Baltimore: Johns Hopkins University Press.

———. 1988. "Adjustment with a Human Face: The Role of Food Aid." *Food Policy* 13(1): 18–26.

———. 1991. "The Many Faces of Adjustment." *World Development* 19(12): 1847–64.

———. 1995. *Adjustment and Poverty: Options and Choices*. London: Routledge.

Stewart, Frances, Sanjaya Lall, and S. Wangwe. 1991. *Alternative Development Strategies in Sub-Saharan Africa*. London: Macmillan.

Streeten, Paul. 1992. "Global Governance for Human Development," Human Development Report Office Occasional Paper 4. UNDP, New York.

———. 1994. "Human Development: Means and Ends." Paper presented at American Economic Association meeting, 3 January, Boston.

Summers, Robert, Irving B. Kravis, and Alan Heston. 1984. "Changes in the World Income Distribution." *Journal of Policy Modelling* 6(2): 237–69.

Svasti, Pongsvas, Naris Chaiyasoot, Waraporn Suvachittanont, and Parinee Masnee. 1991. "Human Development Indicators." Paper prepared for UNDP. Bangkok.

Tatlidi, Huseyin. 1992. "A New Approach for Human Development: Human Development Scores." Institute of Development Studies, Sussex, United Kingdom.

Townsend, Peter. 1979. *Poverty in the United Kingdom*. London: Penguin.

UNDP (United Nations Development Programme). 1988. *The Amman Statement on Human Development: Goals and Strategies for the Year 2000*. UNDP Study Programme and North-South Roundtable of the Society for International Development. New York.

————. 1990a. "Development Challenges for the 1990s." An Anniversary Issue to Commemorate 40 Years of Multilateral Technical Co-operation for Development in the United Nations System. New York.

————. 1990b. "Human Development Country Studies in Selected Countries." New York.

————. 1990c. *Human Development Report 1990*. New York: Oxford University Press.

————. 1991. *Human Development Report 1991*. New York: Oxford University Press.

————. 1992a. *Balanced Development: An Approach to Social Action in Pakistan*. Islamabad.

————. 1992b. *Human Development in Bangladesh: Local Action under National Constraints*. Dhaka.

————. 1992c. *Human Development Report 1992*. New York: Oxford University Press.

————. 1992d. *Making People Matter: Introductory Comment on a Human Development Strategy for Ghana*. Accra.

————. 1993a. *Human Development Report 1993*. New York: Oxford University Press.

————. 1993b. *Rethinking Technical Cooperation: Reforms for Capacity Building in Africa*. New York.

————. 1994a. *Human Development Report 1994*. New York: Oxford University Press.

————. 1994b. *1994 Report on Human Development in Bangladesh: Empowerment of Women*. Dhaka.

————. 1994c. *Philippine Hukan Development Report*. Manila.

————. 1996. "Governance for Sustainable Development." UNDP Policy Document. New York.

UNICEF (United Nations Children's Fund). 1989a. *The State of the World's Children 1989*. New York: Oxford University Press.

————. 1989b. *Strategies for Children in the 1990s*. A UNICEF Policy Paper. New York.

————. 1990. *The State of the World's Children 1990*. New York: Oxford University Press.

————. 1991. *The State of the World's Children 1991*. New York: Oxford University Press.

————. 1992. *The State of the World's Children 1992*. New York: Oxford University Press.

————. 1993. *The State of the World's Children 1993*. New York: Oxford University Press.

————. 1994. *The State of the World's Children 1994*. New York: Oxford University Press.

United Nations Economic Commission for Africa. 1991. "Human Development in Africa." Addis Ababa.

United Nations Economic Commission for Latin America and the Carribbean. 1991. *Sustainable Development: Changing Production Patterns, Social Equity and the Environment*. Santiago.

United Nations Population Fund. 1991. *The State of World Population 1991*. New York.

———. 1992. *The State of World Population 1992*. New York.

———. 1993. *The State of World Population 1993*. New York.

———. 1994. *The State of World Population 1994*. New York.

Uphoff, Norman. 1992. *Local Institutions and Participation for Sustainable Development*. Gatekeeper Series 31. London: International Institute for Environment and Development.

Uphoff, Norman. 1992. *Local Institutions and Participation for Sustainable Development*. Gatekeeper Series 31. London: International Institute for Environment and Development.

Urquhart, Brian. 1993. "A UN Volunteer Force—The Prospects." *New York Review of Books*, July 15, pp. 52–56.

Urquhart, Brian, and Erskine Childers. 1990. *A World in Need of Leadership: Tomorrow's United Nations*. Uppsala: Dag Hammarskjöld Foundation.

van der Meer, Esther. 1993. "L'Indicateur de développment humain." Masters thesis. University of Geneva, Department of Econometrics, Geneva.

van Ginneken, Wouter. 1976. *Rural and Urban Income Inequalities in Indonesia, Mexico, Pakistan, Tanzania, and Tunisia*. Geneva: ILO.

Weiner, Myron, and Omar Noman, 1997. *The Child and the State in India and Pakistan*. Karachi: Oxford University Press.

WHO (World Health Organization). 1989. *Global Strategy for Health for All by the Year 2000*. Rome.

Wood, Adrian. 1994. *North South Trade, Employment, and Inequality: Changing Fortunes in a Skill-Driven World*. Oxford: Clarendon Press.

World Bank. 1986. *Poverty and Hunger: Issues and Options for Food Security in Developing Countries*. A World Bank Policy Study. Washington, D.C.

———. 1987. *Financing Health Services in Developing Countries: An Agenda for Reform*. A World Bank Policy Study. Washington, D.C.

———. 1989a. *Sub-Saharan Africa: From Crisis to Sustainable Growth*. A Long-Term Perspective Study. Washington, D.C.

————. 1989b. *World Development Report 1989.* New York: Oxford University Press.

————. 1990. *World Development Report 1990.* New York: Oxford University Press.

————. 1991a. *Egypt: Alleviating Poverty during Structural Adjustment.* A World Bank Country Study. Washington, D.C.

————. 1991b. *World Development Report 1991.* New York: Oxford University press.

————. 1992. *World Development Report 1992.* New York: Oxford University press.

————. 1993. *World Development Report 1993.* New York: Oxford University press.

————. 1994. *World Development Report 1994.* New York: Oxford University press.

World Bank, African Development Bank and UNDP. 1990. *The Social Dimensions of Adjustment in Africa: A Policy Agenda.* Washington, D.C.: World Bank.

World Commission on Environment and Development. 1987. *Our Common Future.* New York: Oxford University Press.

World Resources Institute. 1990. *World Resources 1990.* New York: Oxford University Press.

————. 1991. *World Resources 1991.* New York: Oxford University Press.

————. 1992. *World Resources 1992.* New York: Oxford University Press.

————. 1993. *World Resources 1993.* New York: Oxford University Press.

————. 1994. *World Resources 1994.* New York: Oxford University Press.

WSSD (World Summit for Social Development). 1995. "Report of the World Summit for Social Development." 6–12. March, Copenhagen.

Wulf, Herbert, 1992. "Disarmament as a Chance for Human Development: Is There a Peace Dividend?" Human Development Report Office Occasional Paper 5. UNDP, New York.

Yudëlman, Sally W. 1987. "The Integration of Women into Development Projects." *World Development*, no. 15 (supplement, autumn): 179–87.

Zhizhou, Cai. 1993. "Human Development in China." Background paper for *Human Development Report 1994.* UNDP, New York.

Zuckerman, Elaine. 1988. "Poverty and Adjustment Issues and Practices." World Bank, Country Economics Department, Washington, D.C.

Remembering Dr. Mahbub ul Haq

'Mahbub ul Haq's...enduring monument is the annual Human Development Report, which he created in 1990 and edited until 1996. It has caught the world's imagination and has served as a model for similar national reports in no less than 197 countries.'

— Kofi Annan
Secretary General
United Nations

'The World Bank owes a tremendous debt of gratitude to Mahbub, who, probably more than anyone else, provided the intellectual impetus for the Bank's commitment to poverty reduction in the early 1970's. Mahbub had the courage to speak out against the conventional wisdom of the time and make the task of improving the lives of the poor the centrepiece of the Bank's mission.'

— James D. Wolfensohn
President
The World Bank

'Mahbub had a burning passion for the idea of Human Development and used his intellectual brilliance and political skills to turn this idea into a crusade with world wide outreach.'

— James Gustave Speth
Administrator
United Nations Development Programme

'Dr. Haq would be remembered for the signal and original contributions made by him to the concept of human development as the goal, and indeed the soul of economic development.'

— Shri K. R. Narayanan
President of India

'Dr. Haq's commitment to development led to him being described in the international media as the "guru of human development" and "a tireless champion of the poor".'

— *The Hindu*

'I deeply admired his intellectual and moral courage, his readiness to speak out without fear whenever he felt it necessary, to focus his analytical skills and vast knowledge on the most difficult issues. The world of development co-operation and activism will not be the same without him.'

— Federico Mayor
Director General
UNESCO

'Simply put, Dr. Haq was the greatest living expert on measuring human progress.'

— Jonathan Power
Khaleej Times

'Mahbub ul Haq constantly challenged the Washington consensus but he did it in a way that was as critical of developing countries who mismanaged their resources as of development countries which were mean in their transfers...'

— Lord Meghnad Desai
The Guardian

'Mahbub's death has robbed us of a great man who contributed so much to his country, the Commonwealth, and the world. He was a uniquely gifted thinker who applied his mind to the most challenging global issues. His dedicated and passionate involvement in the fight against injustice and poverty singled him out as a giant amongst his contemporaries.'

— Emeka Anyaoku
Commonwealth Secretary General